Frontier Naturalist

Frontier Naturalist

Jean Louis Berlandier and the
Exploration of Northern Mexico and Texas

RUSSELL M. LAWSON

University of New Mexico Press ❖ Albuquerque

© 2012 by the University of New Mexico Press
All rights reserved. Published 2012
Printed in the United States of America

17 16 15 14 13 12   1 2 3 4 5 6

LIBRARY OF CONGRESS CATALOGING-IN-PUBLICATION DATA

Lawson, Russell M., 1957–
Frontier naturalist : Jean Louis Berlandier and the exploration of northern Mexico
and Texas / Russell M. Lawson.
p. cm.
Includes bibliographical references and index.
ISBN 978-0-8263-5217-0 (cloth : alk. paper) — ISBN 978-0-8263-5219-4 (electronic)
1. Mexico, North—Description and travel. 2. Texas, South—Description and travel.
3. Berlandier, Jean Louis, d. 1851—Travel. 4. Natural history—Mexico, North.
5. Natural history—Texas, South. 6. Scientific expeditions—Mexico, North—
History—19th century. 7. Scientific expeditions—Texas, South—History—19th century. 8. Naturalists—France—Biography. 9. Explorers—Mexico, North—Biography.
10. Explorers—Texas, South—Biography. I. Title.
F1314.L39 2012
508.72—dc23
2012018873

Book design by Lila Sanchez
Composed in 10.25/13.5 Minion Pro Regular
Display type is Minion Pro

Cover image: Map depicting battle against Isidro Barradas in vicinity of
Tampico, Mexico, in 1829. Copied from the original by Lt. Charles N. Hagner,
Topographical Engineers. Library of Congress.

For Pooh, again.

Contents

Acknowledgments

I WISH TO EXPRESS MY THANKS TO MANY INSTITUTIONS FOR SUPPORT and to individuals for help during the writing of this book. I appreciate the financial assistance of the professional development fund and the support of the administration at Bacone College. I received assistance from archivists and librarians at Gilcrease Museum, Beinecke Library at Yale University, Gray Herbarium at Harvard University, Old Colony Historical Society, Smithsonian Institution Archives, Ewell Sale Stewart Library and Archives at the Academy of Natural Sciences in Philadelphia, and Bacone College.

Thanks also to several anonymous readers who provided helpful criticisms about the manuscript; staff members of the University of New Mexico Press, past and present, such as Luther Wilson, W. Clark Whitehorn, Elise McHugh, and Felicia Cedillos; and copyeditor Lisa Williams.

I wish to thank my son, Benjamin A. Lawson, a PhD candidate in history at the University of Iowa, for drawing the map of Berlandier's travels. My wife, Linda Lawson, read a draft of the manuscript and provided helpful suggestions. This book is dedicated to her.

Abbreviations

BRBML   Jean Louis Berlandier Papers. Yale Collection of Western
         Americana, Beinecke Rare Book and Manuscript Library.

DIBL   Digital images from the Jean Louis Berlandier Papers,
         Beinecke Library, Yale University: http://hdl.handle.net
         /10079/fa/beinecke.berlandi.

GHA   Papers of Jean Louis Berlandier, Archives, Gray Herbarium
         Library, Harvard University.

SIA   Smithsonian Institution Archives.

SIAJLB   Smithsonian Institution Archives, Record Unit 7052,
         Jean Louis Berlandier Papers.

Introduction

𝒟

✛ THIS IS A STORY OF DISCOVERY. THE SETTING IS A LAND OF EXTREMES: in temperature, the heat of the *terra caliente* and the cold of the Sierras; in moisture, the arid lands of the Mexican Plateau and the humidity of the lowlands near the sea; in elevation, ranging from 10,000 feet in the mountains to sea level along coastal waters; in nature, peaceful and calm on summer evenings along *parajes*, camping places next to ponds and rivers, and violent and terrifying when storms from the northern plains roll across the plains to the south and east. This is a story about discoverers: inquisitive, courageous people of constancy and perseverance. Featured are a Frenchman educated in Geneva living in Mexico; an American scientist and soldier, veteran of the Mexican War; Mexican scientists and soldiers; Tejano settlers and American filibusters; and indigenous hunters, warriors, and guides. The northern Mexican and southern Texas frontiers from 1826 to 1853, the chronological boundaries of this narrative, were under contention by different peoples: Comanches and Lipan Apaches, squatters and colonists from the United States, and mestizo settlers from south of the Río Bravo del Norte—the Rio Grande. Among all of these peoples were those who are never content with what is and who one is, who seek to go beyond what is known to what can be known, who are restless to find and, having found, to find again. Discoverers typically have motives that include wealth, glory, and knowledge. The discoverers portrayed herein were of the latter sort, wanting to know for the sake of knowing; to extend themselves outward, restlessly, into the natural environment; to contribute to a broadening of institutional knowledge in libraries, museums, institutes, and associations. Beyond these lofty goals, on the trail discoverers sought to take the best paths to go from here to there, to ensure water to drink, food to eat, shelter from the elements, and protection from enemies.

xiii

The spring of 1828 was a particularly wet one on the northern Mexican frontier. The varied people who inhabited the rivers of Texas, particularly the Colorado, Brazos, and Trinity, had rarely seen the waters rise so high, making tall oaks seem like huge bushes floating on the surface. Freshets inundated entire valleys, destroying crops and farms, impoverishing people already desperately poor. Old Spanish roads that traversed the land from San Antonio de Béxar to Nacogdoches were washed out in some places and soggy, sticky clay in others. Only a fool would travel this way except through utter necessity, and the only travel that made any sense was by mule or on horseback. And yet, to the astonishment of the Tejanos, the Mexicans of the gulf plain of Texas, during April, May, and June of that year a large caravan of soldiers, who did not appear quite like typical Mexican soldiers, sloshed, splattered, and cursed their way along the *caminos* of Texas. What was unusual about this group of soldiers was their stated aim and commensurate behavior, seeking knowledge rather than booty; their wagons, loaded with strange-looking equipment, one decked out in gilded finery; and their members, at least one of whom was not armed, nor dressed in a uniform. This latter member of the troop was constantly straying from the caravan, disappearing into woods and over hills into meadows. He carried a satchel into which he put plants, roots, leaves, and flowers. He frequently halted to write something in a journal he carried, and sometimes he seemed to be sketching something he spied in the distance. The man was young, and he spoke with a strange accent. His English was very poor and his Spanish little better; when he spoke with confidence it was in French. This traveler among the American squatters and colonists, the Mexican immigrants from south of the Rio Grande, and the Indians, most of whom were recent arrivals from north of the Red River, was a native Frenchman, a Swiss scientist, a newcomer to the northern Mexican and southern Texas frontiers: Berlandier.

The lead character in this drama of discovery is Jean Louis Berlandier. His journey to Mexico lasted from 1826, when he joined ship at Le Havre de Grace, to his death in 1851, when he failed to cross a swollen river in northern Mexico—the San Fernando, which he had forded so many times before, just as he had forded the scores of rivers, streams, and arroyos of Texas and Mexico during the preceding twenty-four years. Berlandier packed several lifetimes of travel into two dozen years of scientific and exploring expeditions in Mexico, in and about Teotihuacán and its surrounding peaks; across the Mexican Plateau north to the Rio Grande; across the same river into southern Texas; north and east fording the Nueces, Colorado, and Brazos Rivers to the Trinity River; up the Guadalupe River into the Texas hill country, down the San Antonio River and east to the Mississippi River and the port of New Orleans; in and about the frontier town of Matamoros near the mouth of the Rio Grande; exploring the Laguna Madre of the Gulf Coast; journeying south throughout the Mexican states of Tamaulipas, Veracruz, San Luis Potosí, and Nuevo León; ascending the summits and wandering the valleys of the Sierra Madre Oriental; and crossing and recrossing the Pánuco, Tamesí, Soto La Marina, Pílon, and San Fernando Rivers. Berlandier, trained as a botanist in Geneva, collected thousands of floral and faunal specimens; wrote detailed botanical, zoological, geographical, geological, meteorological, and historical accounts; drew maps of his travels, sketches of what he saw, and watercolors of native plants, animals, and peoples; kept extensive journals of his experiences, observations, and discoveries; and wrote detailed narratives of his adventures.[1]

Varying peoples with disparate interests inhabited the region of northern Mexico and southern Texas in the 1820s and 1830s. The colonists, squatters, and filibusters of the United States of America sought to possess the fertile river valleys of Texas, which Spanish soldiers and Franciscan missionaries had explored and sporadically settled during preceding centuries, control of which the new Republic of Mexico sought to retain by the presence of presidial troops along the roads and in the towns of the valley of the Rio Grande east to the Sabine River. This same land had, however, been occupied and its resources used by dozens of American Indian tribes. Anglo-, French, and Spanish Americans had encountered, though had rarely studied, the varied tribes of southern Texas. The Native peoples, as well as the flora and fauna of the regions watered by the Rio Grande, Nueces, Colorado, Guadalupe, and Brazos Rivers, had rarely given way to the descriptive pen, careful study, and patience to collect and to preserve of the Euro-American naturalist.

Jean Louis Berlandier initially journeyed to Mexico to join the Mexican Boundary Commission (Comisión de Límites), a military and scientific expedition to cross the Rio Grande and to explore Texas to Nacogdoches to discover the region's peoples, climate, geography, flora, and fauna. The commission was led by Gen. Manuel Mier y Terán, an able mathematician and surveyor, who led officers who were trained in medicine, cartography, and surveying, and a host of soldiers who served to guide and protect. The only two civilians were Raphael Chowell, a mineralogist, and Berlandier, who served as botanist and zoologist. Wagons driven with care contained instruments of science to determine latitude, elevation, direction, and to preserve images and specimens. In November 1827 the journeyers left Mexico City, arriving at Laredo on the Rio Grande in early February. Wildflowers were already beginning to bloom, even though the environs of Laredo were dry and sparing. From Laredo they moved north to San Antonio, where Berlandier spent a fortnight botanizing before they moved east toward the Sabine River, crossing the Guadalupe, Colorado, Brazos, and Trinity along the way. Spring rains brought rising rivers and lowland mud that slowed the expedition to a crawl. Worse, the mosquitoes gloried in the wet, humid environment and plagued the men unmercifully. Berlandier and others became ill with the fever and chills of malaria. At Trinity River the botanist was forced to turn back. He spent the summer recovering—first at San Antonio, then at Matamoros— returning to San Antonio in the fall, healthy once again and ready for scientific adventure.

At San Antonio, Berlandier became acquainted with José Francisco Ruíz, an army officer who had spent some years living with the Comanche Indians of Texas. Berlandier, fascinated, used Ruíz as his source of investigation into this and other Indian tribes of southern Texas. He accepted Ruíz's invitation to join him and some soldiers and scores of Comanche on a hunting expedition up the Guadalupe River in the late fall of 1828. Berlandier used the opportunity to botanize and to study Indian culture and customs. His observations became an important basis for his book "Indigenes nomades des Etats Internes d'Orient et d'Occident des territoires du Nouveau Mexique et des deux Californies," which is a wonderful ethnography of the Plains Indians written by a sensitive observer of human and natural history. Berlandier, also an artist (as was his companion of the Comisión de Límites José Sánchez y Tapía, as well as Matamoros friend Lino Sánchez y Tapía), sketched and painted plants, landmarks, and the men and women of various Indian tribes. Years later Berlandier published (along with Raphael Chowell) an account of the Guadalupe journey and the Boundary Commission expedition as a whole.[2]

After his journey up the Guadalupe, during the winter and spring of 1829, Berlandier explored south along the San Antonio River to Goliad, south near the confluence of the San Antonio with the Guadalupe River, and east to New Orleans. He returned to Matamoros that summer, where he made his home for the rest of his life. Berlandier organized his collection of botanical specimens and sent them to the botanists who had sponsored his journey in Geneva. These men, especially Augustin Pyramus de Candolle, were angry about the poor quality of the specimens and branded Berlandier a sloppy, inaccurate botanist. Undeterred, Berlandier used his base at Matamoros for continuing

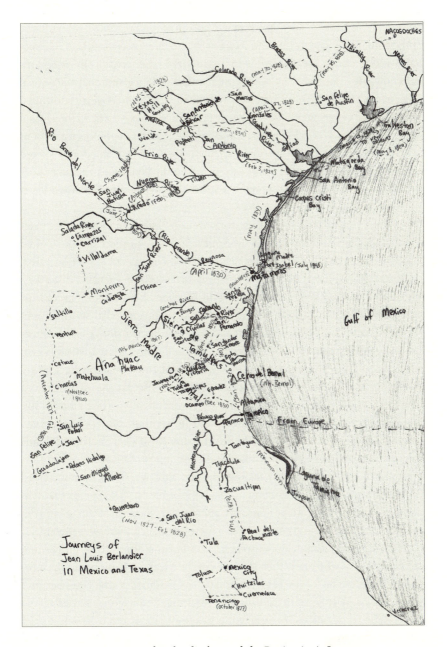

Figure 1. Map of Berlandier's travels by Benjamin A. Lawson.

botanical journeys in northern Mexico, specifically to places in Nuevo León and Tamaulipas, and across the Rio Grande to Brazos de Santiago, Goliad, San Antonio, and other locations in Texas. Berlandier employed his botanical knowledge into building a thriving medical practice and pharmaceutical business at Matamoros; his journeys were made in part to acquire additional materials for his growing *materia medica*. Berlandier experienced the United States invasion of Mexico in 1846 and kept a journal of the occupation of Matamoros. He operated a war hospital to treat the wounded and served as an intermediary between the Americans and Mexicans. Berlandier survived the war but died in 1851 trying to cross the swollen San Fernando River on horseback.

Supporting characters in this story are the American and Mexican soldiers and scientists connected to the Smithsonian Institution and the United States and Mexican Boundary Survey. Most notable was Darius Nash Couch, a talented naturalist who worked tirelessly on behalf of scientific discovery. Through Couch's efforts, Berlandier and his work became known and his extensive collection of flora, fauna, drawings, paintings, and writings preserved. Couch had the support and assistance of Joseph Henry and Spencer Baird, secretary and assistant secretary of the Smithsonian Institution. In addition to Couch and Baird were members of the Comisión de Límites such as Manuel Mier y Terán, Raphael Chowell, José Sánchez y Tapía, and Constantino Tarnava. Also important to this narrative are the nameless soldiers, mule-drivers, local adventurers, and indigenous hunters who served as guides to Jean Louis Berlandier and Darius Nash Couch. These include the *soldado*, a soldier who joined Berlandier on many of his travels as a guide and guard; the *Quicapú*, a Kickapoo hunter and warrior who befriended Berlandier and became his companion on journeys in Texas; and the *ayudante*, a former clerk at Berlandier's apothecary shop in Matamoros who guided Couch on his journey across northern Mexico. Others who play minor roles in this story—muleteers (*arrieros*), simple and honest trail guides and caravan drivers who knew the arid paths of the Mexican Plateau and the dangerous trails of the Sierra Madre; and soldiers assigned to the Mexican presidios who were experts in hunting and tracking. The soldiers, warriors, and guides who led scientists into the wilderness mountains and valleys of southern Texas and northern Mexico were hardly literate—usually illiterate—but, through their willingness to share information, their intuitive ability to find their way, and indigenous knowledge of animal behavior, healing properties of plants, and sources of food when none seemed available, were invaluable informants to scientists who were focused on objective thinking but lacked a tacit understanding of the natural environment. Science is a collective activity. Usually the community of scientists involves trained scholars working in collusion to find over time evidence to support or to deny hypotheses about the workings of nature. The experiences of Berlandier and Couch suggest that the scientific community of nineteenth-century America also involved ad hoc scientists, whose training was neither academic nor apprenticed, but who nevertheless possessed wisdom, acquired by trial-and-error experiences over time, about flora, fauna, directions, climate, and landscape, that cannot be taught but only learned.[3]

Jean Louis Berlandier used the sources of tacit, experiential knowledge derived from years spent on the trail to supplement his formal education acquired from the Geneva Academy, apprenticeship to a Geneva apothecary, and acceptance into a select group of Geneva savants, the Société de Physique et d'Histoire Naturelle de Genève. Berlandier used his pen, pencil, and paintbrush to record his experiences, which provide the core for a hitherto untold story of exploration and science on the Mexican and Texas frontier.

Very little of the natural world of northern Mexico and southern Texas escaped Berlandier's notice and examination. His contributions to understanding this world were many and varied. Berlandier as a physician was a leader of the public health movement in his part of the world. As a medical researcher he discovered what plants worked best for what ailments, relying on reports from various sources throughout northern Mexico and Texas. He learned, for example, that the Carrizo tribe used the *cenizilla* (*Leucophyllum frutescens* [Berl.]) as a febrifuge to relieve feverish patients. He kept extensive notes of his discoveries in "A estudiar en viajes: Histoire naturelle des plantes employees dans la matiere medicals les arts, etc. des Mexicains anciens et modernes" and "Des plantes usuelles chez les Indiens du Mexique," which are preserved in the Berlandier Papers at the Gray Herbarium Archives, Harvard University. As a zoologist, Berlandier made an extensive study of turtles along the Gulf Coast and Rio Grande. He studied and accurately drew the green turtle (*Chelonia mydas*) as well as the Texas Tortoise, which in 1857 Louis Agassiz christened in Berlandier's honor *Gopherus berlandieri*, writing that the turtle was "collected by the late Mr. Berlandier, a zealous French naturalist, to whom we are indebted for much of what we know of the natural history of northern Mexico." Berlandier made other precise drawings of animals, such as the beaver, and painstakingly drew as well the internal organs of various specimens that he dissected. As an ichthyologist he studied flying fish, commenting on interesting pathological phenomena. Berlandier collected a variety of entomological species and claimed to have discovered a dozen unique species of butterflies in Tamaulipas, although these were never published.[4]

Berlandier was as adept and prolific in his study of the physical sciences in the neighborhood of the Rio Grande valley. As a physicist, he experimented on the nature of sound in 1845, enlisting in his experiment the aid of Mexican artillery troops. As an astronomer, Berlandier made experiments on the temperature of the sun, studied the path of comets over the course of nightly observations, and made celestial observations to determine the latitude of various locales. As a geologist he measured heights of mountains, using the barometer and thermometer, in the Sierra Madre, and contributed to the theory of uniformity in geologic change based on his study of volcanoes in Tamaulipas. For more than twenty years, Berlandier made a study of meteorological conditions in and about Matamoros, or wherever he happened to be in Texas and Mexico, recording the speed, direction, and changes in winds; the variances in temperature according to winds, latitude, air pressure, landscape, and elevation; the conditions that resulted in powerful storms, especially lightning storms, and their impact on affected people and places; atmospheric conditions during all seasons; and the prevalence, characteristics, and impact of hurricanes in the Gulf Coast. In the related field of hydrology, Berlandier hypothesized about the power of streams and rivers, wondering about the changes over time of rivers and their paths to the sea. As an oceanographer Berlandier studied coastal waters and the impact of the sea and tides on shorelines and rivers; he developed a theory that the Gulf of Mexico was receding, resulting in increasing tidal lagoons and sandbars along the shore and at the mouths of rivers.[5]

Berlandier contributed to the geographic understanding of southern Texas and northern Mexico through his many journeys describing the lay of the land, topography, soil and geologic history, climate, and pathways of beasts and humans. He repeatedly drew on-the-spot maps of his journeys, forming not only a personal history of discovery but a cartographic record of travels of people and obscure places along the road.[6]

Although Berlandier did not have training as an anthropologist, he became quite a gifted student of human culture through his ability to empathize with other peoples, even those completely distinct from his experiences theretofore. He left behind extensive materials to contribute to the history of American Indians. Because of his many journeys, sometimes in the company of Indians, he became an expert on the Indians of Texas and northern Mexico, acquiring new information on, particularly, the Comanche, coming to understand their inherent intelligence and abilities in natural science.[7]

Berlandier's greatest significance was as a scientific explorer, the first such naturalist to make extensive journeys and commensurate observations in northern Mexico and Gulf Coast Texas. He journeyed into relatively unknown lands, enduring privations and making scientific discoveries. He had the character of a scientific discoverer: he was open, anticipatory, and rootless. He confronted personally through his journeys the ignorance of Europeans in regard to the harsh environment of America and its undiscovered natural history.

Jean Louis Berlandier was able to see the natural environment of America when the land was still wilderness, when nature was largely untouched, little altered by human curiosity and industry. This is the primary importance of his life and work. His vast library of manuscript documents of natural, human, and personal history allows us to peer over Berlandier's shoulders as he lived, worked, and recorded natural and human experience to see, as it were, an America that no longer exists.

CHAPTER ONE

Savant of Matamoros

✵ THE WAR HAD BEEN OVER FOR ALMOST FIVE YEARS, AND AN UNEASY peace had settled upon the region, when Lt. Darius Nash Couch, a veteran of the conflict between the Republic of Mexico and the United States of America, arrived to Brazos de Santiago at the southern extreme of Padre Island, just opposite Point Isabel, at the beginning of February 1853. Lieutenant Couch was on a leave of absence from the army, on assignment with the Smithsonian Institution to discover the flora and fauna of northern Mexico and southern Texas. Nash was familiar with the region, having served during the war under the command of Maj. Gen. Zachary Taylor.

Couch had just graduated from West Point and had been assigned as a brevet second lieutenant in the 4th Artillery under Maj. John Munroe when he had arrived at Port Lavacca near Matagorda Bay along the Texas Gulf Coast in the autumn of 1846. The twenty-four-year-old New York native had journeyed through the thick, humid atmosphere of late summer from Port Lavacca west-northwest to Goliad, then had followed the path northwest to San Antonio. In the waning days of October and first days of November, Couch had departed in the company of others, civilians and mounted soldiers, southwest from San Antonio toward the valley of the Rio Grande. They had crossed many rivulets and streams, and fewer large rivers, along the way, all the while on their guard against aggression from the Comanche Indians. Political conflict and war always beget instability and engender further conflict and war; the Comanches had experienced a changing of the guard among the whites several times during the preceding generation. The Texas Revolution resulted in an even greater vacuum of power in West Texas than had existed under the Mexicans and Spanish, and the Comanches had responded assertively, which was the only way they knew during times of instability. Comanche attacks on other indigenous peoples of the region, as well as the Texans and, across the Rio Grande, the inhabitants of Tamaulipas, Nuevo León, and Coahuila, held steady during the 1830s and 1840s. The Comanche reputation for raiding and surprise attacks had grown, which ensured that Couch and the other dragoons on the road to the Presidio San Juan Bautista had been on their guard against attack. Not only had Lieutenant Couch been too late to experience the first battles of the war at Palo Alto and Resaca de la Palma, the American victories of which allowed the advance across the Rio Grande and occupation of Matamoros, but by the time Couch had reached the presidio, he had been terribly ill with dysentery, a disease that would plague him for the rest of his life. While General Taylor's army had marched southwest for Monterrey, then Saltillo, Couch had been transported by wagon to Monclova in the Mexican state of Coahuila, where he would rest and recover.[1]

During the long periods of illness and inactivity, Couch had become fascinated with the harsh beauty of northern Mexico, the green-leafed palms that lined the banks of the slow-moving, broad Rio Grande tinted a yellowish-brown from the runoff of countless acres along its course; the chaparral, or hedgerows of the sparing, twisted, thorny mesquite; the stark, inland peaks of the Sierra Madre; the arid landscape dotted with numerous species of cactus, yucca, and other spiny desert plants; the dry creeks, arroyos, that became unfordable and inundated the parched land during the rainy seasons of spring and autumn; the sudden, violent thunderstorms that swept across the prairies; the deep blue of the sky, misty mornings, radiant sunsets; the conflict of land and river and coast and sea that left large spillover lakes and lagoons mixing freshwater with brine; the immense, unexpected, and unknown number of insects; and the variety of reptiles unfamiliar to an Easterner like Couch. The land had beckoned the young American army officer.

Now years later, in 1853, Couch was intent on scientific rather than military conquest when he returned to the Rio Grande, hoping to reverse the lack of scientific data about this border region. The progress of scientific discovery had moved west across the Appalachian Mountains and the Mississippi during the previous half century but had scarcely advanced south of the Red River and west of the Sabine River. By Couch's time, nascent scientific centers with groups of mostly amateur scientists existed at such growing cities as Cincinnati, Lexington, and Nashville. Faculty such as Constantine Samuel Rafinesque and Daniel Drake made Transylvania University in Lexington a center of collecting and understanding the materia medica of the trans-Appalachian country. Cincinnati boasted several scientific institutions devoted to the collection and distribution of natural history and scientific knowledge. Under the leadership of Philip Lindsley, the University of Nashville was a locus of science in the American South. More itinerant naturalists had been working in the years since the Louisiana Purchase in 1803 in the trans-Mississippi west, as physicians and apothecaries, living near or at frontier forts such as Smith, Gibson, and Leavenworth. Naturalists such as Thomas Nuttall, John Kirk Townsend, and John James Audubon traveled about the little-known regions of the western United States, making discoveries and searching for knowledge. Scientific activity was much more limited in Mexico; what existed was generally centered in Mexico City. The achievements of Spanish and European scientists before independence had not been equaled by Mexican scientists. Nevertheless, the *Flora mexicana*, the product of the Royal Botanical Expedition, remained a useful resource for the Mexican botanist, as was the Royal Botanical Garden of Mexico City. Scientists seeking information on the Rio Grande region and tributaries had to rely on the reports of ad hoc scientists such as Captain Zebulon Pike and his companion Dr. John Robinson; better was Alexander Humboldt's *Political Economy of New Spain*, which was nevertheless limited in its description of the northern regions of New Spain and the lower Rio Grande. American scientists that had journeyed in the direction of the Rio Grande included Peter Custis, who had ascended the Red River to near the Great Raft in 1806, and scientists such as Thomas Say and Titian Peale of the Stephen H. Long expedition of 1820, who likewise never journeyed into Texas. Maps of the Long Expedition referred to the south-central plains as the Great Desert, and so it seemed in respect to the lack of fertile achievements in science. An exception was Thomas Drummond, who journeyed to Texas in 1832 and studied the natural history, particularly botany, of the Brazos and Colorado River valleys. But Drummond's work was not well known, as few narrative accounts of his life and travels survived him. Twenty years later, after the Texas Revolution and the Mexican War, the paucity of scientific data remained. Like many others of his time, Couch was encouraged by the inauguration of the Smithsonian Institution, which he hoped would become a reservoir of scientific data. He had a much healthier respect for American scientists than their Mexican counterparts, and he believed that whatever data and specimens he could acquire should be preserved by Americans rather than Mexicans.[2]

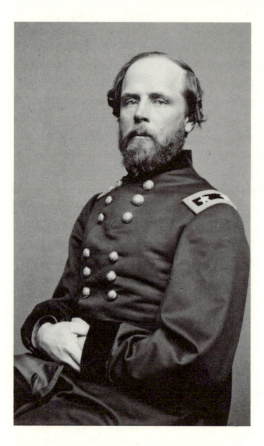

Figure 2.
Portrait of Maj. Gen. Darius
Nash Couch, officer of the
Federal Army. In the Brady
National Photographic Art
Gallery (Washington, D.C.),
Library of Congress.

The experiences of the war were brought back to Couch when he arrived at the valley of the Rio Grande after so many years and looked upon the sites of battle where so many had died. Navigation continued to be funneled through Brazos de Santiago as it had been seven years before; for most sea captains, the mouth of the Rio Grande was too uncertain to risk an attempt. The entrance to Brazos de Santiago, a narrow strait between the southern extreme of Padre Island and a peninsula of the mainland, was like the mouth of the Rio Grande: shallow, six to eight feet deep. Brazos de Santiago was a little deeper, depending on the wind and the tide. Fort Brown had become a small village, incorporated as Brownsville in honor of the fallen Maj. Jacob Brown. Across the river, Matamoros, with over three thousand inhabitants, was more populated than it had been during the war, when the inhabitants had fled the destruction and rapine of undisciplined American troops.[3]

Couch stayed in Brownsville while he wrote letters to correspondents and made inquiries among the locals about where to hire the best guides and mules. Couch was among many naturalists, some in the military and some not, who journeyed for the Smithsonian Institution in the early 1850s to discover the natural productions and exact boundaries of the newly acquired lands north of the Rio Grande and west to the Pacific. Capt. George B. McClellan, for example, preceded Couch to lower Texas by a few months, collecting for and communicating with Spencer Baird, of the Smithsonian Institution. The Topographical Corps of Engineers of the U.S. Army engaged in exploring and surveying lands of the western United States in the years during and after the Mexican War. Lt. J. D. Webster surveyed the Rio Grande valley from near its mouth to near its source in 1847. R. H. Kern explored the Pecos River in 1850. Maj. William Emory, who had traced the route from Fort Leavenworth, Kansas, to California from 1846 to 1847 as part of a military reconnaissance led by Gen. Stephen Kearny, became the leader of the United States and Mexican Boundary Survey, which lasted for half a dozen years, concluding in 1856. Lieutenant Couch's independent natural history survey was in the same spirit as the more sophisticated, organized, and expensive expeditions undertaken by the army. Couch had some support from the Smithsonian, though generally he was his own sponsor. For a fortnight Couch traveled in and about Brownsville, collecting birds, animals, insects, and snakes. "Although I have been here fourteen days," he wrote Spencer Baird, "I have done but little. Some 25 or thirty birds badly put up, a few snakes, quadrepeds [sic], and insects is all I can show—and yet I have worked." His insect collection was minuscule, for which he blamed the weather. He had not collected fishes, because a comrade in arms and exploration, Capt. Stewart Van Vliet, was so engaged on the Brazos River. Couch hired a Mexican servant to assist and inquired of him and others where to look for specimens.[4]

Couch's inquiries paid off a hundredfold. He learned from his servant of a local savant named Berlandier, recently deceased, who had lived at Matamoros and who was well known throughout the valley for his journeys and writings; observations about the multiple fields of natural history; collections of flora, fauna, artifacts, and specimens; drawings, watercolors, and maps; and skill as an apothecary and a physician. Couch's Mexican servant was the former assistant, or ayudante, to the savant. He informed Couch that the widow of the savant of Matamoros still retained the collection—how complete and in what condition was uncertain. Couch's servant took him to

Matamoros to the widow's home. She was Mexican, though Couch understood that the savant had been Swiss. They had been together many years,
though married only in the last few, and had children; a daughter had married a Mexican infantry captain. Although almost two years had passed since
her husband's demise, the widow had maintained the collection, the extent,
variety, quality, and singularity of which excited Couch, who felt on his several visits that he was entering a museum when he walked through the door of
the dwelling of physician and wife and apothecary shop. The widow showed
Couch an extensive, well-preserved collection of insects in glass cases—this
collection alone occupied the space of a small room. Couch counted 150 bottles in which specimens of birds, snakes, lizards, turtles, and other invertebrates were preserved in alcohol. There were many boxes (75 cubic feet) of
plants—some well preserved, some not—and minerals of all types. The savant
had extensively and precisely catalogued his entire collection. Couch discovered that the savant was an artist and cartographer as well; he examined the
many drawings and watercolors of landscapes, plants, birds, and indigenous
peoples. There were dozens of maps of locations in Texas and Mexico that
the savant had drawn on his journeys. There were as many sketches of landscapes he had seen along the way. Meteorology, astronomy, and geography
had interested the savant as well, as illustrated by the many journals and
manuscripts recording measurements of latitude with the sextant; temperature readings in Fahrenheit, Celsius, and Réaumur; barometer readings from
heights and valleys; celestial observations of planets and moons; measurements of the blueness of the sky by the cyanometer; and varied descriptions
of landforms and landscapes in Mexico and Texas. Also amazing were the
"piles of manuscripts"—extensive journals recounting journeys to various
river valleys in Texas; to locations along the Texas and Mexican Gulf Coast;
to the Mississippi River and New Orleans; to the Sierra Madre Oriental, specifically the Sierra de Tamaulipas; to the towns of the states of Tamaulipas
and Nuevo León; to Tampico from Le Havre de Grace, from Tampico to
Mexico City, from Mexico City to Laredo, and from Laredo to San Antonio.
There were also diaries of specific events, such as the American occupation of
Matamoros in 1846. The many essays on natural history included "Animals of
New Spain"; "Invertebrates"; "Notes on Zoology of the State of Tamaulipas";
"Notes on Animal Temperature"; "Physiology"; "Reptiles and Amphibians";
"Zoology"; "Botany"; "Fishes"; "Mammals"; "Birds"; "Insects"; "Meteorology
and the Physics of the Globe"; "Meteorology: Means of Observations and
Computations"; "Coyote of Mexico"; "Natural History of Plants Employed in

the Art of Medicine from the Ancient Mexicans to the Moderns"; and "Plants Used Among the Indians of Mexico." Accounts of human history in the savant's collection included "Gazetteer of Mexico"; "Mexican Antiquities"; "Notes on the Mexican Revolution"; "Notes Useful for the History of the Internal Provinces"; "Principal Periods in the History of Mexico"; and "Notes on the Coast Lands between Matamoros and Refugio." The manuscripts were written in French or Spanish.[5]

Lieutenant Couch asked what amount of money would convince the widow to part with the collection. The savant had wished his collection to go to Geneva, where he was once a student, or at least to Mexico City, perhaps to be archived at the library. But the widow was in need of money; she responded to Couch that $1,500 would purchase the collection. Couch thought about it for several days, then sent a note by the ayudante with a counteroffer of $500; the widow declined but sent her daughter's husband, the *capitán*, to counter Couch's offer; Couch declined. On February 15, the widow sent word that she would accept Couch's offer of $500. Even if he got his price, the amount was still exorbitant for the soldier. But he convinced himself of the collection's ultimate value to science, that it would be scattered and forgotten if it stayed with the widow, and that the Americans, especially the scientists and archivists at the Smithsonian, would take better care of it than the Mexicans. "I purchase it," he told Baird, "because it's too valuable to general science to let remain and rot in Matamoras." Couch fully expected that many new species would be found in "the collection," which "is a labor of 24 years and ranges from the Sabine to California." Even though Couch was the owner, he would not steal the fire of discovery from the dead—the savant of Matamoros would receive full credit for his discoveries.[6]

Spencer Fullerton Baird of the Smithsonian was justly excited by Couch's news: "I fully expected when you left that you would be instrumental in securing to our country such important material for developing its history." The importance of the collection and the best plan for preserving and publishing it were still to be decided. Determining so many insect species would take, perhaps, years. Baird wrote explicit instructions on how to pack and ship the collection. "Ship right off," he wrote. "Be careful in packing, not to put tender and coarse articles together: for instance don't pack minerals with plant bottles! Better take the specimens out of bottles and put in Lino bags. And by all means have the kegs and vessels perfectly full." Couch's acquisition, which made Baird "feverish" in expectation of seeing it, ensured that Couch would be able to have a considerable extension to his leave of absence from the army.

"I can now accomplish anything I desire," he told the lieutenant, respecting the impact of Couch's discovery on the Washington political and scientific community, "in regard to this matter."[7]

Couch, meanwhile, in the few weeks after his purchase, packed the glass cases of insects, invertebrates suspended in bottles, plants well preserved, mineral specimens, and scientific data and some drawings, preparing a total of three dozen boxes for shipment to Washington via New Orleans. "One box of valuable manuscripts, paintings, &c is . . . left behind," kept with himself, because of their apparent worth, and perhaps because Couch wished to make use of them in his own journey. "Unfortunately for me," Couch confessed to Baird, "the manuscripts are in French or Spanish, neither of which I read well." Fortunately, Berlandier's script was easy to read, notwithstanding the language, and he often illustrated his narrative with maps and drawings.[8]

A slight man with deep-set eyes, a receding hairline of brown hair, and a full beard, Couch was energetic and impatient with delays and frustrated by his own lack of accomplishments. Although he had achieved quite a coup in purchasing the savant's collection, he still wished to make his own discoveries. He planned an extensive excursion south to Monterrey and west to the Mexican Plateau. He hired two mules and another servant, along with the ayudante. Berlandier's former servant impressed Couch; the ayudante had learned from his association with the savant and knew something about the materia medica of the region. The three men set off toward Monterrey around the first of March; Couch left the three dozen boxes of the collection in the care of friend and fellow naturalist Captain Van Vliet, who shipped them to Washington in Couch's absence. Before he departed, Couch heard that some Mexicans were displeased with the widow Berlandier for selling the materials; an offer of the original $1,500 asking price was also floated about; but Couch was convinced that the collection was too important to science to remain "unknown"—he would not sell. The mules hired for the journey were uncooperative, forcing Couch's return after a fortnight to Brownsville because, Couch wrote Baird, the "pack mules did not work well, and now am to do what Captain Vliet first proposed to me, take wheels," that is, wagons. Such delays weighed heavily on the naturalist, who perchance took to trying to make out the sense of some of Berlandier's journals.[9]

Couch and his Mexican guides set forth from Matamoros for Monterrey on March 15, 1853. The ayudante eschewed the most direct route overland through Tamaulipas to Nuevo León, opting to parallel rivers, first the Rio Grande, then the Río San Juan. One gathers from Couch's barely legible and partially lost journal that he chose a leisurely pace, taking the time to search for birds, snakes, and lizards, collecting any that in his estimation would be new to science. Ticks plagued the men. The sun beat down and browned their skin. "The whole line of the road to the San Juan is ugly and uninteresting," Couch wrote; "in April when nature should be decked out in its gayest attire the dry hills and parched valleys paint a picture of desolation and sadness." The people along the way were more interesting, and Couch pronounced the men of the San Juan valley to be strong, courageous, and patriotic, having fought well, he recalled, during the war under Gen. Antonio Canales Rosillo. Arriving at China, also situated on the Río San Juan, Couch wrote that it was a "village of about 800 or 1000 people—houses of sandstone adobe and stakes in the suburbs, all miserably constructed having the reputation of extreme poverty." Couch, a young soldier and bachelor, constantly commented on the comparative attractiveness of the local population. He thought most women along the San Juan valley were not attractive; however, at China "some few seen going to church on a feast have quite pretty faces and walked gracefully." Couch stayed a few days at China while a religious festival was going on, which he eschewed though his guides probably attended; meanwhile, he roamed about the woods, noting the vegetation, such as acacia, mimosa, and cypress trees, reminding himself, parenthetically, to consult the Berlandier manuscripts for further details. From China they pursued the path to Monterrey by way of Cadereyta and Montemorelos, journeying southwest over an arid land with little in the way of food for man or beast. Heat, dust, rattlesnakes, and, according to the ayudante, bandits, were, however, plentiful; Couch had a run-in with a rattlesnake but not a bandit. He also had occasion to join muleteers around the campfire; he agreed with Berlandier that "the faithful muleteer forgets his daily toil God bestows upon him so many blessings. This class of people are perfectly trustworthy and genuinely brave. Treasure or valuables placed in their hands for transport will be safely delivered to its destination unless overpowered by robbers. Generally of mixed blood their habits are identical with those of the same craft in Old Spain." In recent years, muleteers hitched their mules to wagons, many of which were left behind by Taylor's army when the fighting stopped. Haciendas often took the place of villages. These huge plantations covered thousands of acres and employed hundreds of the poorest class of Mexican, the peon, who worked from dawn to dusk and slept in adobe hovels, "compared to which the [slave] cabins on the lower Mississippi are palaces." The inhabitants, and therefore visitors such as Couch, ate tortillas and frijoles. Arriving at Cadereyta, a city of about twelve thousand, Couch found himself in the shadow of the Sierra Madre. As they did his predecessor on the trail Berlandier, the peaks and valleys fascinated Couch, who spent much time observing and estimating heights and distances. Staying at a rancho (called Boguello), a small settlement of various families formed for mutual defense and economic benefit, he took time to ascend one of the peaks. Couch and his guides followed the descending Río San Juan, upriver, toward Monterrey. At one stop, they accompanied the locals to a cave filled with bats that served as a sanctuary for mass.[10]

They journeyed north of the Sierra Madre on the "Camino Real," which was "a thoroughfare of considerable trade," accompanied by muleteers and other travelers. They finally reached Monterrey, "which contains about 25 thousand inhabitants generally industrious," Couch wrote in his journal; "since the American war it has greatly increased in prosperity and wealth (an air of thrift and business pervades rarely seen in a Mexican city). In every quarter new buildings are going up and old ones remodeled; large trains of wagons and pack mules fill the streets bringing imported goods." Couch examined the city strategically, as if it were still 1846 and he was positioning his cannon for bombardment: "As the road approaches Monterrey the surface becomes more even; at 5 or 600 yards from the plaza a gentle surface swell would have given General Taylor an excellent position for sinking a battery and bombarding the city at his pleasure." The old fort that defended the town against the American advance was in decay, as was the palace of the Roman Catholic bishop. At Monterrey, Couch organized his working collection gathered along the way; it was hardly satisfactory. For so much work, he had little to show: half a dozen snakes, a "tolerable collection" of lizards, a few frogs, and fishes. He feared that much of what he had collected would be lost, because of inadequate supplies for preservation. He was more successful in locating different species of birds. He found his guides trustworthy, even if they did little of the work; Couch complained to Baird that "my servants are gentlemen, am I the servant"? His daily regimen was to rise at five in the morning, "eat two or three cold tortillas," then go exploring until noon or afternoon, when he returned to quarters exhausted. He stayed for a fortnight in and about Monterrey, exploring, collecting, observing, and recording. An injury to his shoulder caused him constant pain—the same "rheumatism" had bothered him six years before on the eve of the Battle of Buenavista, southwest of Monterrey. The people distrusted "los Americanos," particularly one who was a former soldier; Couch's propensity to examine the landscape from the perspective of a military officer looking for the most strategic advantages did not counter the opinion that the inhabitants formed of him. Couch nevertheless found them civil and hospitable. He was heavily dependent on the knowledge and guidance of the ayudante and the other guide. Couch continually relied upon the ayudante to help him with the materia medica of the land, often because he himself needed the healing relief of salves and analgesics.[11]

From Monterrey, Couch and his guides journeyed southwest toward Saltillo, negotiating the same gorge of rising elevation that Berlandier had passed through going the opposite direction, twenty-five years earlier. After visiting the town of Santa Catarina, Couch, the ayudante, and the other guide proceeded "southeasterly a couple of miles or so" to "a break or pass through [which] flows Rio de Monterey for a half a mile by impassable cliffs; after passing through this gap we found a continued succession of chains or ranges of the Sierra for 20 miles; a few ranchos are here and there sprinkled, inhabited by mestizos or pure Indians," which Couch branded as "the most villainous set of people imaginable. To them murder is not crime if a foreigner is the victim; it's a meritorious act; of a wealthy native a confession is made only when Charon rings his last bell for the trip across the Styx." The men ascended toward the Mexican Plateau. Along the way Couch questioned the ayudante about his former employer. The onetime apothecary's assistant told Couch that Berlandier had related bits and pieces about his life: how he had come to Mexico from Switzerland years before, when he was in his early twenties, sent on a mission by other savants in Geneva who wished to have a complete botanical collection of the flora of northern Mexico. Couch, who was clearly interested in finding out more about this man who had spent so many years creating a natural history and museum of the Rio Grande valley, had begun to peruse Berlandier's own story, related in the pages of the manuscript journal *Voyage au Mexique.* Couch would have found Berlandier's autobiographical comment that he had been "born in misery, accustomed to all of life's privations."[12] How could a person born in poverty rise to become someone of such learning and wisdom, a savant?

In April, Lt. Darius Nash Couch and his two guides and companions set out from Saltillo journeying west into the state of Coahuila toward the town of Parras. The route was somewhat familiar to Couch, as he had come this way in late 1846; the Hacienda de Buenavista, where the battle of the same name was fought in February 1847, was just a few miles to the south.

Saltillo, the capital of the state of Coahuila, was fertile and pretty, its buildings painted in different colors, its churches beautiful. Couch had spent time in convalescence at Saltillo in the first few weeks of January 1847, under the care of Capt. Charles Hitchcock, an army physician who had been looking after Couch ever since the lieutenant's arrival to Mexico. Hitchcock was a young West Point graduate like Couch and had been deployed to Mexico at the same time as Couch. After the Battle of Buenavista, Couch had explored the town in the spring, noting that Saltillo had a "bountiful supply of running water" that produced "gardens" that, he recalled, had been "smiling in fresh Spring flowers." The image of "the prettiest senorita" stayed with him still. Saltillo was in a snug valley between two cordilleras. Arroyos cut deep trenches, called *barrancas* by the locals, into the ground. The landscape continued to fascinate Couch, just as it had during the war, when he wrote in his journal: "There is a world of cacti in this region, growing in immense size some of them, and such cruel spikes, which will penetrate leather." He recalled that the ground of the Battle of Buenavista was such a cactus world, devoid of all trees. In the weeks after the battle, while Zachary Taylor's army was encamped in the region around Saltillo, Couch had explored the surrounding mountains with "a six-shooter in my belt and a sharp sabre by my side"; he had discovered a "scenery" that "was wild and beautiful" and had seen "new animals, birds, and plants," resolving someday to return and, as a naturalist rather than a soldier, discover them anew.[13]

Couch estimated the journey to Parras at 185 miles. The arid landscape between Saltillo and Parras was, like much of Mexico, an ironic mosaic of utter poverty experienced by the majority of the inhabitants contrasted with the magnificent wealth of the few grand landowners. Fantastically large yucca trees, their bayonet-like leaves piercing the air, provided visual diversion for the weary travelers. Prickly pear was everywhere. Couch continued to collect samples of flora and record his experiences and observations. "Between Saltillo and Parras," Couch wrote Baird, "the people were in continual alarm from the incursions of Northern Indians; this state of things greatly impeded my labors." By the time they reached the valley town Parras, Couch had, perhaps, struggled with his mediocre French in reading *Voyage au Mexique* to know, at least, that the ayudante was correct in asserting that the pilgrim Berlandier had joined the Comisión de Límites, which Couch understood to be similar to the United States and Mexican Boundary Survey, in which the secretary of war sent expeditions of topographical engineers and other scientist-soldiers to survey the post–Mexican War boundary between the United States and Mexico.[14]

The unnamed ayudante who traveled with Darius Couch through Mexico in the spring of 1853, and who had begun to inform him about the savant of Matamoros, doubtlessly felt a little like the savant Berlandier had decades before. The ayudante was a young man in his early twenties, as was Berlandier in 1827. Like Berlandier, who had traveled with the military-scientific Comisión de Límites, the ayudante was traveling on a scientific expedition with the soldier-scientist Darius Couch. And, like young man Berlandier, the ayudante had learned from a savant about botany and materia medica. The ayudante did, however, lack certain qualities of his mentor, such as perseverance, constancy, and courage.

Couch and guides arrived at Parras (Parras de la Fuente) in early May. The surrounding landscape was fertile and rich, enclosed by mountains of varying elevations that were generally barren of vegetation. Parras had fine buildings and homes. Couch recalled that when he had first seen Parras in December 1846, some of the inhabitants had a haughty, aristocratic demeanor. Departing Parras west to the Bolsón de Mapimí, Couch, the ayudante, and the other guide heard continuing reports of Indian aggression from the isolated rancheros of the Chihuahuan Desert; indeed, the Bolsón de Mapimí was a traditional camping site for the Comanche in their raiding expeditions from the Rio Grande. Couch was, however, unrelenting. The two Mexican guides finally grew too frightened to continue and demanded that they return to Parras. Couch had no choice but to turn back. From Parras they marched back to Saltillo and then Monterrey, where Couch, the ayudante, and the other Mexican parted ways. It was not just the American Indian threat that had impelled the ayudante to break with Couch; there was also Couch's worry over the security of his personal possessions, which erupted into suspicion about the supposed criminal designs of his guides. Couch's sextant-chronometer, which he used to calculate longitude, although it did not properly work, was such an object of fascination and temptation for thievery among the local people (and perhaps his companions?) that it was not worth carrying. More concerning was that Couch narrowly escaped "being murdered," by whom it is not clear, except that his journey from Saltillo west was an object of suspicion by the local authorities, one of whom, wrote Couch, "openly said that my intentions were not pacific, my true object being to search out their strong points in the mountains." Couch's condescending attitude toward the Mexicans perhaps opened himself up to such charges. "I am the first American of standing," he wrote Baird, "that has been through here publicly [since] during the war, and the mass are very bitter against the Americans." The ayudante could hardly have felt comfortable, or even above suspicion himself, traveling with and assisting an American soldier. Couch confided to Baird that he was disappointed by his apparent failure and wished that he had obtained "a commission from the [Smithsonian] Institution and gone to the City of Mexico first" to acquire official sanction for his journey so to forestall the attempts by local authorities to interfere with his plans. Couch was not the type to quit so easily, however. Although the relationship between Lieutenant Couch and the ayudante was at an end, Couch had learned much about the savant Berlandier from the ayudante, knowledge that he would continue to refer to in the coming months and years.[15]

At some point on the trail, the ayudante informed Couch that after the Comisión de Límites was dissolved around 1830, Berlandier had settled in Matamoros, where he worked as a physician and an apothecary. The ayudante further stated, as Couch recalled in a letter to Spencer Baird in November 1854, when he had returned to active duty and was stationed at Fort Leavenworth, that Berlandier "was universally beloved for his kind amiable manner and regard for the sick poor of that city, being always ready to give advice and medicine to such without pay. He followed a very general custom in that country, living with a woman as his Mistress, but married her a short time before his death. The result of this connexion was several children—one of them being married to a Captain of Mexican Infantry." Couch had met this capitán when negotiating with the widow to purchase her husband the savant's collection.[16]

Of the many details about Berlandier's life that Couch had learned from the ayudante—that a young pharmacist's apprentice from Geneva, Switzerland, had journeyed throughout Mexico and Texas, had hunted with the Comanches, had several times escaped death from violence and sickness, had settled down to become a respected physician in the city of Matamoros— none was as astonishing as what the ayudante told Couch about Berlandier's role during the two-year war between Mexico and the United States from 1846 to 1848. Couch learned that Berlandier had held an officer's commission during the war; that he had met with Gen. Zachary Taylor in March 1846, "previous to [Taylor] crossing the [Arroyo] Colorado and order[ed] him to remain on the left bank of the river" and not to approach the Nueces; that he had served several Mexican commanders as a close adviser—General Arista, who had recognized the scientist's talents as a "geographer and statistician," had used Berlandier "in making maps, sketches, etc. of the country adjacent to the Rio Grande"; and that Berlandier had been a war surgeon "in charge of the hospitals" in Matamoros.[17]

Notwithstanding the loss of the ayudante as his guide, Couch refused to give up. In Monterrey he found two more wilderness guides to assist him, the first an unnamed "muleteer . . . said to be without fear," a necessary trait for one about to enter a dangerous wilderness; "besides," Couch wrote Baird, he "will replace my mules without cost if they should tire out." The other was "an educated German" by the name of Jacob Weare, who "is of undoubted bravery and has a knowledge [of] Mexican customs." Weare would "be a sort of companion" for Couch on his "natural history" journey to the lands "west of Parras." As before, Couch was to proceed to the Mexican hinterland armed with "a small box of medicines," besides making it his "*entire* business to collect plants for medicinal purposes, with doctoring now and then." It was not to be, however. Probably because his new servants heard more alarming reports of Comanche aggression, Couch again had to change his plans; he dropped the proposed western journey for a southern one through Tamaulipas across the Pánuco River into Veracruz and west into the "Huastacea country," as he wrote in a letter to Spencer Baird. But it never came about. Rather, he recalled in a letter over a year later, "it became expedient to cancel the journey and return to the United States." Long nights on the road and by sea from Monterrey to Matamoros across the Rio Grande and back home to Massachusetts were spent, one imagines, in vicarious journeys to Tamaulipas and beyond, courtesy of the journals of Jean Louis Berlandier.[18]

After his foray into Mexico, Couch married and was reassigned to Fort Leavenworth, where he continued to stay in touch with Spencer Baird and to peruse the Berlandier materials in his possession. Couch even tried his hand at translating Berlandier's account of his journey with the Comanches on a hunting expedition west of San Antonio in the autumn of 1828. He reworked his journal kept on his 1853 expedition to Mexico, editing and adding material, with the aim, never realized, of publication.[19]

Having donated the largest part of the Berlandier collection to the Smithsonian, Couch offered to sell the remainder, which included manuscripts and paintings, to recoup his initial $500 investment. The restrained budget of the Smithsonian would not allow the purchase, so Couch went elsewhere, selling parts of the collection to other interests. Through the agency of Asa Gray, Professor of Natural History at Harvard University, botanist C. W. Short purchased botanical specimens and manuscripts that became the basis for the Berlandier collection at the Gray Herbarium. Short and Gray were disappointed by the quality of the plants; Gray asked Baird for a character portrait of Berlandier, which Couch provided in a letter of

November 16, 1854. Although Couch had a positive appraisal of Berlandier's life and character, Gray chose to pay more attention to the literary complaints of Augustin Pyramus de Candolle and his son Alphonse, who branded Berlandier a liar and sloppy scientist.[20]

Jealous scientists and angry patrons make for a skewed view of a person's character. Berlandier was a scientist who was fascinated more by nature than himself. He left behind precious few details of his life and character, which can be reconstructed only by a close attention to his journals and other writings. The figure that emerges is of a man who sought knowledge rather than power, an understanding of nature rather than wealth, a life of an obscure savant rather than fame, the activity of exploration rather than the passivity of contemplation.

CHAPTER TWO

Lock of the Rhône

⚘

⚘ DURING HIS YEARS LIVING AND TRAVELING IN MEXICO AND TEXAS, the savant of Matamoros, Jean Louis Berlandier, returned to the images of his youth as the standard for comparison of human culture and society and natural history. He examined and analyzed the mountains of America according to his recollection of the Jura Mountains and the Alps of High Savoy, and American rivers next to the standard of the Rhône and Arve. The Rhône in particular had lodged itself completely in his mind, indeed was one of the foundation memories of his youth. In adolescence and adulthood, after Berlandier had gone to Geneva to work and learn, he knew the Rhône as the great source of the crystal waters of Lake Geneva; many times he had walked next to the Rhône where it emerged from the lake, soon to join with its muddy counterpart, the Arve, arriving from Savoy and the highlands of Mont Blanc. His more fundamental childhood memories were of a narrow defile, a gorge of forbidding walls of stone, at the bottom of which a narrow river flowed toward Lyons, Marseilles, and the sea. Here the mountain walls opened slightly to allow the river through. In a past geologic age a key, as it were, had been inserted into the mighty limestone mountains that formed an impenetrable barrier between Switzerland, Savoy, and France; the turning of the key opened the lock, creating a gap in mountain walls through which the river could flow. The place was known as l'Ecluse, The Lock, and for thousands of years it was a place where peoples fought and died to have the power to turn the key.[1]

Berlandier lived in Geneva after the defeat of Napoleon, at a time when the city had been freed from French domination to become an independent republic, part of a confederation called the Helvetic, after the ancient Germanic Helvetii peoples. The Roman general Julius Caesar, in his *Gallica*, provided one of the earliest accounts of the Helvetii trying to force the lock of the Rhône. The Helvetii were a warlike people who sought to migrate west into Gaul through the pass in the Jura Mountains, and to cross the Rhône from south to north. Caesar fortified the banks of the Rhône from Lake Geneva to l'Ecluse, which prevented the Helvetii from crossing the Rhône, though Caesar could do little to prevent them from passing through the lock along the southern banks of the river. Eventually, downstream, the Romans and Helvetii met in battle; the Romans were victorious. Berlandier, whose subsequent literary and scientific talents revealed that he was a gifted child, doubtless knew the story of the Helvetii as Caesar told it. The image of tall Germanic warriors facing the disciplined, well-armed Roman troops provided the stuff of imagination for many young Savoyans, Swiss, and French who lived along the Rhône valley. The romantic mind recalled other deeds of the heroic past, such as the attempts to hold the pass by the dukes of Savoy for centuries during the medieval and early modern periods. When Berlandier was growing up during the Napoleonic years, the fort served as an important key to defending eastern France. In the wake of the destruction of Napoleon's army that ensued as it retreated from Russia in 1812, the Austrians were emboldened to pursue the advantage against a weakened France; they stormed Fort l'Ecluse in 1814, repulsing the French defenders, some of whom were old or otherwise decrepit and unfit for regular service.[2]

Such are the fragmentary records of Jean Luis Berlandier's life that it is unclear whether he lived on the grounds of Fort l'Ecluse, and if he did, when and why. His mentor Augustin Pyramus de Candolle, the Swiss botanist, years later in his *Mémoires* provided scant details of the lives of his former students, including the tidbit that Berlandier had grown up in the neighborhood of Fort l'Ecluse. His intelligence and accomplishments as a student in Geneva make it doubtful that Berlandier was the son of peasants. His later interests in military affairs and easy familiarity with common foot and horse soldiers of northern Mexico and southern Texas are persuasive evidence that he was the son of a French soldier at Fort l'Ecluse. The Mexican soldiers of frontier presidios, such as at Laredo and San Antonio, were rarely paid, and even when they were, the money was insufficient. Berlandier empathized with the impoverished soldiers and their families, perhaps because they reminded him of his own father and mother. Soldiers of the remote outpost of Fort l'Ecluse were similarly poor. When the Austrians destroyed l'Ecluse in 1814, Berlandier was about ten years old. Perhaps his innate curiosity had compelled him to watch from the stony fort as the Austrians marched in the wake of Caesar, having descended the Arve to the Rhône and followed it the short distance to the defile held by the French. The French under Napoleon had improved upon the already formidable fortifications of the fort. Nevertheless, after intense fighting lasting over twenty-four hours, in which both sides suffered many casualties, the French were forced to surrender.[3]

By the time of its destruction, the fort was already an ancient edifice of stone standing imposingly over the Rhône. A stone fortification of some sort had existed at the site for at least five hundred years; before that, religious recluses had found the sublimity of the peaks and valley, with Mont Blanc sitting grandly to the south, a perfect place for lonely spiritual contemplation. The angle of the slopes was, according to one observer, seventy-five degrees, hence difficult to ascend. The northern slope rising almost perpendicularly above the stream was part of the Jura mountain chain that extended southwest to northeast, forming a natural boundary between Switzerland and France. The Rhône separated the Jura from hills known as La Vuache, part of the mountainous terrain east of the Rhône River that divided Savoy and France. Fort l'Ecluse was in some ways typical for its time. The passageways were dark and narrow, the bare stone cold and damp. Stone masons had fitted large and small stones neatly to form seamless walls built into the rock of the mountainside. Gun turrets enclosed small cannon, while smaller turrets secured small-arms fire. A massive iron gate kept attackers out. The fort had a commanding situation, looking out upon the Rhône valley.[4]

Growing up amid the small peaks of the Jura Mountains and La Vuache, Mont Blanc always looming in the distance, Berlandier felt at home in a mountainous environment, whether in the Alps of Europe or, later, the Sierra Madre of Mexico. As the great sixteenth-century Swiss naturalist Konrad Gesner discovered, the heights of hills and mountains give the naturalist a vision of the diversity and perspective of the Earth, changing elevations echoing changing seasons, rivers winding through mountains in artistic relief, the sun rising earlier and setting later, clouds and constellations seemingly at arm's length. The naturalist, armed by the powers of vision and perspective provided by height and distance, senses the expansion of space, the symbiotic workings of the environment, the smallness of the individual human. Such awareness inspires a further quest to seek and discover, to acquire knowledge. At the same time, the alpine environment in which Berlandier matured suggested the wonders of the minutiae of nature, the smallest flower holding its own in the contrary mountain weather. Alpine flowers such as edelweiss have inspired many a young nature lover to discover the inner workings and external utility of such beauty. Humans have for millennia found in simple plants of unassuming beauty growing in the most unlikely of places, even rocky alpine summits, the means of curing illness, relieving pain, countering depression, and preventing sickness. The materia medica of mountainous environments became the object of study for many young French, Swiss, and Genevan students; Jean Louis Berlandier during the second decade of the nineteenth century became one of these prospective pharmacologists.[5]

How Berlandier became apprenticed to a Genevan apothecary is lost to time. Perhaps his parents had such wisdom and foresight, recognizing their son's intellectual abilities, that they sent him to Geneva. Perhaps the Berlandier family, in the wake of France's defeat, relocated to the Swiss city, where the boy was apprenticed. The institution of apprenticeship was, before the Industrial Revolution, the means by which poor children could learn a craft from a master. The apprentice lived with the master's family, repaying the master with work. Apprenticeship in Geneva during the centuries before the beginning of the Industrial Revolution was typically in the craft of watch- and clock-making. The chance to become an apprentice in the exclusive manufacture of watches in Geneva was often reserved for Genevese. That he was Protestant rather than Catholic, and possibly arrived in Geneva before 1815, when the Swiss city was under French authority, perhaps allowed Berlandier an easier time integrating himself into the old Calvinist capitol. Berlandier had a work mentality that fit Geneva quite well. Max Weber's idea of the Protestant ethic was inspired by such Protestants as the people of Geneva, who devoted their lives to work, production, and profit. The city had extensive trade, even outside of Europe, the Rhône being the means of exporting timepieces. The citizens of Geneva were wealthy, in part because they knew how to use the labor of the surrounding poor of the Jura and Savoy regions. Perhaps members of Berlandier's family had at times worked as *ébaucheurs*, contractors who manufactured some of the metal components of Genevan watches. The ébaucheurs were exploited, but it was work. Geneva was, then, a wealthy city toward which the young Berlandier journeyed at some point during the second decade of the nineteenth century.[6]

Berlandier, living in Mexico from 1827 to his death in 1851, was a prolific scientist, writer, explorer, and physician; his habit for hard work was doubtless learned or at least honed during his lengthy residence in Geneva. The city was a place for the independent thinker. During the years of French control, when Napoleon ruled, the Genevese refused to acquiesce, blatantly favored the English, and served in French armies only with reluctant despair. Geneva was, nevertheless, French-speaking, as it was long an asylum for persecuted Huguenots. The city was fortified by an encircling wall, the gates of which closed precisely at ten o'clock p.m. After the fall of Napoleon, when Geneva was a member of the Helvetic Confederacy of Swiss states, the canton was open and egalitarian, befitting the romantic movement in Europe. Geneva's climate and natural beauty brought artists, poets, and writers such as Mary Shelley and Lord Byron. Travelers commented on the narrow streets of the city and its pedestrian malls. The climate, like most mountain locations, was usually foggy, misty, rainy, or snowy. On fair days, sunrises and sunsets were spectacular. Mary Shelley, residing at Lake Geneva in June 1816, gloried in the rosy horizon as the sun set behind the Jura Mountains. The population, nearly thirty thousand when Berlandier lived there, was noted for its culture, literacy, and learning; young people such as Berlandier attended the excellent Geneva Academy, which featured a classical liberal arts education. Geneva was an intellectually cosmopolitan city that combined a strong Protestant religious tradition with a skeptical Enlightenment scientific worldview as well as the focus on sentiments and feelings characteristic of the European romantics. Geneva savants included Jean André de Luc, the meteorologist, geologist, and alpinist; Horace Bénédict de Saussure, the physicist, geologist, and author of *Voyages dans les Alpes*—Berlandier used Saussure's cyanometer on his journey to Mexico to register the extent of blue in the sky; Jean Pierre Vaucher, theologian and botanist; and Pierre Prévost, the noted classicist, philosopher, and physicist. Prévost, who developed basic principles of heat exchange, became one of Berlandier's mentors. Prévost was in his youth a friend of philosopher Jean-Jacques Rousseau, who like Prévost was born in Geneva, though Rousseau spent his life elsewhere in France. The French philosopher and writer Voltaire retired in Geneva, and visitors constantly sought out his chateau.[7]

Berlandier mirrored intellectuals and writers of his time. Like fellow Genevese Rousseau, Berlandier combined skepticism toward traditional religious and scientific dogma with an emotional response to the beauties of nature and human thoughts and feelings. A form of rational Protestantism suggestive of Arminianism subtly hides between the lines of Berlandier's journals. He was particularly suspicious of religious superstitions, such as those practiced by Spanish priests throughout the Mexican dominions. Praying to the saints and the Virgin or saying prayers over holy relics, Berlandier believed, could do little to cure disease and hasten recovery. He criticized the ostentation of Catholic parish buildings that loomed above the huts of impoverished peasants in European as well as Mexican towns. Farmers' tithes and gifts to enrich the church sacrificed their family's material needs to guarantee eternal reward; parish priests and missionaries, ostensibly vowed to poverty, welcomed such gifts to lessen the cares of life.[8]

The most celebrated Genevan scientist during Berlandier's residency was Augustin Pyramus de Candolle, Berlandier's mentor at Geneva Academy, where Candolle taught from 1816 until his death in 1841. Candolle was an original thinker and a superb scientist, and he knew it—his *Mémoires* is an indulgent exercise in vanity. A native Genevese, Candolle studied in Paris under the likes of Georges Cuvier and Jean-Baptiste Lamarck, taught briefly at the Collège de France, and for eight years at the University of Montpellier, during which he began his *Prodromus Systematis Naturalis*, an encyclopedic work and labor of many years, in which Candolle classified and systematized the extent of the world's flora as then known; Candolle continued to produce volumes of the *Prodromus* until his death in 1841. After the fall of Napoleon, Candolle returned to Geneva, where he taught at the Academy. Candolle was a descriptive botanist who, like his student Berlandier, focused on morphology, system, and symmetry rather than physiology and function. Candolle was interested in changes and irregularities in plants, in which he anticipated Darwin, if slightly, though he was devoted to the philosophy of "constancy in species."[9]

Candolle, like all nineteenth-century botanists, worked in the shadow of Carl Linnaeus, who had developed the binomial classification of plants according to genus and species, distinguishing plants largely by sexual properties. Linnaeus believed in a broad community of science and had scientific correspondents around the world, especially in America, a virgin land for the botanist. Linnaeus cultivated protégés whom he sent on voyages to America, Asia, Africa, and elsewhere, collecting specimens that were identified in subsequent editions of his *Systema*. Some of these traveling students had great success, such as Peter Kalm, who journeyed to America in 1748. Others were not so successful, such as Daniel Solander, who accompanied James Cook on his worldwide *Endeavour* expedition from 1768 to 1771, and who never sent Linnaeus any specimens. Augustin Pyramus de Candolle like-wise encouraged protégés whom he could send into the world on botanical expeditions. His most famous was a young student at the Geneva Academy whom Candolle, like Linnaeus, sent on Herculean tasks. Candolle would subsequently wallow in disappointment when the ideal of perfect specimens sent back by the dozens was not accomplished. Candolle, in his *Mémoires et Souvenirs*, published posthumously in 1862, condemned Berlandier for send-ing dried-up and worthless specimens from the Mexican frontier. Others—Candolle's son Alphonse de Candolle and Harvard professor Asa Gray—also branded Berlandier a dishonest failure. All the while, until his unexpected death in 1851, Jean Louis Berlandier faithfully traveled throughout the Mexican frontier, participating in numerous expeditions into wilderness, treacherous country inhabited by the Comanches and Apaches, suffering repeated privation and risking death again and again, establishing himself as one of the great scientists of northern Mexico, a prolific writer on numer-ous scientific subjects, and an expert on the indigenous American tribes.[10]

Candolle had himself journeyed on botanical expeditions into the Alps and Jura Mountains. To be sure such journeys could bring about suffering and fear, even disaster—but these were in the neighborhood of Candolle's youth and adulthood. Berlandier, however, experienced two lives, as it were: one in the familiar alpine regions of France and Switzerland, the other in an altogether different environment, with a different geography, climate, culture, human history, and natural history.

Initially, under Candolle's mentoring, Berlandier had proved his met-tle. He taught himself Latin and Greek and worked tirelessly to understand plant morphology. He joined Candolle on numerous field trips and became involved in the Société de Physique et d'Histoire Naturelle de Genève. Candolle and the other Geneva naturalists of the Société sent Berlandier on a mission down the Rhône to Marseilles to "receive a live ostrich" and return it to Geneva. Berlandier read his paper "Du mode de reproduction par fecon-dation de quelques vegetaux de la famille des Campanulaiees," before the naturalists of the Société in January 1825. This success was followed the fol-lowing year by the publication of this study on gooseberries in the Société's *Memoires.*[11]

For centuries, since the European discovery of the Americas, aristocratic naturalists had spared little expense in contriving to import plants and seeds from the New World. Philadelphia botanist John Bartram had during the mid-eighteenth century earned a living from exploring and gathering and selling seeds to rich European botanists who wanted their own American gardens in London, Paris, or Geneva. The Royal Society of London was a leader in such acquisitions of American floral species. It was natural, then, for the Société de Physique et d'Histoire Naturelle de Genève to have the same institutional aspirations, to compete with the Royal Society, the Société d'Histoire Naturelle de Paris, and similar societies throughout Europe, by acquiring unique floral specimens for its own museum. The problem was, of course, that the acquisition of flora from the New World required active agents working on behalf of European science. The history of American botany has numerous examples of such agents, many of whom were exploited, working in the name of science for the fame of European patrons. John Bartram, for example, explored much of the Appalachian Mountains gathering seeds to ship to his chief European correspondent, Peter Collinson of London. Bartram's son William journeyed to the American southeast under the patronage of John Fothergill, a London physician. Merchants of Liverpool sent English naturalist John Bradbury to America to acquire seeds, especially of cotton species, in 1809; Bradbury explored much of the Missouri valley. Glasgow botanist William Hooker patronized Scottish botanist Thomas Drummond's journeys in Canada and the American South in the 1830s. Frederick Pursh of Germany explored the West Indies and Canada under the patronage of both Europeans and Americans. The work of European and American explorer-botanists resulted in a growing collection and understanding of American flora by the early nineteenth century. Manasseh Cutler explored the northern Appalachians, specifically the alpine environment of Mount Washington, in 1784 and 1804. William Dunbar and Peter Custis explored the Red River and tributaries in 1804 and 1806. Englishman Thomas Nuttall explored the Ohio, Mississippi, Missouri, Red, and Arkansas Rivers in 1818 and 1819. Thomas Say joined the Long Expedition and explored the Canadian River in 1820.[12]

The naturalists of the Geneva Société knew that a relatively unknown aspect of American flora was the region of northern Mexico. Botanists had discovered much about the flora of Latin America. Swiss botanist and Candolle student Heinrich Wydler journeyed to the West Indies, specifically Puerto Rico, in 1827. Wydler was, however, unable to satisfy Candolle's expectations. An associate of Candolle and member of the Geneva society, Marie-Philippe Mercier, had also botanized in the West Indies and was a close correspondent of the Venezuelan botanist José María Vargas, who identified much of the flora of his native land. The Spanish naturally were on the forefront of botanical exploration in their possessions of the Philippines, Peru, Chile, New Granada, and Mexico. The Real Jardín Botánico de Madrid, under the direction of Casimiro Gómez Ortega, its first director in the late eighteenth century, along with Martín Sessé y Lacasta, sponsored a series of scientific expeditions, the Royal Botanical Expedition, throughout Spanish colonial holdings. From 1787 to 1803, Sessé directed a variety of expeditions to specific sites in Mexico, work that culminated, eventually, in the *Flora mexicana*, on which he collaborated with other botanists, such as the Mexican José Mariano Mociño Suárez Losada. Mexican botanist don Vicente Cervantes helped Sessé establish the Royal Botanical Garden of Mexico City, at which Cervantes became professor of botany. (Berlandier visited the Botanical Garden in 1827 and met Cervantes.) The Royal Botanical Expeditions became a model for subsequent expeditions, such as the Mexican Boundary Commission that Berlandier accompanied.[13]

One result of the Royal Botanical Commission was several thousand drawings of plants compiled by Sessé and Mociño, which were brought back to Spain but never published. After Sessé's death, Mociño in France in 1816 chanced to meet Candolle, to whom the old man showed his drawings. Candolle recognized their merit, though they had some inaccuracies, and requested that they be studied and reproduced by the Geneva scientific community. Eventually, Candolle hired a talented artist, Jean Christophe Heyland, who reproduced some of Sessé and Mociño's drawings. Heyland worked for Candolle as botanical illustrator for twenty-four years; one of his students was Jean Louis Berlandier, who perfected his own talent for drawing and painting plants under Heyland's mentorship.[14]

After the many years of mentoring and tutelage, Augustin Pyramus de Candolle arranged for Jean Louis Berlandier to journey to Mexico. Why Candolle selected Berlandier and why Berlandier accepted are questions open to speculation. Berlandier's writings over the course of his lifetime reveal a somewhat rootless personality who looked for opportunities to be on the move. Berlandier, who identified with the great explorer-scientists of the past and his own time, such as the Prussian Alexander von Humboldt, with whose works Berlandier was familiar, wished to imitate their accomplishments. Perhaps Berlandier found the society and culture of Geneva limiting, as he was not native Swiss, which could have presented barriers to advancement, especially since Berlandier was a person without rank, born into poverty. Moreover, his writings reveal a thinker with broad rather than narrow interests, one who would eschew a specific lifetime labor such as Candolle's *Prodromus,* rather seeking a broader range for his interests, embracing all of nature. Whereas Candolle anticipated the increasing development during the nineteenth century of the professional scientist who sought an expertise in one clearly defined object of inquiry, Berlandier's style of scientist mirrored a past time of the gifted amateur who tried not to ignore any worthy object of inquiry, in the end achieving general knowledge about much, expertise about little. Such a thinker must have, in part, a practical personality, must be able to see beyond the immediate object of inquiry, to anticipate what is to come, to encompass the many paths of life and ways to know. Candolle might not have had the awareness to understand Berlandier's wanderlust or broad interests in nature, but he doubtless could tell that Berlandier was more than just a botanist and would never be able to devote his life to one work. What better type of person, among his many students, could be expended from the important work in Geneva to go to a faraway place of uncertain people, potentially hazardous environment, and questionable specimens?

A small but active scientific community had weathered the revolutionary storms that had culminated in Mexican independence in 1821; five years later there continued to be clouds on the horizon warning of imminent conflict and disorder. Candolle had been in correspondence with Lucas Alamán y Escalada, a former student who in 1826 was the Mexican minister of foreign affairs concerned with the distant frontier of Texas, which the Mexicans, like the Spanish before them, struggled to administer and keep. Alamán worked with others similarly worried, such as Gen. Manuel Mier y Terán, about American movements across the Sabine River into Texas as well as the increasing number of Indian tribes migrating from north of the Red River into Texas. Alamán decided to put together an official commission to journey from Mexico City north across the Rio Grande to investigate the problems and potential in Texas. He sought a life scientist to join the expedition, and Candolle suggested Berlandier, who was then in his early twenties. Alamán agreed that Berlandier would, upon arriving in Mexico, join the Mexican Comisión de Límites that was to journey to the territory under dispute between the governments of Mexico and the United States. The commission was to be captained by General Terán and was to include soldiers, artists, mapmakers, and the lone biologist Berlandier.[15]

On an early October day in 1826, Jean Louis Berlandier bade farewell to Geneva, the Rhône, the Arve, l'Ecluse, and Mont Blanc, for, he believed, a couple of years, promising to return to his family, friends, and colleagues after a successful voyage to the New World. Rather like his scientific hero Alexander Humboldt, who explored the Alps and journeyed to America as a young man, to make brilliant discoveries for which he earned great acclaim, returning in triumph to Europe, Berlandier set forth from Geneva intent on making his fortune. He was, however, never to return. It was a final farewell, he would discover, but only years later. Candolle recorded in his *Mémoires* that Berlandier departed Geneva's scientific community with hard feelings, the result of some jesting at his expense; the master suggested that the student was so selfish as to sabotage the scientific goals of the journey, never fulfilling his responsibility to return well-preserved specimens to the Geneva scientists. Berlandier might have been in ill humor at his departure, but his subsequent work and writings do not support the contention that he thereafter childishly refused to cooperate. Rather, the landscape of America imposed upon the expectations and assumptions of Europeans who never traveled there—Berlandier would not be the first scientist or explorer who had his or another's ideals dispelled by the reality of the New World.[16]

From the beginning of his journey Berlandier kept detailed notes. European travelers in America and American travelers in Europe likewise kept and often published their journals of travels. Berlandier also wished to keep a scientific record, a natural history, of his journey to America. His journal became many volumes covering many years and many travels.

The route Berlandier took from Geneva to Paris is uncertain. Perhaps like a contemporary traveler, William Buell Sprague, who made the same journey in March 1828, Berlandier crossed the Jura by wagon or mule, journeyed into Burgundy through the large town of Dijon and the more modest town of Montbard, where the naturalist Georges-Louis Leclerc, Comte de Buffon, had lived, then on to Montereau, where he took passage by boat to Paris on the Seine. After staying in Paris for a few days, he continued by boat down the Seine to its mouth at Le Havre de Grace in Normandy, the great harbor on the English Channel, arriving on October 11. It took a few days for Berlandier to find a ship going to Mexico taking passengers. Captain Reling of the American ship *Hannah Elizabeth*, a schooner taking a load to the Pánuco River in northeast Mexico, who was willing to take on as well a few passengers, signed among others the young scientist. They departed October 14.[17]

Figure 3. Halibut schooner in summer rig. Two topmasts up and all sails spread.
Drawing by Capt. J. W. Collins. NOAA National Marine Fisheries Service.

CHAPTER THREE

Río Pánuco

⚘

✦ JEAN LOUIS BERLANDIER BEGAN HIS JOURNEY TO MEXICO WITH A cloud of anxiety and doubt hanging over him. The uncertainty of his future, the questions that arose about his abilities, or lack thereof, to accomplish the tasks set forth by Augustin Pyramus de Candolle, and the dangers of a long sea voyage to an unknown land mingled with the excitement he felt about journeying across the Atlantic to Mexico to take part in an important scientific expedition. Anxiety so often translates into fears about minor incidents, which befell Berlandier when the ship was ready to sail. Examining his luggage, his mind on the science to come, he could not find a microscope presented to him by Professor Prévost of the Academy before his departure. Prévost had taken the time to instruct Berlandier on the kind of zoological observations he wished the young scientist to make with the microscope, which Berlandier now realized, when it was too late to rectify his mistake, he had neglected to bring. Immediately, Berlandier penned a hasty note to Jules Paul Benjamin Delessert, a botanist who lived in Le Havre, asking him to send for the microscope and forward it. Despite Delessert's efforts, Berlandier never received the microscope. Berlandier nonetheless began his observations as soon as the ship left the Bay of the Seine, entering the English Channel, where while land was still in sight he saw numerous jellyfish.[1]

A strong easterly carried the schooner quickly away from the land of Berlandier's birth, a place he "cherished." Notwithstanding his sense of loss, he was happy to discover that the rough waters of the channel did not disturb his stomach, as it did so many other passengers, who experienced recurrent and violent seasickness. The botanist and former apothecary's apprentice took on the role of physician, attempting to comfort and relieve the nausea of other passengers. One person in particular, a nameless man who suffered the entire voyage to America, received Berlandier's constant attention and prescription. Through trial and error the ad hoc physician discovered that a small amount of champagne helped settle the man's stomach, at least momentarily or until the wind blew and the ship pitched again. He theorized that the small amount of acid in the fluid was efficacious. The first night, the wind died and a calm settled on the channel; the plain of the sea seemed somehow more awe-inspiring than the tumbling breakers of day. Berlandier's mind became restless, and he felt a profound loneliness for the past tempered by an optimistic hope for the future. He spent the night contemplating the sky, the constellations moving toward morning, when the eastern rays settled upon low-lying clouds, bringing with the passing minutes wonderful changing hues. Berlandier, who knew enough English to make out what the sailors were predicting about the day's weather, commented in his journal about the ability of the humblest mariner at sea or farmer on land to use the rising and setting of the sun to prognosticate the day's precipitation and temperature, usually with great accuracy. The mariners used the habits of sea creatures as well to predict meteorological changes. Dolphins skimming the waves in the same direction as the schooner led to the prediction that the wind would change from stern to bow, and indeed it happened a few hours later; dolphins, said the mariners, always swim in the direction of a coming headwind.[2]

The ship made rapid progress exiting the Channel, keeping Brittany to port, a strong following wind filled with rain driving the ship forward into the rough seas of the Bay of Biscay. Land birds such as crows hovered about the ship, which worried the superstitious sailors that such an evil omen presaged an unfavorable voyage. Following the northerly winds and currents through the Bay of Biscay, the ship skimmed past Cape Finisterre and the inland mountains of western Spain, sailed parallel to Portugal, then southwest, making their way toward the trade winds, keeping south of the Azores. After another week cruising through the mid-North Atlantic, they crossed the Tropic of Cancer, a notable event in Berlandier's mind, and he took note of meteorological changes and their effect on human physiology. He had brought along a fine Celsius thermometer, which showed a rise in ten degrees from Le Havre to the Tropic of Cancer. Fortunately, it was November; the sun's rays, approaching the southerly Tropic of Capricorn, were oblique rather than direct. The crossing of such distance resulted in an average of one degree increase for each five degrees south latitude. The physiological effects from such a slow increase in temperature were, Berlandier reasoned, negligible, as the human body was adaptable to such slight changes. A fortnight later they had passed through the Sargasso Sea and approached the New World. Spying land November 20, but stalled for the day by contrary winds, they waited in suspense to see what land they lay abreast. The captain of the *Hannah Elizabeth* supposed it was Puerto Rico, but upon realizing it was one of the outermost of the Virgin Islands, he grew uneasy because of the darkness of the night, uncertainty of position, and known shoals that made such waters dangerous. The next few days were harrowing attempts to evade shipwreck in dark nights and unfavorable winds. The captain navigated their way north of the Virgin Islands, keeping St. Thomas astern, until they spied the mountainous heights of Puerto Rico. The *Hannah Elizabeth* cruised past, with Puerto Rico to port, then turned southwest through the Mona Passage, at which point they were hit by a strong squall. The captain of the *Hannah Elizabeth* had seen the storm approaching but refused to trim sail until it was almost too late. Skirting Hispaniola to its south, the schooner entered the unpredictable waters and winds of the Caribbean. Sometimes within just a mile or two, the winds would arbitrarily change, grow calm, then blow again in the opposite direction. Along the way Berlandier sketched some of the islands they passed, for example, Isla Beata, which lies just south of Hispaniola; later he put his drawings to watercolors. The last week of November they passed Cape Tiburón, bearing north, while the schooner continued west toward Jamaica, an island rich in history and tragedy. Berlandier recalled the story of Columbus's shipwreck, which kept the sailor marooned on the island for a year, while he became increasingly ill with malaria. Other maroons, escaped slaves who hid on the island, experienced tragedy of a different sort, when the English rooted them out using bloodthirsty hounds.[3]

The tragic life of one of the most beautiful of nature's creations, the flying fish, also fascinated Berlandier, who found that the Caribbean was a place that hosted countless numbers of them. Berlandier had read the works of Humboldt and Etienne de Lacépède on fishes and agreed with their assessment that the fish not only glided but beat their fins like wings. Constantly hunted, which caused their soaring attempts to escape, rarely could they escape the jaws of the dolphin and dorado, which delighted in the fish, or gulls that soared from above to take those missed by the dolphin or another predator, the booby. After the sailors happened to catch a dorado, Berlandier dissected the fish, observing its peculiarities and a strange disease that kept it slender despite its being pregnant. Off the coast of Jamaica, the sailors caught a barracuda, a fish that was reputed to castrate bathers in the surf of Caribbean islands. The barracuda's flesh tasted better than the dorado's, in Berlandier's opinion. A few days later, the sailors captured a shark, which the sailors disemboweled and the scientist studied.[4]

With the coming of December, the *Hannah Elizabeth* sailed northwest through the Yucatán Channel separating Yucatán from the westernmost point of Cuba, Cabo San Antonio, entering with the gulf stream into the Gulf of Mexico. The days continued warm and monotonous, the sunsets astonishingly beautiful, the winds contrary. When a strong rainstorm lasting two days battered the schooner, sailors told Berlandier the winter months are typically stormy on the Gulf of Mexico, when sailing is hazardous, and finding adequate anchorage along the shore foolish. In such storms the ship must sail with the wind, "close-hauled", and ride it out—this is precisely what the captain of the *Hannah Elizabeth* did. After entering the Gulf of Mexico, the schooner sailed due west toward Mexico; on December 9 they spied hills in the distance, a range of small mountains, the Sierra de Maratines, and further south, the bold peak of Bernal de Horcasitas. The mountain rose from the stingy land with sheer walls of rock, an uneven pinnacle jutting from earth. Berlandier would one day attempt the ascent of Bernal, but now, after weeks at sea, he looked upon the mountain as a landmark of their destination. The sailors told the scientist that Bernal is just north of the Pánuco River. Notwithstanding that Bernal is a comparatively small mountain, it was visible far out at sea—Berlandier estimated seventy-five miles. As the winds were contrary, blowing from the west and then the east, the shore and distant peaks beckoned, then disappeared, then beckoned again. The captain and crew had their work cut out for them, as the contrary breezes continued for days, and whenever they approached land before an easterly, they could not make out the river's mouth. Besides Bernal, there were no other landmarks, no lighthouse or large fortification for bearings, and the land surrounding Pánuco was flat and, to Berlandier, not "agreeable." Patience and trial and error paid off by the thirteenth, and the ship came to anchor. Soon river pilots appeared in their small craft, making Berlandier think (anxiously, perhaps, at first) of brave but doomed warriors of the past who confronted Hernán Cortés when he first approached the Mexican coastline in 1519. The mouth of the Pánuco was very wide, though the water was shallow, and a sandbar blocked shipping at low tide or when the winds were contrary. An English traveler who journeyed to Tampico less than a year earlier, in February 1826, described the bar as a horseshoe shape, formed by the continuing battle between sediment from the river meeting the tide of the Gulf. The river pilots, mestizos who dressed the part of coarse and crafty sailors, enjoyed the power of guiding foreign ships into port according to their own whims and schedules. Nevertheless, the *Hannah Elizabeth* was successfully navigated into the mouth past small fishing villages and a makeshift fort, Pueblo de la Barra, made of old tree trunks and guarded by a few ill-clad soldiers. Ship and passengers proceeded upriver past the old port of Pueblo Viejo, then on to the revived port city of Tampico.[5]

Tampico, also called Santa Anna de Tamaulipas, was a small cosmopolitan port city with a long, confusing history. The native Huasteco peoples had for centuries lived along the Pánuco valley. Berlandier, who supposed that few pure blood natives still lived in the region, after so many centuries of intermarriage with outsiders, believed that the people of the Pánuco valley were largely mestizos, a mixture of Indian and Spanish. There were many mixed-breed *costeños* (coastal dwellers) as well. The Huastecos were originally from the Yucatán, and known as makers of fine crafts. Like many regional tribes, they came under the authority of the Aztecs in the late 1400s, which enabled the Spanish later to enlist the Huastecos as allies in their conquest of the Aztec Empire. After Columbus's voyages and the establishment of the Spanish Empire in the Caribbean, Spanish governors such as Francisco Garay of Jamaica and Diego Velázquez of Cuba began the exploration of the lands and waters to the west and north, in part to discover the Strait of Anian, the hypothetical water passage through America that connected the Atlantic and Pacific Oceans. Explorers such as Juan de Grijalva and Antonio de Alaminos explored the Gulf Coast of Mexico as early as 1518. A Spanish fleet under the command of Alonso Alvarez de Pineda sailed in the waters of the Gulf of Mexico along the Mexican coast in the autumn of 1519, around the same time that Cortés was making his historic journey from the coast to Tenochtitlán. Spanish rivalries for power and gold made the Pánuco valley, like so many other places in America under Spanish hegemony, a battleground among conquistadors. Cortés, believing the Pánuco valley to be commercially and strategically important, drove both Francisco Garay and Pánfilo de Narváez from the region and established the town of San Estévan del Puerto, the forerunner of Tampico, in 1522. The struggle for power, however, continued for years, with the native Huastecos caught in between. The conquerors initially intimidated, slaughtered, and enslaved the natives, then, once conquest became ordered government, institutionalized control. Missionaries such as Andrés de Olmos converted the Huastecos to Christianity. Imperial rivalries with the English and French in the Gulf of Mexico and Caribbean forced the Spanish Crown to reinvigorate control over the region north and south of the Pánuco valley. During the mid-eighteenth century, Castilian José de Escandón recolonized the region, renaming it Nuevo Santander. During the Mexican War for Independence from 1810 to 1821, dislocation of trade at Veracruz led to increasing trade through the mouth of the Pánuco; Tamaulipan authorities decided that the port town of Pueblo Viejo, which had an inadequate harbor for expanding trade and larger ships, had to be supplanted. In 1827, the town of Tampico was renamed Santa Anna de Tamaulipas; merchant vessels such as the *Hannah Elizabeth* were directed beyond Pueblo Viejo to the rejuvenated port, which was situated on high ground near the confluence of the Pánuco and the Río Tamesí.[6]

Mexico in 1826 was a new republic with all of the typical signs of political birth: intrigue, party politics, civil conflict, economic disruption, and the insecurity of a young country beset by the intrigues of stronger outside nations. Mexico had gained independence from Spain in 1821 after over a decade of sometimes bitter conflict that involved numerous revolutionary leaders and movements and battles between rebels, royalists, and, along the Rio Grande, American Indian tribes. The movement for independence occurred as an appendage to world events. The American Revolution of a previous generation provided some ideological inspiration to the Mexicans; the consequent expansion of the American empire across the Mississippi into the Louisiana Territory was of concern to the Spanish and, after 1821, the Mexicans. The shadow of the meteoric rise to and fall from power of Napoleon Bonaparte in Europe continued to fall upon America long after Napoleon's death. Napoleon had in 1800 forced the Spanish to give up the Louisiana Territory, which Spain ostensibly had controlled for almost forty years, for the sake of an imagined new French empire in North America; in the end Napoleon sold the territory to the United States, which had its own designs on Louisiana. The problem was that the extent and boundaries of Louisiana were unknown and under contention by the Americans and Spanish. Was the Red River the southern boundary, or was it farther south at the Nueces or Rio Grande? Was the Sabine River the western boundary, or did it extend farther west to other rivers, perhaps even the Rio Grande

in New Mexico? Even after Spain and the United States settled the issue
in 1819, when the Adams-Onís Treaty marked the boundaries between the
American and Spanish empires at the Red and Sabine rivers, many land-
hungry and nationalistic Americans, called at the time filibusters, continued to interpret the boundaries of the Louisiana Territory according to a
vague impression on the part of the French that Louisiana extended to the
Rio Grande.[7]

Little of this dispute involving the conflict of empires concerned Jean
Louis Berlandier upon his arrival at Tampico, but over the course of his
journey to Mexico he found himself becoming emotionally and politically
embroiled in the dispute between the Mexican and American governments.
This would not be for quite some time; first he had to make his way to Mexico
City, join the Comisión de Límites, which was still a shadowy affair in his
mind, and journey over the course of many weeks from Mexico City to the
Rio Grande, and Texas. For now, Berlandier journeyed about Tampico. He
saw merchants and ships from Europe and America. Trade and newcomers transformed the city, which was busy and cosmopolitan. Fortunately,
Berlandier arrived in December, when the weather was mild and the climate
healthy, rather than in the sickly heat and humidity of summer months.
Tampico was a city of the impoverished, of loathsome sights and smells, of
human misery at its most dire. The town lay within the crook of an elbow
on the northern banks of the winding Pánuco; the rise and fall of the tide,
low elevation, haphazard flooding, and uneven ground resulted in stagnant
pools and lagoons wherein vermin multiplied and diseases were engendered. The Laguna del Carpintero lay just north of the center of town; during the months of spring it sometimes dried up, leaving behind decaying
carcasses of fish, reptiles, and amphibians; a miasmic stench arose from
the lagoon, threatening the health, Berlandier believed, of the populace.
At such times flocks of vultures descended upon the ooze to feed. In the
spring of 1827, while Berlandier was in residence at the city, there was no
rainfall for months, and the lagoons dried up; fever epidemics occurred soon
after. Freshwater for the feverish was a rarity in Tampico. The tidal Pánuco
was saline, the water rarely good or fresh. Water merchants made a fair living retrieving water from the Río Tamesí, which flowed from the inland
Sierra Madre, merging with the Pánuco just to the west of the town center.
Berlandier thought the Tamesí was more beautiful than the Pánuco, as it had
more of the character of a mountain river, like those of Savoy and Jura. The
waters of the Tamesí were sweet and drinkable before arriving at Tampico;

its division into numerous small lakes and lagoons before merging with the Pánuco made for delightful river scenery.[8]

By contrast most inhabitants of Tampico lived in huts of adobe or bamboo, some of the latter like cages, without enclosed walls. Locals blamed the utter poverty of the people on indolence engendered by the constant heat and humidity that bled energy from the inhabitants. Berlandier believed the climate provided a partial reason, though the upriver Huastecos were subject to the same heat and humidity but were less indolent than the costeños and mestizos of Tampico and the lower river. Recurrent breezes, from inland in the morning and from the sea in the evening, provided scant relief. Many mornings moisture lay over the city, especially the mangrove jungles along the lagoons and swamps, like a suffocating blanket. The mangrove thrives in water with high salinity, so adapted well to the lagoons of the Pánuco valley. Mangrove roots dug deep into the muddy lagoons and estuaries of the Pánuco region. Although it was winter, the region was a lush tropical forest. Even during times of drought, during spring months, the fogs descended upon the hapless people. Ironically, the fertility of the surrounding jungle could provide everything humans needed with a small amount of work. One of the prime staples of the diet was the banana, which grew wild in the Pánuco valley. Pimentos and chili peppers were plentiful as well, growing without attention to cultivation. Large numbers of fish and game birds inhabited the rivers, estuaries, and shores of river and gulf. Berlandier particularly enjoyed observing the roseate spoonbill nesting among the mangrove trees. Caiman were also present and could be dangerous, though Berlandier discovered when his canoe sank in the Laguna del Carpintero and he had to wade to shore that the caimans left him alone.[9]

Diseases thrived in the Pánuco valley, though the infrequency of virulent epidemics surprised Berlandier. The physician-to-be observed at Tampico pulmonary complaints (pleurisy); various boils, sores, and ulcers (herpes); skin problems (*chicote*); and a variety of fevers, particularly yellow fever (*vomito prieto*). Berlandier subscribed to the theory current at the time (before the discovery of microorganisms) that unhealthy air could cause fevers. Logically, the decaying vegetable and animal matter of the dried-up lagoons in and about Tampico caused an unhealthy air, miasma, that could bring about fever, especially among those who lived in impoverished hovels.[10]

As Berlandier was not expected in Mexico City until the summer, he spent leisurely winter and spring months at Tampico and environs. The extent of the town was modest, so the pedestrian Berlandier could walk from one end of town to the other in just a few minutes. As with many Spanish and Mexican cities, Tampico had been laid out with orderly city blocks and streets meeting at right angles. There were places of interest Berlandier was wont to visit, such as the customs house situated at the southern edge of town next to the river. Here the captain and supercargo of a ship would present their papers and declare their cargo; Mexican customs officials had a reputation for corruption, to which Berlandier attested in his writings. The depth of the river adjacent to the customs house was about three fathoms, sufficiently deep for merchant vessels to lie at anchor while longshoremen unloaded the cargo. Upriver from the customs house was the cemetery. The town boasted quite a few merchants' houses from various countries. There was a plaza named for muleteers and another named for the English, in both cases revealing the dominant presence of drivers and merchants. When Berlandier first saw Tampico in 1827, the town had few defenses, save a ramshackle battery, Pueblo de la Barra, situated at the mouth of the river. In 1832, as a result of civil conflict and the Spanish invasion, Tampico became heavily fortified with a line of walls, entrenchments, turrets, and blockhouses. Berlandier saw these when he visited Tampico in subsequent years; he made several drawings in which he precisely illustrated the fortifications.[11]

In February, Berlandier journeyed with a local merchant south to Tuxpan. They traveled through Pueblo Viejo, the port eclipsed by the revived Tampico, south to Tampico el Alto, a small town near the Gulf, then east to the Laguna de Tamiahua, a long, shallow tidal estuary that paralleled the coast. The thin leaves of the huisache tree (*Acacia farnesiana*) provided some shade on the path; the plant's golden globe flowers provided a delightful perfume. Berlandier and his companion hired a pirogue, or hollowed-out log canoe, manned by three local natives—or, Berlandier thought, people as close to natives as anyone was in that region. The boatmen tirelessly rowed the small pirogue south, hugging the east shore, a thin peninsula called Cabo Rojo. To the west was a small mountain chain, La Cuchara, and behind it, the distant Sierra Madre. Days were warm but the night breeze coming off of the water reminded Berlandier of the frigid air descending from the Alps. When the boatmen needed rest, they camped on shore amid coconut and banana trees and cacti. As the lagoon narrowed the current picked up, imitating a river; indeed the locals referred to it as Río de Tamiahua. Lagoon masquerading as a river eventually narrowed to shallow bayous hidden from view by mangrove trees. It took many years of experience and a discerning eye for the boatmen to navigate the winding water amid the jungle. The suffocating atmosphere was humid, and the air was·rank with the pungent smell of decaying organic materials. Berlandier was only too glad to emerge from the bayous into larger lakes along the coast leading to Tuxpan. These lakes were also estuaries, salty and shallow.[12]

Tuxpan, like Tampico, was built near the mouth of a river, the Río de Tuxpan; fresh water from inland mountains descended through the jungle, picking up sediment until it reached the tidal zone, where river water competed with the incoming tide to create estuaries and lagoons that surrounded the town. Tuxpan had a large mixed-race population, and quite a few Spaniard expatriates. Berlandier thought Tuxpan was cleaner, better kept up, than Tampico, but less orderly in original design, being built according to the happenstance of time. There were far fewer signs of criminal activity and places of ill repute. The water of the town was salty, and well water little better. Berlandier had in his luggage various chemicals that he used to test the impurities and salinity of the water. He kept careful records of temperature and observed the culture of the town and agricultural productions. Locals harvested pimento and sarsaparilla, a reputed cure-all. Cochineal insects, from which a beautiful red dye is extracted, inhabited the various nopale cacti (*Opuntia cochenillifera*) of the region. Citrus trees abounded, as well as coconut, banana, avocado, and the vanilla orchid (*Vanilla planifolia*). Berlandier found Tuxpan quite a beautiful city and enjoyed his brief stay there. Shrove Tuesday, the day preceding Ash Wednesday and Lent, was a time of hilarity when the Tuxpanecos played tricks on one another. Practical jokes of all types were played on both friends and strangers. Berlandier was pelted with eggs, for example, which he appears to have received good-naturedly.[13]

After returning to Tampico from Tuxpan, Berlandier gave himself up to study for a while to develop a theory based on his observations of the Laguna de Tamiahua. Berlandier analyzed many of the maps of the Gulf Coast produced by Europeans such as Humboldt and Americans such as John Robinson (Zebulon Pike's companion). The maps varied in accuracy, but those he tended to trust pictured the Laguna de Tamiahua as more of a bay, with a direct outlet to the sea, than an enclosed lake. He interviewed older inhabitants of the coast to obtain their recollections of the topography of land and estimates of the depths of estuary and river mouth over time. His natural history argued for a growing presence of sandbars at the mouths of rivers such as the Pánuco and Tuxpan and the enclosure of tidal estuaries into lakes and lagoons; the Gulf of Mexico clearly was receding, creating sandbars, which disrupted navigation, and wilderness lagoons such as the Laguna de Tamiahua.[14]

In time Berlandier would further test his theories on the recession of the sea. Until then, he had before him a long overland journey involving over a year, in which he ascended the Pánuco valley to Mexico City, then journeyed north as a member of the Mexican Boundary Commission.

After Berlandier arrived in Mexico, he relied on the advice of Lucas Alamán y Escalada, the Mexican Secretary of the Interior and former student of Candolle, who had arranged for Berlandier's appointment to the Comisión de Límites. Alamán suggested that Berlandier leave before the heat of summer came to Tampico, and take a generally less traveled route to Mexico City. Berlandier as a consequence joined a mule caravan taking goods to Mexico City. Before he departed Tampico, Berlandier packed two cases of thousands of specimens and sent them to Candolle in Geneva. The scientist Alamán suspected that the botanist would wish to make good use of his time on the journey, so he directed Berlandier to take the mule paths through the Huasteca, which was the highlands and valleys of a vast network of rivers that flowed into the Pánuco. Several rivers, such as the Moctezuma, Tempoal, and Calabozo, flowed north from the mountainous regions of the Sierra Madre Oriental toward the Pánuco. The valleys of these tributaries would be Berlandier's route for the month of May in 1827. His guides the muleteers (*arrieros*) had grown used to traveling the narrow, winding route through the Huasteca ever since Mexican independence and the refusal of the Spanish to evacuate San Juan de Ulúa, a fort the occupation of which closed the port of Veracruz for several years, until 1825. The closing of Veracruz had forced merchants to find alternative routes from the Gulf of Mexico to Mexico City, which had made Tampico an important focus of trade. Even after the opening of Veracruz, trade routes continued to go through Tampico and the Pánuco, and muleteers continued to make the month-long journey from the Pánuco to Mexico City.[15]

The exploring naturalist in Berlandier's time had to travel with a variety of equipment used to discover, capture, collect, prepare, and preserve flora and fauna. If traveling by wagon or mule—the latter of which was the preferred means of transport, because of the many streams with deep banks found in northern Mexico and Texas—the naturalist's gear had to include containers, preferably leather panniers that could be slung across the mule's back; several gallons of alcohol with which to preserve insects, amphibians, reptiles, and animal skins; arsenic for preserving animal skins; absorbent and stiff paper, the former for plants immediately upon collecting, the latter for preserving plant specimens when dry; a paper press to press stiff paper and plants contained therein; bags made of flax ("lino bags") with strong cords to tie the top end securely for preserving dry or wet specimens; copper containers, especially in which to keep alcohol; wooden kegs for general storage; glass bottles of varying sizes with corks for preserving small specimens in alcohol; a glass bottle containing ether to kill insects; a set of small scalpels and knives, useful for dissection; nets to capture birds, insects, and fish; cotton cloth for drying and preservation; needle and thread for sewing bags and skins; and shotguns with fine shot for bringing down birds with the least injury to their bodies. Added to this equipment, Berlandier brought plenty of pencils and paper for the many drawings he made in the field.[16]

On his journey to Mexico City, Berlandier put himself in the hands of muleteers, who were the jack-of-all-trades of the camino real, as they euphemistically called the narrow wilderness trails through the Huasteca. They were at the same time caregivers of their animals and their human charges, which they protected from the elements at night, building bivouac-tents; the muleteers provided the security of knowledge of the route and its hazards. Berlandier at first found it difficult to trust armed men (the muleteers carried daggers in their belts), but it did not take long for him to discover these men to be utterly trustworthy. Even so, when they had been on the trail several days in early May and had irrevocably departed from the sea, Berlandier felt a sense of loss. The feeling came upon him late at night under a clear sky where the constellations so familiar to him from his youth were far to the north, replaced by unfamiliar star designs. The full effect of his departure from Europe, from youth, for adventure in an unknown land, overwhelmed him, and he "was given up to the saddest of reflections" as he sensed that never again would he return home.[17]

Berlandier's mental malaise was brief. The next day they traveled in a thick jungle of palms, through which sun rays rarely penetrated. Berlandier realized the wonder he felt on the trail and sensed the vagabond in himself, a feeling that no matter where he might be, as long as nature surrounded him he could be content with the moment. It is not the destination, he thought, and not the future, but rather the experience of the moment that preoccupies the traveler. The pleasurable moments of past journeys are never forgotten by the aging traveler, but readily relived.[18]

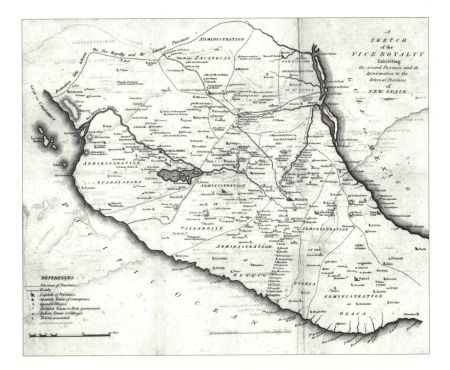

Figure 4. A map of the Internal Provinces of New Spain by
Zebulon Montgomery Pike. Library of Congress.

Palms and bamboo made the jungle almost impassable. The waterlogged
environment of dense humidity and stagnant pools formed watery barriers
on the trail, which forced the muleteers to exercise their skill and experiences
discovering alternative routes. The vegetable world supported a prolific number of herbivores and birds of all kinds, which attracted as many carnivores,
especially jaguars and other wild cats. These animals performed the same
role the caimans did along rivers and coast. Indeed as soon as hunters made
a kill, the window of opportunity to retrieve the prey was so brief that often
upon arrival they found it partially devoured. If the wild animals of the jungle
were not enough to discourage the traveler, the profusion of insects guaranteed annoyance and disgust. Ants, flies, and mosquitoes were a plague, as
were chiggers, called *nighuas* by the locals; but nothing could equal the tenac-
ity and irritation of ticks, which were ubiquitous and attached themselves in
great numbers to any exposed skin. A bite would become a small sore, which
turned into a lesion if not cared for; flies deposited eggs in open sores, which
led to infection and, often, death.[19]

As the muleteers and their charges traveled from rancho to rancho, heading into higher elevations, they halted for nights where hospitable rancheros welcomed them, charmed by the novelty of such visitors. Berlandier reported that at the Rancho de Tanseme, for example, the inhabitants were equally fascinated by the travelers' percussion-lock firearms (as opposed to flintlocks) and the botanist's habit of pressing plants between boards and paper to preserve them. Berlandier, exhausted the night of May 7, dreamed he was in the Alps, traveling from one to another charming chalet; shepherds sang melancholy songs to calm their sheep. Suddenly noise erupted from an unexpected quarter, awakening him; the rancheros, stimulated by drink, had decided on a fandango in the hours after midnight. Guitars, violins, and drunken guffaws accompanied the otherwise beautiful sounds of the night. The inhabitants of this region approaching the Mexican Plateau lived sparingly, with little abundance of even the necessities. Trees blooming in the spring weather included the mimosa (*Albizia julibrissin*) and the huisache; Berlandier often found the differences between these two trees, as well as the mesquite (*Prosopis glandulosa*), confusing, perhaps because, he wrote, "the name of Mitsquitl or Mesquite is applied by the Mexicans, the creoles and the Spaniards to different plants of the immense tribe of Mimosees." Water was hard to come by in this land, and Berlandier's wish to slake his thirst with fresh goat's milk remained but a wish. The inhabitants slept in the humid night air with a bamboo portico over their heads.[20]

Outside of the town of Tantoyuca they arrived along the shores of a tributary of the Pánuco, the Tempoal (Tampio), near its confluence with the Calabozo. Here the muleteers bivouacked to allow the animals to graze and the men to rest. The Tempoal was clear and inviting, and Berlandier enjoyed his first freshwater bath since leaving Europe. Willow, sycamores, and other verdure invited travelers to stay. The forested Tempoal valley was hot and humid; the inhabitants were Huastecos, some of whom spoke Spanish, others their own tongue. The locals were generally shy before travelers, who with difficulty found provisions. With each day the journeyers moved deeper into the forested plateau, crossing small streams, mostly dry, that fed the tributaries of the Pánuco. Muleteers led the troop into the mountains, up and down one called Santa Teresa, in the Huautla range; they spent the night in a mountain village called Coacollote, where Berlandier could detect a familiarity in the surroundings and people that reminded him of the Alps. For the first time in Mexico he found the native women attractive and feminine. Clouds hovered about the forested peaks; rain fell hard in the night. Hills and valleys, jumbled as far as the vision extended, appeared like the landscape of Savoy. They followed a mountain stream of clear rushing water called Cañada de Tlacolula, which coursed through limestone walls. They had to cross and recross the stream dozens of times, which wet their clothes but enlivened their spirits. Berlandier climbed a peak or two and stood among the vast Sierra Madre Oriental, a cordillera almost equal in extent, distance, and majesty to the Alps. As in the Alps, trees were increasingly coniferous the higher the elevation—but the Mexican peaks lacked snow. Also familiar was the constant evidence of the eroding action of swift water on bare rock, which had interested Berlandier since his youth along the Rhône. The maze of sheer walls cut by cool, clear mountain streams coursing over limestone and other rocks; the occasional natural basin with cool, green water; distant peaks ceaselessly emerging in the direction of travel; hoary and unassailable walls of stone rising perpendicularly: all of these scenes reminded Berlandier of home. Besides familiar sounds of wind-blown trees and rushing water, Berlandier heard new songs of brightly colored tropical birds mixed with the repetitive songs of the muleteers. Berlandier and his future friend the Mexican naturalist Pablo de la Llave would in time seek to publish (without apparent success) the name of one of these exotic birds as *Cassieus fuscus* (*Gymnostinops montezuma*). Along the way Berlandier was introduced to the fermented juice, *pulque*, of the maguey (the agave plant—*Agave americana*), the grayish-green spiny plant found so often on their journey. The lovely purple petals of the melastoma (*Melastoma candidum*) was diverting, as was a multicolored species of croton (*Croton*). Berlandier saw sweet clover (*Melilotus officinalis*) as well as the graceful black willow (*Salix nigra*). The cañada was so winding that though it generally flowed from west to east, at times they were following a northerly or southerly course. Frequently they had to supplement their meager food with stone-ground tortillas of the villagers, which few of the newcomers (such as Berlandier) found palatable. Fortunately, parish priests in some villages made money on the side as shopkeepers, so necessities such as flour and sugar could be obtained. One exhausting day of travel, men and mules crossed the cañada an astonishing fifty-six times. On May 14, they departed the Cañada de Tlacolula and ascended Monte Pinelco, a peak covered with pines and oaks, steep but with an easy trail to follow. Whenever Berlandier had the chance, he took the barometric pressure of peak and valley, which though not precise gave him an estimate of comparative heights. From the valley of the Cañada de Tlacolula, for example, to Monte Pinelco the ascent was about

eight hundred meters; beyond Pinelco among the heights on the road to
Zacualtipán they ascended another three hundred meters. Here the wind
was sharp and fresh, the view vast and grand; the chill of mountain heights
once again greeted Berlandier, who had not felt such a familiar sensation in
over a year. The cordillera of the Sierra Madre was so different from the hot
and humid valleys that he felt as if he had been transported back in time
or to a different, European, location.[21]

This feeling continued when they reached Zacualtipán, a large mountain town of seven or eight thousand Indians. The high elevation and temperate climate suggested the climate of Geneva; flora likewise resembled that
of Europe. For example, Berlandier found species of horehound (*Marrubium
vulgare*), cabbage rose (*Rosa centifolia*), a plant species resembling the water crowfoot (*Ranunculus*), willows, and a similar species of the family
Amentaceae that produces catkins. After resting for six days, Berlandier set
out moving southwest toward Atotonilco el Chico. The route, rocky and steep,
went through an arid region of mesquites and cacti. Valleys amid peaks featured a humid, wet environment where figs, maize, and the Peruvian pepper tree (*Schinus molle*) grew tall and thick. The route took them to several
mining towns of the Sierra Madre, first Atotonilco el Chico, then Real del
Monte. Berlandier was sufficiently interested to take tours of the mines. The
tall peaks of the region featured familiar arboreal vegetation, such as pines
and oaks. From Real del Monte on the Pachuco Road to San Mateo, approaching Mexico City, the landscape became a broad plateau subject to frequent
mirages because of the cool air of the mountains descending to the warmer
air of the plateau. Even as they approached Mexico City, they were still in the
Pánuco system of waters, as the Tula River formed part of the northeastern
drainage of the lakes in the north of the city, originating in (according to
Humboldt) the Arroyo de Tequisquiac then flowing into the Moctezuma, and
eventually, the Pánuco.[22]

The approach to Mexico City from the northeast was over a marshy
valley frequently inundated with floodwaters. A broad causeway guided
the visitor into the city's environs. Distant steeples rose among the smaller
buildings. Berlandier had long anticipated his entry into the city and was
quick to record his impressions in his journal. The sights and sounds, great
buildings and beautiful architecture, were duly recorded. His order and
description are close to Humboldt's in *Political Essay on the Kingdom of
New Spain*. Berlandier, a Protestant, had the typical suspicions of his age
respecting the superstitions and rituals of Catholics; even so, he could

appreciate the beauty of Catholic cathedrals and churches. Indeed, his travels in Mexico showed that as in European villages, every small town, no matter how impoverished the inhabitants and how dismal their lodgings, had an immaculate church, even grander than those of Europe. Berlandier sought out convents and missions partly for the architecture and holy images, partly because they tended to inspire a meditative state of mind. He toured the mint, the Royal and Pontifical University of Mexico, and the National Palace, relying heavily on local guidebooks to make extensive descriptions. The latter edifice contained one of the city's two botanical gardens. Berlandier naturally made the acquaintance of the celebrated botanist and founder of the Royal Botanical Garden (El Real Jardín Botánico), Vicente Cervantes, as well as his protégé, Miguel Bustamante. Cervantes, the longtime director of the botanical garden, had worked with the Royal Botanical Expedition led by Martín Sessé; indeed the two men had inaugurated botanical lectures at the university in the 1780s. Cervantes was also a chemist of note, translating into Spanish Lavoisier's *Treatise on Chemistry*. He was the leader of a cadre of young botanists working to develop the natural history of Mexico that included Bustamante, Lucas Alamán, and, now in 1827, Jean Louis Berlandier. After Cervantes's death in 1829, Bustamante became Mexico's leading botanist, taking chairs of botany and natural history at the National Museum. Berlandier got to know Bustamante and Cervantes well. He went on an excursion with Cervantes, for example, after his arrival in the city, to the hill of Chapultepec on the outskirts of the city. There, amid the grand cypresses (*Taxodium mucronatum*) of the hill, overlooking Mexico City, Berlandier saw what led Humboldt to compare the Valley of Mexico to the gorgeous valleys of Switzerland. To the southeast, Berlandier spied the huge volcanoes Popocatépetl and Iztaccihuatl. He had not seen snow-covered peaks since he had departed the Alps a year earlier. This sight, along with the beauty of the valley and the culture and customs of the Mexicans, so heavily implanted with European ideas, forms, and rituals, helped Berlandier feel not so far away from home. During this visit with señor Cervantes, Berlandier began the practice of taking regular measurements of the blueness of the sky with the cyanometer, originally conceived by the French scientist Saussure. Berlandier used a cyanometer built by Cervantes, and he began the journal record "Observations Cyanometriques," which he kept for the next several years, from the time he was in Mexico City to his journey north through Mexico across the Rio Grande and throughout Texas.[23]

Awaiting the formation of the Boundary Commission, Berlandier kept busy exploring and studying. He journeyed with Gen. Manuel Mier y Terán and Miguel Bustamante to the Peñon de los Baños, north of the city, a porphyritic hill with well-known thermal baths. The likes of Baron Humboldt and the Mexican geologist Andrés Manuel del Río had visited and studied these hot springs, and Berlandier had educated himself in preparation for this and other excursions by reading Humboldt's *Political Essay on the Kingdom of New Spain* and del Río's *Elements of Orictognosia, or Knowledge of Fossils*. He spent time also at the library of the University of Mexico, where he studied Aztec antiquities and hieroglyphics mentioned by Humboldt. Accompanied by General Terán and Pablo de la Llave, Berlandier studied the remains of a mastodon unearthed near Lake Texcoco. He familiarized himself with some of the classic works of history of the Valley of Mexico, such as Bernal Díaz del Castillo's *History of the Spanish Conquest of New Spain* and Francisco Javier Clavigero's *Ancient History of Mexico*.[24]

By early October 1827, leaders of the Mexican Comisión de Límites, organized under the auspices of Lucas Alamán with General Terán in command, were making final preparations to depart for the Rio Grande. Berlandier, who had been collecting thousands of botanical specimens and seeds, and a much smaller number of zoological specimens, since his departure from Tampico the previous spring, organized his collection and, on October 8, shipped two cases to Geneva. The cases included the fruits of his labors during the previous four months exploring the environs of Mexico City. Learning that a further delay in the commission's start would give him another few weeks to explore, Berlandier decided to journey to the mountains surrounding the city to the west. Accompanied by a Frenchman he had met by chance in Mexico City, Monsieur Bordier, Berlandier journeyed through small villages to Toluca, on a high plateau amid lofty peaks. Here, Berlandier gathered plants and observed the tree of hands (*Chiranthodendron pentadactylon*), which Humboldt had previously described. From Toluca, Berlandier journeyed south and east toward Cuernavaca, stopping at various picturesque locations along the way. At Tenancingo, he visited an old monastery from which he could spy Pico de Orizaba far to the east. At the Hacienda de Miacatlán, Berlandier joined locals, including the owner of the hacienda and a parish priest, in a journey to the ruins of Xochicalco, an ancient fortress that had been long abandoned but that still revealed the power and engineering brilliance that the Toltecs had once enjoyed. Dating back perhaps a millennium, Xochicalco had a square fortification of ancient walls, hieroglyphics, and sculptures of mythical figures. The ruins of the structure impressed Berlandier, who wrote that "the sides of the parallelogram situated at the summit are perfectly oriented towards the four cardinal points of the compass." The journey from Miacatlán to Cuernavaca was along low-lying mountains punctuated by gorges (cañadas) carved by the action of descending streams. Cuernavaca was not a beautiful city, despite its age and fame as a crossroads of trade. Situated in the shadow of the Sierra de Huitzilac, its climate was humid, its people prone to disease. The evening of October 19, while Berlandier was supping at a tavern in Cuernavaca, a local Indian staggered in the door, desperately ill, beyond help; he died soon after. In such an unhealthy environment, it was of course necessary for botanists and physicians to know what local resources of materia medica were available to healers. Berlandier did not learn until much later, after he had begun his apothecary and healing business at Matamoros, that Cuernavaca was at one time known for the presence of the begonia (*Begonia*), an excellent plant to combat syphilis, used by the indigenous inhabitants of Mexico as an analgesic as well as a strong purgative, a method often used to combat fever. Berlandier had learned about the begonia by reading the writings of Francisco Hernández, the sixteenth-century Spanish naturalist and physician, as well as the letters of Mexican botanist J. J. Laxarsa to Augustin Pyramus de Candolle.[25]

The morning of October 20, Berlandier set out from Cuernavaca for the return to Mexico City, accompanied only by a guide, as Monsieur Bordier remained in Cuernavaca. Journeying north, Berlandier ascended the Sierra de Huitzilac to a great height; at the village of Huitzilac he found only Aztec-speaking *indigenes* (as Berlandier liked to refer to North American Indians). The highest point, La Cruz del Marqués, was ten thousand feet; here a cold rain blew from the north, obscuring distances and chilling the traveler. Berlandier and his guide became lost in the mountains, turning up at an Aztec town called San Miguel de Topilejo. There, Berlandier spent the night, the next morning attending mass, observing the polite and friendly behavior of the local people toward one another and even to strangers like himself. The morning of October 21, he ascended to Xochimilco, from which he could spy the Valley of Mexico, had the cold rain not obscured much of the view. Mountain heights and cold moisture reminded Berlandier very much of home. He continually experienced the mountains surrounding Mexico City from the perspective of Switzerland. The climate was different, warmer, more like the south of Italy. Mexico City, like Geneva, was built amid lakes that gathered the descending waters of surrounding peaks. Before the arrival of the Spanish, the indigenous peoples of the Mexican Plateau had built a thriving civilization in a watery, flooded environment. The Spanish, however, did not want a Mexican Venice, and had sought ways to drain the waters of five lakes that surrounded the city. The most ambitious project was the Desagüe de Huehuecota, begun by the Spanish in 1607, which was the means by which the waters of the Valley of Mexico became linked to the Pánuco valley.[26]

Upon Berlandier's return from his brief excursion in the mountains surrounding Mexico City, he found preparations completed for the departure of the Boundary Commission.

CHAPTER FOUR

The Arms of God

✣ THE COMISIÓN DE LÍMITES DEPARTED MEXICO CITY, TRAVELING
north, on November 10, 1827. Led by soldier, mathematician, and surveyor
Gen. Manuel de Mier y Terán, members included officers Lt. Col. José Batres
of the medical corps, Lt. Col. Constantino Tarnava of the corps of engineers, and artillery lieutenant José Sánchez y Tapía, who served as cartographer (and artist), and scientists Raphael Chowell, the mineralogist, and Jean
Louis Berlandier, who served as a geoscientist, anthropologist, historian,
zoologist, botanist, and artist. The wagons of the commission contained
instruments of science to determine latitude, elevation, and direction, and
to preserve images and specimens. An escort of cavalry provided protection. The official purpose of the Comisión de Límites was to journey across
the Rio Grande to territory that was under contention between the governments of Mexico and the United States. Spanish authorities suspected that
American scientific expeditions up the Red, such as that led by American
scientist William Dunbar in 1804 (which departed from the Red to the Black
and Ouchita Rivers) and James Freeman and Peter Custis in 1806 (which
Spanish troops intercepted and turned back), were veiled attempts to reconnoiter the area for American invasion. Open aggression by American filibusters such as James Long in 1819 confirmed Spanish and Mexican fears
that Americans would stop at nothing to acquire Texas. Even after the
Adams-Onís Treaty of 1819 settled the boundaries at the Red and Sabine
Rivers, American diplomats sought to renegotiate the treaty shortly thereafter, when Mexico gained independence from Spain. Mexican statesmen,

49

justifiably wary of American intentions toward Texas, decided on a combined military and scientific expedition to the region to study, on the one hand, the flora, fauna, geography, and climate of Texas as well as, on the other hand, the varied human elements, such as Indians and Americans residing in Texas and representing a threat toward Mexican sovereignty. Terán, an able soldier and a fine scientist who disliked the American presence in Texas, was a good choice to lead the commission. More questionable was the decision to outfit an exploring expedition with cumbersome wagons, including the general's own gilded one.[1]

Foretelling the pattern of the entire trip, the first day on the road a wagon broke a wheel, which necessitated a delay at Cuautitlán. The wagon repaired, they set out again on November 12, only to be halted at Huehuetoca by another wheel breaking on another wagon. Terán, deciding that such slow progress required the contrast of usefulness, ordered Berlandier and Chowell to investigate the works of the Desagüe de Huehuetoca. This canal, built to provide an artificial outlet of the waters of Lakes Zumpango, Cristóbal, and Texcoco, hence to prevent the Valley of Mexico from recurrent flooding, was cut in the limestone base by thousands of workers over the space of several centuries. To the west lay the Cerro de la Bufa, which formed the watershed of waters flowing west and east. Berlandier and the commission journeyed among the headwaters of the Pánuco. Their route was an old, ill-maintained road, El Camino Real de Tierra Adentro, that historically connected the capital with the presidios of New Mexico; journeyers followed the road north from Mexico City along the high plateau toward San Luis Potosí and Saltillo. The way north was waterless, save for recurrent dry arroyos, with a few desert plants, cacti and huisaches; the few farmers in the region practiced dry farming of necessity. The path continued to the small town of San Juan del Río, where Berlandier climbed a small mountain, which was bare on top due to lack of moisture rather than elevation. At the base of the mountain were desert plants such as mesquite and tree morning glory (*Ipomoea arborescens*). The town was named for a tributary of the Tula River. On the road to Querétaro the next day, he found a species of milkweed (*Asclepias*). Querétaro delighted Berlandier, who enjoyed thinking about its past as a fountain of revolution, its reputation for industry, its many monasteries, and its aqueduct. The path from Querétaro to San Miguel de Allende was through a mountainous desert; small towns lay in the valleys amid peaks soaring to almost eight thousand feet. One valley held the pretty town of San Miguel de Allende. The town had been known as San Miguel until only recently, when the people decided to honor one of their inhabitants, Ignacio Allende, who died in the early stages of the revolution. General Terán, wishing to go through Guanajuato on the way to San Felipe and San Luis Potosí, divided the troop, taking a few dragoons and Berlandier with him to Guanajuato, while the majority of the men with the wagons took a more direct, less mountainous route to San Felipe. Terán and Berlandier took an uncertain route through mountainous, largely uninhabited terrain. Berlandier preoccupied himself with discovering species of sage (*Salvia*), moor grass (*Molinia*), and specimens of the heath family (Ericaceae). The mining city of Guanajuato appeared unexpectedly, cradled in the mountains, the entrance along a gorge now dry, but in the rainy season a torrential cañada garnering the collective waters of the surrounding mountains. Despite the absence of beautiful architecture and tree-lined mountain slopes, Guanajuato reminded Berlandier of Swiss towns nestled in the Alps. The journey north of Guanajuato was through a wilderness of peaks rising over eight thousand feet, dotted with a variety of hardy oaks, mesquites, and flowering butterfly bushes (*Buddleia davidii*). Berlandier discovered a species of the vine *Passiflora*, which he thought was a new discovery. Coming to the northern edge of the sierra, atop an unnamed peak, Berlandier looked out upon a vast, uninhabited plain that represented the route to San Felipe. The desolation of the landscape engendered a feeling of loneliness, of loss of all that is familiar, of uncertainty as to how to react to a wilderness so foreign to one's experience. At San Felipe the group rendezvoused with the other members of the commission who had been awaiting their arrival, then forged on toward San Luis Potosí. The road they took was one, in Berlandier's words, formed by nature; the way was slow and tortuous through a dry valley that received enough water in the rainy season to support palms, huisaches, mesquites, oaks, and pasture. The extremely large Hacienda del Jaral relied on the latter for raising horses renowned throughout Mexico. They pursued a path between sierra through the small town of San Francisco to San Luis Potosí.[2]

San Luis Potosí was built upon a high plateau surrounded by mountains. The elevation made the air cool, though the climate was largely dry, and water descended from the surrounding slopes irregularly. The treeless mountains, Berlandier believed, did not generate as much moisture as forested slopes. In this arid environment, cacti, maguey, and species of chili (*Capsicum*) were profuse, and there was sufficient grassland for herds of sheep and goats. A short distance to the southeast, less than ten miles, lay the headwaters of the Pánuco: Río Santa María and Río Verde flowed east from the mountainous plateau, soon merging with Río Tamesí, Río Salto, Río Tempoal, and Río Moctezuma, forming the Pánuco. Berlandier sketched the town, highlighting its orderliness and the public buildings, churches, and adobe dwellings amid an arid and stark environment.[3]

North of San Luis Potosí the valley narrowed into a stark defile; the surrounding mountains were of limestone and porphyry. Berlandier collected specimens of the creosote bush (*Larrea tridentata*), which was in flower even though it was December. Passing through a narrow defile that led to the Hacienda de Bocas, they entered into a vast arid plain that led north-northeast to Ciudad Venado. Proceeding in the same direction on December 17, they traveled between two cordilleras to the west and east, arriving at Hacienda de Charcas. Berlandier noted that the mountains were more rounded, less like two volcanic peaks, appearing as buttes or mesas, to the south, from where the men had journeyed. December 19, Berlandier joined General Terán, Raphael Chowell, and José Batres on an excursion east to the mines of Real de Catorce. They journeyed through small haciendas until the plain opened up to the jagged hills of the mountains of Catorce, the highest of which were over nine thousand feet; they were dramatic, bald peaks that dominated the horizon. Clouds frequently surrounded the peaks, sometimes producing frost and snow. The work of the mines had deforested the mountains. Descending toward Hacienda de Vanegas to the northwest, they found species of milkweed, horehound, yucca (*Yucca*), and creosote bush. But the route from Vanegas to Salado was a stingy desert of no water, few plants, and little shelter from the sun. Significantly, one of the few plants Berlandier found was the saltwort (*Batis maritima*), which can withstand soils of high saline content. At the Hacienda de Salado there was likewise little vegetation, little potable water, and little reason to stay. They moved on quickly to the northeast through a valley between long, narrow cordilleras lying north-south or east-west. They went from arid hacienda to arid hacienda, although on December 27 they passed through a place of lush growth, the Hacienda de Buenavista, made famous during the Mexican War, from which they could see Saltillo. The Hacienda de Buenavista signaled that the soil was becoming less impregnated with salt, so hosted a more diverse flora. Berlandier found banana yucca (*Yucca baccata*), a species of vetch (*Vicia*), another of aster (*Aster*), and pine and sycamore trees.[4]

At Saltillo, Berlandier and his companions were finally exiting the Mexican Plateau and descending to well-watered plains, where they would leave the mountains behind and enter a realm of vast rivers flowing from north-west to southeast. First, however, they had to reach Monterrey, the road to which from Saltillo was through a gorge lying somewhat perpendicular to the remaining cordilleras of the Sierra Madre. January 5, 1828, they traveled by moonlight toward Monterrey; the beauty of the moon shining upon the mountains bathed in billowing clouds astonished Berlandier. Although not as tall as the Alps or snow-covered, the mountains reminded Berlandier of Switzerland, because of rugged features, triangular, piercing peaks, and deep, narrow gorges. The gorge leading from Saltillo to Monterrey passed through the Rancho de los Muertos, situated at the foot of a hill known as the Slope of the Dead, from where once not long before the Toboso Indians raided travelers. The presence of buzzards fit appropriately with the place, more so when the soldiers of the commission found a decomposing body. The road was a pockmarked punisher of wagons, which broke down repeatedly. Berlandier and Constantino Tarnava decided to leave the others behind and reconnoiter the path to Santa Catarina. Instead, they became lost and wandered about half the night. Finally they found their way to Santa Catarina, where the rest of the commission had already arrived. A clear mountain stream of the same name emerged from the slopes descending through Monterrey, shortly thereafter merging with the San Juan on its way to the Rio Grande. The environs of Monterrey had flora to interest the botanist. Flowers bloomed even in January. One unidentified plant reminded Berlandier of the dwarf willow (*Salix herbacea*) he had seen in the Alps. At the foot of the cordillera, Berlandier found an evergreen-oak, the Texas Live Oak (*Quercus fusiformis*), which was exclusive to the region of northern Mexico and southern Texas.[5]

The last week in January the commission departed north from Monterrey; Berlandier wrote that their exact destination on the Rio Grande was uncertain. Coming upon two dragoons sent from Gen. Anastacio Bustamante, the commander of the region (Eastern Interior Provinces), they informed General Terán of General Bustamante's wish that they rendezvous at Laredo; the dragoons were to escort them. The trail went north through a continuing arid environment with smaller mountains still about. They came to Salinas Victoria, where they crossed the small Río de Pesquería, a tributary of the Río de San Juan. They made slow time on the path, which was not a road, but an ad hoc route to Laredo. Continuing north, they arrived at Hacienda de Mamulique, situated adjacent to a rocky terrain to the north. Near Mamulique they found members of the Carrizo tribe camped by a creek. The Carrizos were a small, relatively defenseless tribe that inhabited the region on either side of the Rio Grande. They were terribly poor, but friendly, and Berlandier, who described them as "demi civilisés," *half-civilized*, was surprised to discover the extent of their materia medica. Berlandier sketched a male and female, portraying the latter in a full dress and barefoot, the former with bow and arrow and rifle, clothed only in a breechcloth. In "Indigenes nomades," he branded the men and women of the tribe as "dirty"; the latter, he added, were "utterly disgusting." The Carrizos did not practice agriculture but lived off their hunting and gathering abilities. They frequented white settlements for charity and protection and had been baptized Christians.[6]

From Mamulique, the commission moved north by northwest through a narrow valley toward Villaldama, the Lion's Mouth, a mining town situated on a small stream, the Río Sabinas, which flows into the Río Salado. Beyond Villaldama in the midst of a range of mountains, the men arrived at Carrizal, the place of the cane, which was another feeder stream of the Salado. They explored the peak and cave of Carrizal, and made geological observations about erosion and stratification. From Carrizal the men continued north in an arid, rocky environment to the presidio of Lampazos. This was the best-known route from Mamulique to Laredo, but so infrequent were travelers, and so remote the trail, that the men feared an attack by the Lipan Apaches or Comanches, who were known to frequent the area. That they did not have a run-in with Indian warriors was due, perhaps, to the presence of the presidio at Lampazos; though not imposing, the presence of such a village and soldiers in this desert environment impressed Berlandier. Paralleling a small stream took them northeast to Barranca; the same stream led to the Río Salada. The last day of January, the tortoise-like speed of men and vehicles journeying northeast of Barranca was too much for Chowell and Berlandier, who impatiently rode ahead toward the Río Salada, notwithstanding the possibility of Apaches or Comanches in the area. The two men camped next to the river, which was mostly dry, awaiting their companions. Whatever water was present in the river hosted some mussels, which the locals of Coahuila harvested and extracted freshwater pearls for jewelry. Chowell and Berlandier also found numerous turtles in and out of the water, the latter sunning themselves on dead tree branches above the surface. The entire troop proceeded onward, as the Salada's water was salty and there was no other fresh source. The path was at times almost impenetrable due to mesquites and huisaches; the soldiers used their swords to cut a path. They set out before sunrise the morning of February 2, under a full moon. By midday the lack of fresh water and the heat of the sun made their thirst "unbearable," José María Sánchez wrote in his diary of the journey, "and we were unable to rest as there was not a single tree under which we might stop. A plain that seemed to be on fire stretched before our eyes and our despair increased." But then they spied in the distance the first major goal of the journey, the Río Bravo del Norte, the Rio Grande.[7]

They crossed the river into an environment, topography, and climate wholly new to Jean Louis Berlandier. Hitherto the Pánuco valley had the familiarity of a vast river system that flowed from lofty peaks inland. Even in the humid environment of Tampico, Berlandier knew that the river was like that of his youth, the Rhône, which gathered the clear waters of the Alps and carried them forth through lowlands to the Mediterranean. Arid and never snow-covered, with bald tops over which hot winds blew, nevertheless the cordilleras of the Sierra Madre were the closest thing that Berlandier had to remind him of home. Had these Mexican mountains been snow-covered, the grand rivers they would produce from melting snow would make the Mexican Plateau as lush as the valleys watered by the Alps. Even the Rio Grande, though sluggish and filled with sediment at Laredo, still brought forward to the fertile imagination the memory of the snow-capped peaks of the Rockies. Memory was the only recourse Berlandier henceforth had to experience the grandeur and sublime solitude of distant peaks. He felt a "pang" of regret when entering Texas, departing the vistas of the Sierra Madre.[8]

Trying to accommodate himself to this limited visual experience, Berlandier began to search for as much information as he could about the Rio Grande and lands to the north. He acquired information about the river's natural history from local residents, knowledgeable soldiers, and hunters and trappers. He discovered that the river rises in the Rocky Mountains north of Santa Fe and is fed by numerous clear streams and rivulets until it descends to lower elevations, where its water becomes more sluggish. When it enters Texas it receives the waters of the Conchos, Pecos, Salado, and San Juan Rivers. Berlandier learned that the river is called Río Bravo del Norte until it arrives at the lowlands of Texas, where locals know it as the Rio Grande. The river at Laredo, with its brown shallow water and rapid current, reminded Berlandier of the Arve before it merges with the Rhône flowing from Lake Geneva. Besides this, Laredo could offer the Swiss scientist little else that reminded him of Helvetia, as he was fond to call home.[9]

Some of the men who traveled with Berlandier had similar misgivings based on what they left behind and what was to come. They knew that increasingly as they journeyed north and east they would enter into a land more remote from Mexican society, culture, and government, a land of inhospitable climate, rivers, prairies, and forests under contention by

Mexicans, colonists and squatters from the United States, and American Indians. The leader of the commission, General Terán, was a pragmatic, analytical thinker given to scientific inquisition and mathematical determination. A melancholy soul as well, his mind often ruminated on past scenes of conflict between Mexicans and Spain and among the violent political parties of independent Mexico. Questions concerning the unfinished and problematic Mexican Revolution worried him. Could Mexico achieve political and economic stability, or would civil conflict continue to haunt the country? Could permanent Mexican independence be realized in the face of continued aggression from the Spanish and other European powers? Would Mexico be able to hold on to Texas, or would American filibusters and colonists achieve their clear goal of creating an independent Texas? Would the aggressive and expansionistic U.S. government to the north keep its hands off Texas? Was Mexico even a part of their grand imperial designs? Recent personal tragedy caused Terán the most melancholy: just before the Boundary Commission set out, his two-year-old son unexpectedly died. After only three days of mourning, duty forced Terán to leave his wife of three years and journey north, uncertain when he would see her again. Memories of death and departure henceforth tainted whatever joy in life Terán experienced. He looked for solace in work, and elusive tranquility in study. Terán wrote in January 1829 of the melancholy enveloping him as he traveled through the Texas wilderness.[10]

Lt. José María Sánchez was similarly given to rumination. A dreamy, romantic thinker, a skilled artist and thoughtful writer, Sánchez wrote in his journal that he was frequently perplexed about his own insignificance compared to the grandeur of the creation. He was, like Terán, haunted by the immediate past; images and recollections of his loved ones, whom he dearly missed, pulled him back toward Mexico even as he journeyed north and east into Texas. His mind mirrored the experiences of the journey, reflecting the emptiness of the wilderness and the privation of its inhabitants. The journals of Berlandier and Sánchez have similar reflections on the interaction of humans and the wilderness, which sometimes yields strength and perseverance, which was the experience of Sánchez, and at other times weakness and surrender, which Berlandier, against his will, experienced.[11]

Laredo was hot, windy, dirty, the inhabitants shiftless and lazy, the location "dreary," the floral specimens scarce and uninteresting. Berlandier loved trees almost as much as mountains, but Laredo had few trees; this was due in part to the climate, in part to the lack of will of the inhabitants to plant trees, even when willows, sycamores, and poplars could stabilize the riverbanks to prevent the river's constantly eating away at its banks and carrying the soil downstream. One matter of interest to Berlandier and his companions was the presence of the Lipan Apaches at Laredo. During previous weeks traveling from Monterrey to Laredo, Berlandier had heard about the former depredations brought by the Lipans upon the small haciendas and towns of northern Mexico. The inhabitants of Laredo had similar stories to tell. The Apaches and their enemies the Comanches had previously harassed Laredo; since Mexican independence, however, the Indians had spared Laredo and other Rio Grande valley settlements from serious attacks. Part of the reason for peace with the Apaches was their leader, Castro (Cuelgas de Castro), who had made peace with the Mexican government after years of supporting attempts by rebels and filibusters to detach Texas from the Spanish Empire and Mexico. Castro had allied himself with Mexico against the Comanches. Berlandier saw Castro and thought him "urbane" and "civilized," unlike his counterpart, El Cojo, the Lame One, who was "ferocious" and "treacherous." Another chief, Pocaropa, "speaks fairly good Spanish." Lieutenant Sánchez, who like Berlandier was an accomplished artist, sketched the Lipans during their visit to Laredo. A watercolor based on his sketch, executed by Matamoros artist Lino Sánchez y Tapia, shows an elegantly dressed couple, the female with her hair nicely pulled back, wearing a skin poncho covering a skin dress; she appears modest and pretty. The male wears the garb of the warrior, shirtless with a mantle thrown over his shoulder; he is naked save for a breechcloth and long leather leggings rising to the upper thighs. He is armed with rifle, bullet pouch, and powder horn. His face is painted with vermilion. He wears his hair in a queue almost to the ground; Berlandier learned that the Lipan warriors tied women's or horse hair to their own to effect this length. The Lipans were few in numbers compared to their enemies the Comanches, who had driven the former south and prevented the Lipans from hunting buffalo. Nevertheless, the Lipans were fierce and feared warriors, wily and treacherous, and excellent horsemen who while riding bareback could disguise themselves by grabbing the horse's mane and using the strength of their legs to hold on to the side of the horse, making it appear that the horse was riderless. The unsuspecting observer, Berlandier wrote, "believes he is looking only at a herd of wild horses. Then, when close enough, [the Lipan warriors] fall on their enemies with an extraordinary velocity." While at Laredo the Lipans performed a song and dance whereby they marched slowly in single file, shuffling their feet to make a loud marching noise, all the while holding a buffalo robe sufficiently taut that it could be struck like a drum, and singing in accompaniment with a wide range of high and low notes.[12]

Figure 5.
Lipan warrior. In: "United States and Mexican Boundary Survey. Report of William H. Emory. . . ." Washington. 1857. Volume I. P. 79. 1857. NOAA Library Collection.

Berlandier's sojourn at Laredo was too brief to know fully the river; he would in time spend more than twenty years living at Matamoros near the mouth of the Rio Grande—then he would know the river better than any other, even the Rhône. Until then, there were many rivers to cross, some shallow and easy to ford, others deep, ferocious, and deadly. Berlandier would discover in the coming months that the rivers of Texas were generally of the latter sort. The Spanish had christened many of the natural phenomena of New Spain with names of faith and devotion. The San Antonio River recalled the great desert saint of old; the Trinity River honored the Father, Son, and Holy Spirit; the San Juan River was named after the great Apostle. Then there was the Río de los Brazos de Dios. The explorer, journeying through Texas in spring months, when rains were plentiful and floods recurrent, inundating the surrounding valleys, learned precisely why the unknown Spaniard who christened the river called it *the arms of God*. This river, like other Texas rivers such as the Colorado and Trinity, embraced with cool waters to irrigate the land and slack the thirst of man and beast and at the same time smote with uncontrollable waters that flooded and destroyed. Pious inhabitants could sense the reach of the divine, giving and taking, blessing and cursing. These Texas rivers were long and winding, gathering the clayey, salty waters of distant plateaus, rather than crystal waters of snowy mountains. One could hardly expect otherwise once the commission departed Laredo and began the path along the arid desert between the Rio Grande and the Nueces River. Berlandier noted that Texas rivers change the course of their direction befitting the curve of the Gulf Coast. Rivers such as the Nueces enter the Gulf from the west; as the traveler goes farther east, rivers such as the Brazos enter the Gulf from the north-northwest; the Trinity, the easternmost river that Berlandier reached, flows due south.[13]

The route from Laredo to San Antonio was along a trail-turned-road, the Old Bexar Road, frequented by muleteers, shepherds, soldiers, and Indians. The February climate reminded Berlandier of spring in southern Europe. There were few trees or hills, but the ground was covered with a "pleasant, spring-like verdure." Whenever they bivouacked for the night at a spring or pond, Berlandier collected interesting plants and set to preservation work. He found rushes, cane, a flowering wild cabbage, and a flowering legume plant. Shepherds and others that they passed proclaimed their fear of Indian attack, even though there had been recent peace between the Mexicans and Lipans, and Mexicans and Comanches. The noise of the wagons, horses, and men appeared to scare off all but the most foolhardy prey. Deer were elusive; turkeys were too slow to elude the good aim of the soldiers, who provided fresh poultry to enliven their meager diet of corn cakes, *pinole*, and salt beef. They also purchased a lamb from the shepherds. Vultures hovered about, though only a starving man would dine on these disgusting creatures. Many years later, in his manuscript on birds, Berlandier wrote that vultures "prefer dead and stinking prey, and carry with them the odor of putrefied flesh. They are covered with lice. Their flight is majestic and without noise." Soldiers and travelers often used the bird as a means of communicating, nailing a dead vulture to a tree with a note attached, which could scarcely fail to be noticed by others on the trail. Berlandier and companions could hear but rarely see the *tiburón*, or bullfrog. Sánchez, for one, found the bullfrog's constant croaking during the night a cause for sadness. Coyotes were sufficiently curious (and hungry) to come close to camp and were recalcitrant to leave. Catfish populated streams and ponds. Camping the night of February 21, the men were astonished by the clear midnight blue of the heavens, which "kindled the imagination" in Sánchez, leading him "to reflect upon the great mystery of the unknown and the boundless power of the Supreme Being that brought everything out of chaos by His infinite power." Berlandier shared thoughts similar to Sánchez's. The farther north and closer to the Nueces River they traveled, the greater the greenery of the plains and fertility of the land. The sky was still stingy with its moisture, so that they found the Nueces to be largely dry, with a shallow current, known from the distance not by its valley but by the willows and ash trees that hovered along its banks. Berlandier made no mention of pecan or other nut trees, even though *nueces* is, literally, "nuts." The Nueces was relatively clear; the river where they crossed flowed northeast after having dipped like a horseshoe after a long descent southeast from its western source. The wagons forded the Nueces on a makeshift bridge, contrived by several soldiers who had been sent ahead a few days. They were near the confluence of the Atascosa flowing from the north, the Frio flowing from the west, and the Nueces. It was a short journey from the Nueces to the Frio. The Texas prickly pear (*Opuntia lindheimeri*) dotted the ground; Berlandier observed another species of cactus, *Opuntia leptocaulis*, which he thought, incorrectly, was a new discovery, and which he called tasajillo. Berlandier found flowers from the genera *Ranunculus*, *Physalis*, and *Anemone*. Deer and wild horses roamed on the land, which was becoming more hilly. Although it was late February, the air was warm and sultry. The Frio River, which they crossed February 25, was largely dry, though the watermark on trees lining the bank indicated the massive flood that the river could, in the rainy season, produce. Over the course of his many journeys into Texas, Berlandier would see the Frio at times when the river had a full but not flooding bed of water, which could be cool and clear, and good to the taste.[14]

They made camp along a stream called San Miguel on February 26. A soldier named Balboa, who commanded the military escort provided by General Bustamante and who had lived in this region long enough to become familiar with the almanac of the winds and sky, had been observing meteorological phenomena during the course of the day; he noted the calm at the surface but power of the south wind in the upper atmosphere, followed by, after dark, the growing force of the north wind. He approached Berlandier and Sánchez and informed them that a prairie thunderstorm was approaching. But there appeared to be little evidence, and Berlandier and Sánchez were suspicious of his confidence. Berlandier later realized from experience that the weather of Texas is predictable in its many changes. The unusual heat of the day brought by the powerful south winds invariably gives way to the cooling norther that is escorted by flashes of lightning, torrents of rain, pelting hail, and destructive winds. Balboa turned out to be right. As the evening progressed, a wall of dark clouds appeared in the northern horizon accompanied by a dazzling display of cloud-to-ground lightning. Sánchez wrote that the imminent storm "inspired a certain sadness not unmixed with terror." Soon the storm was upon them: a drenching rain accompanied by tremendous gusts of wind and piercing blasts of light. Hailstones as large as walnuts pelted the ground, the animals, and the men, some of whom were protected by tents that the wind ripped from the temporary pegs holding them down. The natural phenomena resembled, Sánchez and Berlandier thought, "the grandeur and magnificence of the mighty spectacle in which nature seemed to battle with itself." Once the storm passed, a cool north wind, a clear sky, and complete silence remained for the night.[15]

On the bright morning of a new day they set forth from San Miguel to another creek, called La Parrita. The verdure of prairie plants had been heightened by the rain; leaves in the elm, ash, and oak forest surrounding the creek looked healthy and green. La Parrita was a stream of clear, good-tasting water. Upon arriving in the evening they crossed the stream just in case rains upstream caused rising water overnight. Berlandier botanized, collecting species of herbs and grasses. They spent a tranquil evening next to La Parrita. The only sounds to interrupt their repose were the melancholy cries of coyotes and the screech owl, which, according to the soldiers, resembled the communication of Indians planning an attack. Berlandier, who frequently collected his thoughts at night, looking into the night sky and beyond to the stars, reflected on his long journey of over a year in Mexico, and the moments of anxiety, longing for home, dread, anticipation, and excitement. He declared to himself that he was as content on the wilderness trail as in "the bosom of society." In time, however, the fatigues of continual journeys combined with the cares of growing older forced Berlandier to make a decision to settle down.[16]

The last day of February the commission journeyed north toward the Medina River on their way to San Antonio. Hickory and oak trees decorated the land. The Medina was a narrow, clear river lined with cypress (*Taxodium distichum*), cedar, and oak trees. Here the commission was met by the commandant of the presidio of San Antonio, Lt. Col. Antonio Elosúa, who provided a military escort for Terán and his men. Downstream the Medina joined the San Antonio and eventually the Guadalupe Rivers. The first day of March, they began the journey that took them to San Antonio. The landscape heralded spring with plum, pecan, willow, and poplar trees. Sánchez, joyful that they were nearing San Antonio, exulted in the "landscape dressed in the most vivid colors of smiling and budding spring. Everywhere delicately tinted tapestries of living flowers were visible, while the shrubs and evergreen oaks, the walnuts and other trees, formed a superb background that lost itself in the horizon, charming the eye and filling the heart of the spectator with an unknown joy."[17]

The land advertised its first fruits: tender young shoots, leaves glistening with dew, slowly dripping, marking time, as winter retreated before the daily movement of the sun's rays becoming more direct. May apples opened, their small, umbrella-like leaves sheltering the soil and their own budding blossoms from the pelting rains of spring; the green fruit would not appear until late April or early May. Tender blossoms, white petals enclosing a center of yellow or purple, appeared among the first flowers of spring. They lined the humid, damp forest floor. Water pooled in random forests, streaming slowly under the midday sun; the air became warm and sultry. Songbirds raised their song above the ground, and the trees resounded with their choir. Squirrels chattered warnings against intruders; crows cawed at hawks and other birds of prey investigating opportunities for food.

The path took them near the missions of San Antonio: La Concepción, La Espada, San José, San Juan, and San Antonio de Valero, the latter known as the Alamo, after the military company stationed there. The missions were scattered on opposite sides of the San Antonio River. They saw the southernmost mission, Espada, but skirted around Concepción, San José, and San Juan. All were built of stone and in various states of ruin. Espada had an imposing, arched entrance. This mission, along with Concepción and San Juan, were relocated in 1731 from the Colorado River to the east to the San Antonio River, where the missions San José and San Antonio de Valero already had been founded, in 1720 and 1718 respectively. Espada and San José were located along the west side of the river, opposite to Concepción and San Juan. For a half century the missions had been abandoned and were falling into ruin. Huddled about the old buildings were the hovels of poor farmers, who had for a century looked to the missions for protection in this life and the next. The missions were fortresses, all save San Antonio de

Valero privately owned and allowed to decay; the structures still served to protect the people when Indians attacked. Although ostensibly at peace, the Comanches raided farmlands lying outside the presidio. The threat of attack gave the inhabitants an excuse not to pursue farming to any great extent. San Antonio was therefore a poor presidio, a town with little beauty save for the mission San Antonio de Valero, which was a large defensive structure surrounded by tall, strong walls. Berlandier believed that the chapel within "could pass for one of the loveliest monuments of the area." Berlandier thought (and Sánchez agreed) that the inhabitants of San Antonio were, like the inhabitants of Laredo, lazy and fun-loving, given to dance rather than to work. They eschewed farming lands near the town as requiring too much work to irrigate the soil, whereas several miles away, beyond the protection of the presidio, they planted their seed and dry-farmed—though they were rarely able to harvest the crop because of the frequent Indian attacks. The soldiers could scarcely stop the Indians, because they lacked the equipment and ambition; the government of Mexico rarely paid them, and they had little incentive to risk their lives. If they had horses, their mounts were inferior to those of the Indians, which, in a culture devoted to horses, must have been frustrating to many caballeros. The American Texans, unlike the Mexicans, were (according to Berlandier) hardworking, taking advantage of the land's resources. Whereas the Mexicans were apt to use whatever trees they could find for building and fuel, the Texans looked to the future, planting trees to ensure forests for their posterity. The primitive technology of the Mexicans also surprised Berlandier; their wagons looked like centuries-old relics of medieval Europe.[18]

During their month-long stay at San Antonio to rest and reconnoiter, they planned to journey to the source of the San Antonio River. On their first attempt (March 4), they did not have a sufficient escort to defend against an Indian attack, so they delayed until March 10, when enough troops could be gathered. The river's source, a spring that issued from limestone, was but five miles from the presidio; the river's course to the town was rapid through a narrow channel. Initially the water was clear before it joined, downriver, the Medina, eventually the Guadalupe. The San Antonio furnished turtles, frogs, catfish, gar, and foot-long shrimp that were, unfortunately, rare. The hills in the environs of San Antonio supported green grass and wildflowers, such as the beautiful purple petals of species of verbena (*Verbena*) and lupine (*Lupine*), as well as a multitude of budding and flowering trees such as the mulberry, persimmon, cherry, poplar, laurel, elm, oak, hickory, pecan, and pine.[19]

General Terán took time, during the sojourn at San Antonio, to pen a letter to the president of the Republic of Mexico, Guadalupe Victoria, on the state of affairs in Texas. Much of the letter dealt with the people of Texas, especially the Indians, many of whom were newcomers to the land, having been driven south and west by the advance of American civilization. Terán learned from Col. José Francisco Ruíz, who befriended Berlandier as well, that the Comanches dominated Texas Indians, being the most feared and the best warriors. Terán was worried less about the Indians, however, than he was about the Americans, who daily encroached on Mexican land west of the Sabine and south of the Red River. Indeed, he had planned to write President Victoria at large about his concern later, after his anticipated arrival at Nacogdoches, but information acquired at San Antonio compelled him not to delay. The extent of American immigration into Texas was alarming. Besides the legal immigrants, arriving under the auspices of Stephen Austin, forming the colony of San Felipe, were numerous squatters and filibusters, who disobeyed the laws of Mexico, crossed the borders, particularly the Sabine River, and squatted on Mexican soil. Mexico did little to discourage the immigrants; the small number of Mexican troops in Texas could scarcely repel such a subtle invasion. The soldiers were at any rate rarely paid, their esprit de corps was consequently low, and the economy of the presidios was stagnant. Soldiers did not engage in farming—neither did many of the inhabitants of the presidios—hence the poverty and malaise of the populace. Several months later, writing from Nacogdoches, Terán had a greater sense of the American threat, and he urged President Victoria to enhance the presidial troops at San Antonio and Nacogdoches.[20]

The commission departed San Antonio on April 13, traveling northeast on the "Middle Road," to distinguish it from the Upper Road connecting San Antonio to Nacogdoches and the Lower Road connecting Goliad with Matamoros. The Middle Road was sometimes called the Gonzales Road toward the Guadalupe River, and, after that, the Atascosito Road. A mere path in the wilderness, it was often indistinct from animal traces and other apparent paths. Texas Americans had fortunately notched trees at intervals to help travelers find their way; some trees even had the mileage from Gonzales notched in their trunks. Lieutenant Colonel Elosúa provided an escort of dragoons that would accompany the Comisión to the Trinity River. The men bivouacked at various creeks along the route, first at the Arroyo del Salado the evening of their departure, where they listened to the hoots of owls and eerie cries of the cuckoo. On April 14, at the Arroyo del

Cibolo, they camped next to a deep channel with freshwater. Buffalo once roamed the area, but not since the increasing numbers of white settlements during recent decades. The landscape was hilly and wooded, with frequent oak and hickory groves; blooming wildflowers, such as species of verbena, larkspur (*Delphinium*), and narcissus (*Narcissus*), abounded, as did butterflies. Berlandier busied himself in making significant collections of flora and fauna. They crossed numerous gullies, arroyos that would swell with water in a heavy rain, which made for a fatiguing journey. Also fatiguing were the malicious plants of nature, particularly the bull nettle (*Cnidosculus texanus*) and poison ivy (*Rhus toxicodendron*), which locals called evil woman, *mala mujer*. Travelers found by experience that some people, when in contact with mala mujer, would unexpectedly get an itchy rash that would swell with pus and spread across the body; if it reached the male genitals, the testicles swelled. The irritation easily spread through scratching, which was unavoidable except for the most self-controlled of men. Strangely, some members of the commission, such as Berlandier, were free from the effects of mala mujer; some soldiers rubbed bear grease all over themselves as a preventative from rash and itching (if not from smell).[21]

They arrived at the Guadalupe River on the evening of April 16 after having traversed a dry, hot, and barren land. The valley of the Guadalupe was beautiful in the flowers and trees of its banks, refreshing in the clear, cool water of its current. The arboreal welcome to the sojourners included cottonwood (*Populus deltoides*), various types of oak, mimosa, mesquite, willow, and red buckeye (*Aesculus pavia*). Berlandier discovered a species of *Clematis*, a thin vine that invades trees and bushes. The multitude of grasses that they encountered along the way had suggested a fertile land, which the Guadalupe valley confirmed. The colony of Gonzales, founded by Green C. DeWitt two years before, had taken very little of what the land offered; there were a few wooden cabins housing somewhat dissolute inhabitants. Indian attacks and the harsh climate of Texas had hitherto rendered the colony largely impoverished. The inhabitants cooked and dined on a bottom floor and slept in a room above; the habitations if not the environs reminded Berlandier of the chalets of Switzerland, though there, on the slopes of the Alps, the houses had to be made more secure against the wind, and the chimney was a central feature dominating the house. Sánchez recorded strange, conflicting sensations in his journal, a product of comparing his life as a soldier with the impoverished squatters who tried to wrestle a bitter existence from the elements. A young American girl elicited contradictory feelings of attraction toward her Arcadian life and wild beauty and revulsion toward what her life held for her, and the elusiveness of beauty and youth in a land of hardship. Berlandier experienced similar feelings the day they departed from Gonzales. They journeyed through a dense forest, the new growth of which covered the wilderness road; soldiers had to cut a path with ax and machete to enable the forward progress of the wagons. Proceeding in this slow and tortured fashion, they came upon a small cabin amid the oak forest; two American women who were part of the DeWitt colony and who were filled with immediate anxiety because of the approach of strangers while their husbands were away clearing land, lived, Berlandier discovered, under a daily apprehension of their situation in life and the constant threat of Indian attacks, especially from the Comanche. Berlandier could understand their fear; he too felt alone and small because of "the solitude of the forest; the silence of that majestic nature, interrupted solely by birdsong; the cry of the screech owl; the hoariness of oaks covered with Spanish moss." For the rest of his life Berlandier would recall the mixture of awe and fear, wonder and confusion, and attraction and revulsion at the savagery of the wilderness compared to the structure and artificial order of civilized society.[22]

There was such a profusion of plants along the banks of the Guadalupe that it took Berlandier the better part of the morning of April 17 to order and preserve them. They consequently got a late start and traveled a short distance along a path so hidden by the new growth of spring that they strayed from the way several times. Marshes and ponds yielded beautiful flowers such as lilies and a hapless caiman, defenseless before the soldiers' firearms. In the early afternoon they were forced to bivouac at the Arroyo de los Tejocotes, where the road descended a steep bank to the creek that impeded the passage of wagons. While soldiers worked to lessen the slope, Berlandier botanized, examining closely the stands of poison ivy as well as a more fearsome plant, the bull nettle, the spines of which are extremely painful to the touch. That night a fierce thunderstorm pelted man and beast with a driving rain. The next day, April 18, their progress continued slowly due to rainy weather and another steeply banked creek. Terán took several observations of celestial phenomena to mark the latitude of the place where they rested, Loma Grande. They feasted on turkey that night. Soldiers told Berlandier that the birds were easy to catch on horseback; once they escaped through flight, upon landing they resorted to running, when they were easily lassoed. With the passing days mosquitoes began to torment the men.

As frustrating was the recurrent breakage of the cumbersome wagons and the increasingly moist, almost swampy landscape through which the road passed. On April 19, after crossing the small river Lavaca, which had little water to impede the way, a disabled wagon wheel allowed Berlandier to explore the plants of the place. He found red buckeye and various species of cacti. Meanwhile, the soldiers fashioned a wagon wheel from sturdy oak branches. After bivouacking April 20, they again set forth April 21, crossing the Navidad River during the course of the day. They camped at a tributary, Cedar Creek, where they met with an old Tonkawa who was hungry and practically naked. He told them of the Tonkawa village a few miles off, which Berlandier, Chowell, and Batres, accompanied by soldiers, decided to visit. Their arrival caused great consternation among the village dogs and children, though the warriors lazily welcomed them. They bartered a few goods, then returned to camp with the Tonkawa chief. The next morning General Terán, Sánchez, and Berlandier repaid the visit. Upon approaching the village one of the dragoons let out a war cry that brought consternation to the village until they saw who their visitors were. They welcomed the Mexicans to the chief's hut made of bowed branches covered with hides. The chief smoked a pipe with a mixture of tobacco and sumac and offered them a thick drink made of the berries of the yaupon (*Ilex vomitoria*). Many tribes of the region used yaupon as a purgative and emmenagogue; Berlandier thought most tribes considered it a cure-all. The Mexican visitors were unimpressed by their hosts' cleanliness, clothing, manners, wealth, and decorum. They branded the women filthy and ugly, and the men little better. A watercolor executed by Lino Sánchez y Tapia, based on the observations of Sánchez, shows the Tonkawa woman as naked save for a breechcloth, her stomach and breasts tattooed; a male similarly attired, with a line tattooed or painted on his face; and another male attired in more formal clothing, with full-length leggings, a mantle, and an ornamented tunic. The latter warrior carries a musket, while the other has a longbow. The men Berlandier saw painted their skin with earthy colors; one warrior had white lines that reminded him of the uniforms of Swiss guards he had seen many years before. The Tonkawa resided in small huts suitable for sitting or sleeping, with a fire burning in the center, the smoke useful for repelling insects. They relied on hunting deer and small game, and what clothes they wore were fashioned from deerskin. The lack of buffalo meat and robes was due to the threat of their hated enemy the Comanche, which kept the much weaker Tonkawa from the buffalo hunt.[23]

Returning to camp and proceeding east, they journeyed but a short distance before another wagon wheel disintegrated, which forced an unexpected camp. A nearby stream and the camp itself were named for Sánchez, because, one gathers, it was a place for the weary of heart. On April 23 they reached the Colorado, the "red river" of Texas. They dined at the house of a wealthy American and camped on the western side of the river, all the while noting that the river was definitely rising; cloudy, foamy spume was accumulating on its waters, and river debris, logs and branches, increasing. April 24, the men ferried the equipment and wagons across the river; they bivouacked for several days to repair the disabled wagon. On April 26, they journeyed east to the San Bernard River, camping among a few small oak trees. The next day they reached San Felipe, spying for some time during the day's fatiguing journey through treeless, swampy land the distant trees that marked the Brazos River.[24]

Stephen Austin had founded San Felipe four years before, in 1824, fulfilling the dream of his father, Moses, of colonizing the land beyond the Sabine, a rich territory loosely controlled by an unorganized and chaotic government born of revolution. The government of Mexico, still beset by political quarrels and violence, sought to impose control over lands it had won in gaining independence. It was a futile effort, however, as the people arriving from the Arkansas Territory and the states of Missouri and Louisiana and beyond were a mercurial people, contradictory, inconsistent, and fickle, yet driven to accomplish and acquire. The men of the Comisión de Límites trusted few Americans that they met on the way to the Sabine, and they uniformly predicted in their respective journals that these shrewd, restless people would one day take this land of Texas from the Mexicans. Sánchez liked nothing about the Austin colony, thought that the empresario, Austin, was duplicitous, and predicted that "the spark that will start the conflagration that will deprive us of Texas, will start from this colony." Berlandier was, like his companion, suspicious and critical of the Americans; but if there was an exception to the mistrust that he felt, it was Stephen Austin. Unlike other Americans, who assumed that empty land without apparent government control was theirs for the taking, Austin respected Mexican sovereignty, and obtained the necessary permissions to establish a colony. Neither did Austin join those filibusters who assumed that Texas was the rightful property of the United States because of the hazy boundaries of Louisiana Territory and the American purchase of 1803. Indeed, men of San Felipe joined Mexican forces in the march toward Nacogdoches to put down the Fredonian Rebellion at the end of 1826 and beginning of 1827. Even so, Berlandier knew that Austin was wily, willing to tell Mexican authorities what they wanted to hear.[25]

San Felipe de Austin was a thriving community of several hundred people of varying abilities, wealth, and status. The town had signs of having been originally laid out in Mexican fashion "with a measuring tape," in Berlandier's words, but most of the settlement that he saw was without planning. Some inhabitants prospered sufficiently to own a cabin in town as well as on their land away from town. Although slavery was banned in the Mexican republic, Austin had successfully lobbied the department of Coahuila y Texas and the central government in Mexico City to allow the colony to use slaves, at least temporarily; according to Sánchez, the inhabitants of San Felipe mistreated their slaves. A few merchants sold the inhabitants their necessities, such as flour, lard, coffee, and liquor; many of the citizens acted as though they relied too heavily on the latter. Sánchez wrote that the Americans practically lived on salt beef.[26]

The Brazos, the longest and most powerful river in Texas, gathers the waters of northwest and north-central Texas as well as the stories and legends of its people. The past evokes images of Spanish explorers dying of thirst rescued by the arms of God. Berlandier disbelieved such stories, arguing that the name of the river derives from its two main arms, the Salt Fork and the Double Mountain Fork. When he arrived at San Felipe, the Brazos was chocolate colored, having accumulated the moisture of land and sky from hundreds of miles inland. Berlandier, ever judging his experiences according to his youth in the Alps, thought the Brazos resembled the Arve as he remembered it just before it entered the Rhône. Massive tree trunks hurried by in the flood. The current of the rising, flooding river terrified those who contemplated a crossing and reminded the pious of the power of God at the creation. The night of April 30 brought a spring storm the likes of which men rarely experience. The fury of the pelting rain, constant lightning and thunder, and unrelenting wind from the north amazed and terrified these sojourners of 1828 who sought comfort in the embrace of the arms of God.[27]

The Boundary Commission departed San Felipe on May 10 at the height of the contradictions of spring along the southern Texas frontier. Wildflowers in bloom such as the delicate bluebonnet (*Lupinus texensis*) were enriched by the noon sun yet battered by late afternoon storms. The wet heat of late spring, oppressive during day and night, at times gave way to the roaring

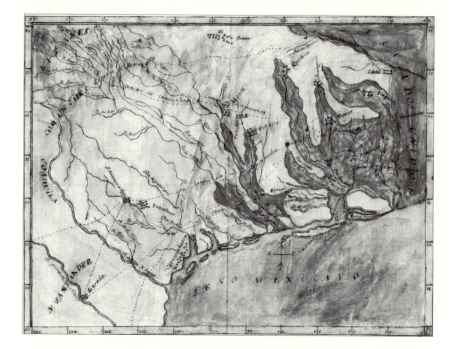

Figure 6. Mapa topográfico de la provincia de
Texas by Stephen F. Austin. Library of Congress.

thunderstorm that drenched and terrified all in its wake only to give way soon
after to the sun made more intense by the steamy air. The surrounding oak
and poplar forest was a rich verdure, the underbrush extensive, still exhibiting the shiny gleam of new growth. The clayey soil was, however, waterlogged,
a soggy mess that surrounded and sucked in whatever penetrated the surface:
men's boots, horse's hooves, wooden wagon wheels.

The expedition under General Terán set forth from San Felipe in the
same impractical fashion as before. General Terán traveled in his gilded
carriage that befit his rank and image but could not have been more out of
place in the wilderness of the Brazos valley. Teams of weary mules battled
to pull through the muck the heavy wooden wheels of huge wagons loaded
with supplies and scientific instruments. Dragoons escorted the commission on horseback, outfitted in tight-fitting uniforms decorated with sashes
and epaulets; swords hung at their sides; they wore helmets with extrava-
gant, bright-colored plumes. Guides and scientists such as Berlandier wore

broad-rimmed hats, coats, and trousers to protect against the extremes of
the wilderness. Berlandier, perhaps, was too preoccupied with botanizing,
collecting, recording, and preserving his observations and floral specimens
to consider the absurdity of such pomp. Intent on his goal of collecting the
botanical treasures of the Mexican frontier, the scientist rarely indulged
in the typical distractions of the journey. Complaints, groans, and curses
filled the ranks as the men battled the heat, mud, and disease-carrying
insects. Yet what was to the soldiers just another duty of exceptional drudg-
ery was to Berlandier the raison d'être, the object of his long sojourn in
Mexico. He reveled in the rich arboreal and floral variety, the collection and
preservation of which would justify his Swiss patrons sending him to this
land. The woods and prairies abounded with the likes of the Texas mountain
laurel or mescal bean (*Sophora secundiflora*), specimens of which Berlandier
successfully preserved notwithstanding the forces of nature working to
the contrary.[28]

The journey of botanist and soldiers from San Felipe toward their destination of Nacogdoches near the Sabine River was halting, burdened by
misfortunes that could scarcely be anticipated. The swollen Brazos barred
their way until May 9, when, with supplies diminishing and time wasting,
Terán ordered the launch of the heavy wagons and their drivers as well as an
escort of dragoons across the river aboard flatboat barges (*chalanas*). Terán
directed the escort to find the road on the opposite side while he waited
with the rest of the men and supplies to cross the following day. The next
day, the river now more daunting, the men boarded a chalana navigated by
one white and three black boatmen, who sang a melody the lyrics of which
were incomprehensible to the Mexicans. They descended the winding river
about six miles and came to a watery inlet, a flooded bayou that, according
to the ferry pilots, would bring them to the rendezvous. They proceeded to
pole the chalana up the bayou, navigating among tree branches, the forest being completely inundated by the flood. It was eerie floating about the
upper branches of oaks, walnuts, and poplars. As daylight ebbed, a heavy
fog overwhelmed the waterlogged environment, adding to the strange-
ness of the situation. All appeared a dense green. The water oozed around
decomposed plants, and the odor of rotting vegetation was pervasive. And
yet it was all immensely beautiful to Berlandier. Soon they reached land,
earth so saturated that it seemed but a sucking sponge. By this time darkness had fallen, and a planned rendezvous with soldiers who had brought
the carriage and wagons over the previous day seemed to have gone awry.

Eventually, they heard the shout of a soldier, who told them that the wagon escort had been forced to separate, because the vehicles had become stuck in the mire. Some of the soldiers had gone to a settler's cabin to spend the night. Terán's men also split, some, such as Raphael Chowell, joining the wagon escort; others, such as Berlandier, stayed with Terán. He regretted his decision throughout the night. Needing rest, the men bivouacked on the boats or whatever muddy spot that had escaped inundation. Berlandier and Sánchez chose to sleep aboard the ferry, while General Terán slept in the woods. The night was long and torturous. Mosquitoes feasted on bare skin. The humidity was oppressive. Although Terán slept under the protection of a tent, neither the "voracious" mosquitoes nor the unbearable humidity allowed him any sleep. Berlandier thought a hundred nights spent at the most humid, bug-infested place in the Pánuco valley preferable to one night in this bayou. The boatmen, used to such conditions, built a smoky campfire to ward off the bugs and sat around it singing homely melodies, awaiting dawn.[29]

The sounds of night, "the silence of the solitude," in Berlandier's words, engendered melancholy reflections on the past and present. The repetitive croaks of frogs, sporadic songs of night birds, and nefarious hums of the mosquito, broke into the daunting silence of the darkest of nights. Rays of moonlight, which could serve as a friendly beacon to scatter the darkness, this night added to Berlandier's sadness, as he could scarcely see the moon through the enclosed canopy of trees and humid air, which added to the overwhelming impression of loneliness. Although the men generally knew where they were, the newness of this experience, stuck in a hitherto unknown swamp, surrounded by caimans and other creatures of the swamp and night, made Berlandier feel as though he had never been more lost, physically and emotionally, in his life. As he listened to the plaintive songs of the slaves, whom he had seen mistreated by their white masters at San Felipe, he thought that even in their worst moments, feeling the pain of the overseer's whip on the bare back, they could not feel more disillusioned, trapped, and lost, with an utter pain in the soul, than he did this night.[30]

Dawn eventually arrived, gray and moist, breaking through the dismal forest and thoughts of the night. Sunlight attempted to penetrate the canopy of hazy verdure. The men were exhausted from sleeplessness. Sánchez thought that the general's face had been "flayed" by the incessant action of the mosquitoes. Berlandier noted that henceforth Terán was bothered by a recurrent fever whenever one of the many bites swelled and filled with pus. This and subsequent days the expedition made slow progress on the muddy path heading east from the Brazos to the Trinity River. Potholes of varying depths challenged the supply wagons as well as General Terán's carriage made less elegant with so many splotches of mud. The land was largely uninhabited save for the random squatter attempting to bring a successful farm from the wilderness. They sometimes met hunters and trappers, often hiring them to pilot the journeyers through the forest. Berlandier learned from their guides that white and Indian hunters alike used the roots of the "beaver tree," or sweetbay (*Magnolia virginiana*), to attract the beaver, prolific in this wet and watery environment, to steel or more primitive traps.[31]

After a long day, May 11, of observations and tedious travel, the expedition halted at the farm of a family who, notwithstanding the botanical riches surrounding them, existed in utter poverty and consequent misery. Camp brought time for man and beast to rest and eat. They bivouacked the next day to repair a wagon disabled by the mud. Berlandier took this chance to look over his collections and carefully preserve floral specimens. He continued his habit of recording daily meteorological readings of wind and temperature, and if the night was clear, he kept track of the positions of constellations and phases of the moon. Terán, a more accomplished astronomer, looked for chances to determine latitude and longitude. He complained to his journal that the opportunities for celestial observation, one of his only emotional comforts during the journey, were rare because of the frequent cloud cover. During the day they could detect among the highest branches a north wind moving the trees but not penetrating to the ground. Exiting briefly from the swamp forest, they traveled through a prairie with spring flowers and Indian tea (*Thelesperma megapotamicum*), a long, thin plant used by local tribes.[32]

The next few days of travel were like the first two. The canopy of oak, poplar, and pecan was reluctant to let sunshine reach the forest floor so to dry it. Mud was ubiquitous; soldiers and animals had to exert great strength just to make the most limited movement. Soldiers wielded axes with frequency to carve a path through the forest; they pulled on ropes harnessed to wagons and mules to extract them from the mud. The days were long, hot and humid, yet the distance in miles traveled between dawn and dusk numbered in the single digits. At the varied meadows along the way, a rich and exotic variety of flowers challenged the botanist to make haste in his collecting. The journeyers lacked supplies, good pasture for their animals, and food for themselves. General Terán ordered Sánchez and Chowell to visit the nearby plantation of

Jared Groce, an early associate of Austin who owned a vast stretch of land on the eastern banks of the Brazos. He operated the ferry that the wagon escort had used to cross the Brazos. Groce told them that the muddy road upon which they traveled was called the Camino de la Magdalena. Groce's plantation grew mostly cotton; he had a cotton gin to separate the fiber from the seed. He practiced girdling, in which incisions were made at the base of the tree to kill it, to prepare the land for cultivation. Sánchez and Chowell found Groce neither hospitable nor appealing, branding him a miser and a vicious man who mistreated his slaves, which numbered over one hundred.[33]

During the second week in May, the rigors of travel forced Berlandier to give up on some of his scientific activities; for example, he took his last observation of the sky with the cyanometer on May 12. May 14 to 16 the men continued their painful march through undulating country of grassy, sandy hills and waterlogged forests. On May 15 they crossed the Navasota River. The labor of pulling wagons (and mules) across the river and through endless mud brought scant reward, and only a few miles a day were gained. For Berlandier, the slow progress meant leisurely botanizing, though it was a struggle to move about in the ubiquitous wet sandy soil. With each step the men's boots sank into the soil, requiring great effort to simply walk. The weather alternated between humidity made torturous by the sun and frequent showers, which scarcely relieved the air of its moisture. Mosquitoes continued to plague the men, with predictable results. On May 16 Berlandier, after a brief repose without shade, experienced dizziness. That night he became terribly ill with a high fever that left him senseless for several hours before dawn. General Terán relinquished his carriage for the sake of Berlandier and another man, the cook, who also became sick. One would scarcely know of Berlandier's extended and severe illness from his journal, in which he continued as best he could to make observations of the environment. Spending days prostrate in the carriage as it traversed the wet, spongy land made it seem like a massive tortoise. To ease the boredom Berlandier betook himself to describing the limestone formations of the landscape and the dicotyledonous nature of the surrounding flora. The men made for the farm of Francis Holland, one of Stephen Austin's associates, a successful farmer who was able to offer the hungry (and sick) men fresh milk and poultry.[34]

On May 18 they set forth from Holland's, crossing a creek (perhaps Holland's or Ten Mile Creek), where one of the wagons broke an axle. Exhausted and frustrated, with two men sickened with the ague, they decided to make camp for a few days to fix the wagon and repair their spirits.

To make matters worse, the general came down with a fever during the afternoon; however, the next morning he was feeling better. Berlandier was not; rather, he was growing worse notwithstanding his best efforts to gather plants known to counter the effects of fever. Berlandier, who had been acquiring information on the traditional materia medica of the Spanish frontier, tried to relieve his suffering with plants of the region between the Brazos and Trinity Rivers. He was familiar with species of dogwood, a tea made from the roots and bark of some species (such as flowering dogwood [*Cornus florida*]) helps relieve fever, chills, and diarrhea. The dogwood has some of the same healing characteristics as quinine. Berlandier learned that the Indian diet included "a species of Nymphaecea which grows wild in all the swamps"—the varied species of water lily (such as *Nymphaea odorata*) have medicinal properties of which, perhaps, Berlandier availed himself as he battled vomiting and diarrhea. Berlandier had gathered specimens of creosote bush on the path through Mexico in December. Perhaps he experimented with creosote tea, which among regional tribes was efficacious in treating diarrhea and stomach ailments. Notwithstanding his attempts to use the resources of the land to relieve his symptoms, Berlandier's condition worsened and he became completely bed-ridden. Raphael Chowell took on the role of physician and nurse. During their forced bivouac, some soldiers worked to repair the wagon, while others were in charge of preparing food. The constant mechanical delays and sickness compelled Terán to ask in his journal, "How can one not despair amid so many troubles and rigors?" May 20, the wagon repaired, they prepared to depart, but rising waters from continuing rain forced another delay. Berlandier grew worse. The next day, the soldiers attempted the creek crossing, which they accomplished after three hours of hard labor during which the mosquitoes of the humid forest mercilessly attacked. Berlandier watched from the carriage. Traveling a brief distance through the oak forest, they came to another creek, named Jaranames after the local Indian tribe. Crossing this creek, the instrument wagon again broke, forcing further delays. More creeks stood in the way, at each of which some misfortune occurred, either the breaking of a wagon axle or wheel, wheels stuck in muck, or dense swarms of large mosquitoes that relentlessly tormented the men. The dragoons, used to such conditions, bore the fatigue and suffering with cheerfulness and resolution. The officers and Berlandier, used to more cultivated lifestyles, were less adaptable. The lack of food affected everyone; the mules and horses as well were famished by the lack of fodder in the wet environment. Mosquitoes were not as troublesome to the animals as the large cleg flies that mercilessly bit the backs of horses and mules, generating sores and restlessness.[35]

Berlandier, besides being ill, dehydrated, hungry, and weak, had his collection of floral and faunal specimens to worry about. The gentle zephyrs from the north and south scarcely alleviated the wet heat of the swampy environment. Berlandier's collection of beautiful floral specimens began to succumb to the humid environment, which spoiled many. Berlandier looked forward to their departure from the unhealthy landscape of swamps formed by the many swollen rivulets and arroyos. He hoped, upon arriving at the Trinity River, to find an easier time collecting and preserving; he also expected that the fresh air and openness of the river valley might bring healing. Until then, Berlandier grew so weak as to not be able to write in his journal. May 23, the men were forced to cross six streams, all very difficult; the worst was the San Jacinto, in which the dragoons had to stand naked in the water, exposed to the unwavering attacks of mosquitoes, for two hours, trying to carry over equipment and maneuver the wagons across. May 24, the vanguard of the band reached the overflowing waters of the Trinity, followed the next day by the remainder of the men and wagons.[36]

The arrival of the men to the flooding river brought a mixture of happiness and grief. The Trinity was one of the last significant geographic challenges the men had to overcome to reach Nacogdoches; to arrive finally, after so many delays and the challenges of the landscape and climate of Texas, brought a tinge of jubilation. Privation, sickness, and despair tempered, however, whatever pleasure the men derived from reaching this important terminus of their journey. The men, their horses, and their mules were without food; the environs of the Trinity brought little hope of finding the means to fill their bellies. The Trinity, like most western rivers with shallow banks during springtime, was in full flood, forming lakes, lagoons, and swamps throughout its valley as it flowed south toward Galveston Bay, and the Gulf of Mexico. The few inhabitants living at this juncture on the road to Nacogdoches had little to offer save "milk, chickens, and lard"; what Berlandier yearned for most, bread, they did not have, rather a "cake made of corn which is absolutely intolerable." Impurities in the Trinity and surrounding lagoons made their water a purgative rather than a refreshing drink. The heat and humidity were incapacitating. The men were weak from hunger, and daily more became ill with fever. Likewise, twenty years earlier, when Capt. Zebulon Pike arrived at the Trinity on his way from Mexico to the United States, he found the Spanish garrison of three hundred men "all sick, one scarcely able to assist another." Among the Comisión de Límites, Sánchez, Chowell, and half a dozen soldiers were well, if hungry. There was hardly a prospect of crossing the Trinity, as the flood swept away most means of conveyance, and the ferryman, an old Mexican who was himself emaciated and ill, could offer no help. Those who tended toward rumination and depression were plunged into despair. Sánchez wondered whether he would ever see his loved ones again and asked for God's mercy. Terán, who was increasingly weak and despondent, fearing that he would soon follow his young son in death, wondered how he would accomplish his mission to reach Nacogdoches. Berlandier despaired of accomplishing his commission to gather the flora of Texas and even to preserve specimens he had already gathered. Indeed, though he was in slow recovery from his illness, he could take little pleasure in the botanical delights of the wilderness, seeing the environment instead, for the first time on his journey, as a malicious barrier to reaching destinations, goals, good health, and a satisfying conclusion to his long journey. The rushing, deep, unpredictable waters of the Trinity were reluctant to allow travelers, especially those in convalescence, to cross. The temptation to dare the river anyway was great; twenty-three years later, in the spring of 1851, Berlandier gave in to the temptation to ford the flooding San Fernando in Tamaulipas. Now, in 1828, he yielded to the wisdom and orders of General Terán, who decided that he and a few select men would press on to Nacogdoches with greater alacrity, which required that the heavy wagons and sick men return to San Antonio, then Matamoros. Here ended Berlandier's pursuit of knowledge of east Texas; he would never return to this region again.[37]

CHAPTER FIVE

River of the Comanches

᠅ JEAN LOUIS BERLANDIER DISCOVERED, AS DARIUS NASH COUCH DID
years later, that a foreign traveler in distant lands was highly dependent
on the guides that he hired or that accompanied him by chance. On his
journey from the Pánuco to Mexico City, Berlandier relied on muleteers to
lead him through the jungles and mountains of the Sierra Madre Oriental
and Mexican Plateau. The Comisión de Límites, journeying through northern Mexico into Texas, relied on men hardened by a life on the trail. Some
of these guides were locals of remote regions, such as Laredo, who were
also soldiers. Other guides of the Comisión, north of the Rio Grande, were
American hunters who knew the wilderness trails leading to beaver ponds,
buffalo plains, and bear haunts. Among American explorers it was more
rare to chance upon American Indian hunters who were willing to join
them on the trail. Some notable scientific explorers, such as the English
botanist Thomas Nuttall, never used indigenous hunters or guides. Thomas
Drummond, on the other hand, the fearless botanist who journeyed through
the Canadian Rockies about the same time that Berlandier journeyed to
Mexico, relied on an Iroquois guide. Meriwether Lewis and William Clark
had frequent intercourse with American Indians, some of whom joined
them in the hunt. Kickapoo hunters, for example, briefly joined Lewis and
Clark shortly after they set out in 1804 journeying up the Missouri River.
The Kickapoos were particularly adept at providing fresh venison to enliven
the spirits of hungry men crowded around the fire at day's end.[1]

Likewise, shortly after the Comisión de Límites split on May 29 at the
Trinity River, while Berlandier, Chowell, and members of the commission
and the majority of the dragoons (including those provided by Elosúa)
marched west, Terán, Sánchez, and half a dozen dragoons proceeding east
happened upon two Kickapoo hunters at an especially important time. The
afternoon of May 31, on their way to Nacogdoches, General Terán became
so weak from hunger and illness that he had to halt to rest. Sánchez worried that Terán had met his end. They heard two shots coming from the
distant woods; soon the two hunters, both extravagantly painted and fierce-
looking, rode up on "excellent horses," upon both of which were freshly killed
deer. They proclaimed themselves as amigos willing to help and shared the
venison before moving on.[2]

The same two Kickapoo warriors amazingly arrived at just the right
time to help Berlandier and the other members of the Comisión returning
to San Antonio. Berlandier and the rest had bivouacked for several days,
putting off departure, awaiting better health and a turn in their fortunes.
Berlandier, while still weak, could not keep from doing a bit of exploration,
if briefly on horseback, around the environs of the Trinity valley. He discovered a rich vegetation, such as the Cherokee rose (*Rose laevigata*), a delicate
white-petaled flower with a gold center. The return trip was to be along the
Upper Road, the Camino de Arriba (or Old San Antonio Road, sometimes
called the Camino Real), on which Berlandier hoped that health would allow
him to discover plant specimens new at least to him. He regretted departing from his friends Terán and Sánchez but looked forward to leaving the
swamps and lagoons of the Trinity for drier and healthier lands, where perhaps game would be more plentiful and hunger satisfied. The soldiers of the
dragoon escort were jubilant to be returning, but they had quite a journey
ahead of them. The hungry and fatigued soldiers and convalescents had no
supplies as they began, and they planned to live off the land the best they
could. The two Kickapoo hunters were a fortunate addition. They kept the
Mexicans and Frenchman provided with venison during the entire return
journey. The leader of the two (called here the Quicapú; his name is not
known) was in pursuit of an Indian who had seduced and carried off his
wife. Although Berlandier did not know it at the time, the two warriors were
to be his welcome traveling companions for well over the next year.[3]

The Quicapú and his companion knew enough Spanish to be able to
converse with the Mexicans. The cuckolded hunter mildly proclaimed his
intention not to seek revenge on the seducer of his wife; he merely wished

the return of his property: the horse his wife rode and the clothing she carried with her. The seducer was a friend, and the Quicapú said this would not change even after he caught up with him. The fierce appearance of the Kickapoos belied their mild behavior. Berlandier discovered them to be trustworthy companions and good friends notwithstanding that they appeared most savage, at least from the perspective and experience of the French botanist. The Kickapoos had shaved heads painted red with vermilion—charcoal, in the absence of the former. A long tuft of hair trailed from the top of the head to the neck. Black and white lines like that of a zebra decorated the face and neck. Armed with a dagger, tomahawk, and rifle, dressed in buckskin and shod in moccasins, they were excellent horsemen, and sufficiently dangerous warriors to provide added security to the dragoons marching into a region where Waco, Tawakoni, and Taovaya warriors often attacked travelers. Berlandier unexpectedly discovered that his Kickapoo companions were useful informants of the ways of the Texas frontier and Indian customs.[4]

The Kickapoo people had in recent years maintained a well-known presence in the region between the Trinity and Sabine rivers. Originally a tribe of the Great Lakes that had participated in the colonial wars of empire between the French and the English, in the America Revolution, and in the Indian wars of the late 1700s and early 1800s in the Old Northwest, the Kickapoo had been initially loyal to the French, then to the British and Spanish, but feared American movement west. The Kickapoo had gained the reputation over the many decades of war for being feared fighters and skilled hunters. Upon the American purchase of Louisiana Territory in 1803, and the subsequent policy of removal of Indians of the Old Northwest and Southeast to the lands west of the Mississippi, the Kickapoo were forced south; many ended up living in the region of the Trinity and Sabine valleys. The Spanish encouraged their removal to the southern reaches of Louisiana in Texas and along the Red River; they invited Kickapoo warriors to Spanish lands, asking that they patrol the vast frontiers. The Texas Kickapoo were inveterate enemies of some tribes, such as the Osage of Indian Territory north of the Red, but friends with such tribes as the Cherokee band led by Chief Bowles, with whom they lived in harmony, sharing the hunt and common enemies.[5]

The motley group of soldiers, scientist, and Indians journeyed west along the Camino de Arriba during the waning days of May and first weeks of June 1828. In the absence of General Terán, Colonel Batres took charge of the commission. Berlandier noted, as they crossed the flooding Navasota River and several smaller streams, such as the Corpus Christi, that the surrounding forest bore evidence of scars from a natural disaster that had happened, he guessed, just a few months earlier. Covering the forest floor were twisted branches of all shapes and sizes, clearly ripped from the tops of trees by some strange phenomenon. The trees lacked their typical graceful, conical crown of branches and leaves; rather, they were irregularly pitted and broken. Huge branches dangled from the treetops, as if the slightest zephyr would dislodge them and they would fall crashing to the ground. Softwood trees such as pines and cedars had been emasculated; hardwoods such as oaks had withstood the event more successfully, yet even some of these had the appearance of massive trauma destroying most of the tree down to the thickest part of the trunk near ground level. Many trees had been completely uprooted and lay prone, the massive trunk, clogged with dirt, contrasting awkwardly with the large pit remaining from its eruption. The windfalls, the scattered branches, the irregular shapes and apparent chaos contrasted with the typical appearance of the southern forest and belied the inherent order of the forest. Berlandier hypothesized correctly that an ice storm during midwinter had laced the trees with water that froze on contact, growing to such thickness that the branches and trunks could not withstand the weight. There were abandoned dwellings nearby, one of which still had corn growing; another dwelling was still inhabited by an old man with his family who had been present during the ice storm when the forest erupted with the sounds of breaking branches, like so many reports of a rifle. The old man had been witness to the unexpected beauty brought about by the natural disaster; once the storm cleared, the tree branches and forest bushes reflected the brilliant sunlight, appearing covered with precious jewels. Small spiculae of ice fell to the ground in consequence of the sun's warmth. Now, months later, the vast majority of the trees were recovering and growing despite the widespread destruction brought about by the storm.[6]

Lacking the most basic supplies, worn out and ill, persecuted by the growing heat and humidity and consequent swarms of mosquitoes, Batres ordered two soldiers to make haste to San Antonio to acquire and bring back provisions while the rest of the men waited, living on the venison supplied by the Kickapoo hunters. They camped next to the old man's house. He was a member of the Austin Colony, who lived upstream from San Felipe, just below the confluences of the Brazos and Little Brazos Rivers. The colonist's crops and dwellings had been ravaged by the recent floods; added to this were the frequent assaults on his property, mostly his livestock, by Waco and Tawakoni warriors. The Waco village was about seventy-five miles north of this spot, situated on the banks of the Brazos; the Tawakoni village was about thirty to forty miles east of the Wacos, also on the Brazos. Both tribes had similar customs, language, beliefs, and lifestyles. They lived in grass huts, except in the winter, when they lived as nomads in skin tents on the trail of the buffalo. Both tribes were friendly with the Comanche, whom they equaled in their abilities as hunters and warriors. Notwithstanding the Indian incursions, the old man welcomed all comers along the road, provided that they were peaceful. While Berlandier and his companions remained camped on the eastern shores of the Brazos, awaiting supplies, numerous Indians arrived along the road and met with members of the commission. In addition to the Kickapoos, represented by the two hunters traveling with the commission, were members of the Bidai, Texas, Caddo, Cherokee, and Chickasaw tribes. The Bidai was an old chief who appeared to have experienced utter privation; Berlandier had seen another of his ilk the previous month at San Felipe remonstrating with Stephen Austin about the misfortunes of his tribe and the injustice practiced by the Mexican government in allowing so many northern tribes to settle on land that, by right of being the oldest tribe to reside in Texas, belonged to the Bidaises. The Texas Indian, also a chief, could doubtless have made a similar claim based on the antiquity of the tribe in east Texas. Berlandier described him as being terribly marked by the ravages of smallpox. The Caddos were a husband and wife who relaxed under a temporary shelter, an awning made of skins, wherein a fire burned continually to ward off the mosquitoes. The man sported a nose ring that supported a silver plaque picturing a cross. Berlandier said nothing about his or her dress, though in his "Indigenes nomades" he remarked on the relatively urbane dress of the Caddos, notwithstanding their propensity for gaudy jewelry and the adoption of the men of the same style of hair and paint as the Kickapoos. It is not known whether the Caddos resting at the camp along the Brazos carried small mirrors with which to admire themselves, as Berlandier claimed was the habit of these people. Berlandier admired the culture if not the bearing and habits of the Cherokees. The man he met at the Brazos was intoxicated, which Berlandier claimed was quite a problem with a people who were otherwise urbane. Their dress had a certain elegance; Cherokee maidens reminded Berlandier of the peasant girls he knew in his youth.[7]

The air continued moist and hot during the first week of June. While some of the men of the commission tried to regain their strength, others ferried the wagons and supplies across the Brazos, making several trips. Clearing the road on the opposite shore of windfalls and other obstructions also occupied the dragoons. The temperature of both air and water was in the eighties on June 8. The men sweltered and the mosquitoes feasted. The plains and forests delighted in the wet heat, and vegetation was prolific. Berlandier noted a beautiful species of pond lily, for example. Also prevalent were small caimans, lying in stagnant pools or arroyos with little current, their snouts barely creasing the surface, lying still in wait for prey. These Texas caimans reputedly preyed only on small mammals, especially dogs. They eschewed the pursuit of humans, contrary, Berlandier had learned, to the much larger caimans of the Pánuco River. His Kickapoo companions, experts in animal calls, having contrived a small instrument held to the mouth that allowed exact imitations, fabricated the whimper of a small dog, which brought several caimans in the direction of the sound.[8]

Traveling west from June 10 to 12, on their way to the Red River of Texas, they traversed a dry environment broken with sporadic oak and pine forests, prairies, and arroyos with sometimes tepid, disgusting water, and other times with sweet, lipid water. Spring continued to be alive in the blooming flowers and trees and the moistness of an otherwise dry landscape. Berlandier witnessed foxes preying on fawns struggling to learn the best means to survive in the wilderness. The men tried to keep to the road as best they could, which was sometimes impossible, because road and random animal traces were indistinguishable. The evening of June 12 they were forced to bivouac in a pine and oak forest where the latter trees seemed very unstable, as windfalls scattered about the landscape, showing signs of the impact of storms on the soft wood. Hunters and guides informed Berlandier that it was best to camp away from the pine forest because of the danger of a windfall during the night; they found an oak grove to bed down in. The next morning they rose at dawn and sought to hurry toward the Colorado in the early morning hours, but forested hills and sharp declivities delayed their advance. Insects along the way delighted in the humidity. By mid-morning they came to the river, which had clearly been flooding during previous days, to which the surrounding land and trees bore visual witness. Red, frothy spume on the surface of the river announced rising water, which drove the men to hurry to get gear and wagons across. The wagons were safely across when a prairie thunderstorm broke with all of its driving rain, terrifying lightning and thunder, and high winds. Berlandier and his companions had not crossed the river with the wagons and were stranded on the near side. The valley afforded little shelter, and the men suffered through the drenching rain. After the cool rain that drove the bugs away, the sun again appeared, bringing hot, humid air that welcomed back the insects but dried the men's clothes. They crossed the river in the afternoon and made camp; some men went hunting while Berlandier cared for his specimens. He discovered, to his chagrin, that much of his collection was wet, a large part damaged, the sudden rain adding to the slow destruction caused by the constant humidity. Berlandier salvaged what he could. The relentless botanist nevertheless explored the environs for more specimens, discovering the Mexican poppy (*Argemone mexicana*), which he later learned was prized by local inhabitants for its narcotic effect; the plant was also used to make an eyewash. Meanwhile, the two Kickapoo warriors joined some soldiers in a buffalo hunt, at which they were successful. Returning to camp, they spied in the distance Tawakoni warriors, who beckoned them to meet. The Kickapoos and the soldiers were equally suspicious of the intentions of this warlike tribe, which frequently attacked the unsuspecting traveler and had a reputation for a variety of immoral habits. The hunters quickly returned to camp, which at the same time welcomed the dragoons who had gone for supplies at San Antonio several days before. They reported that the Tawakonis had made attacks in the region of the presidio. That evening, soldiers, Kickapoos, and Berlandier feasted on buffalo meat and kept a close guard. One skittish soldier thought he saw a raider and fired his weapon, which only succeeded in awakening the camp and filling them with anxiety until morning.[9]

Typical of summer weather in the southern prairies, the day after a heavy rainfall, dew and fog covered the earth and lower atmosphere, not burning off until mid-morning. Even so, the land they traversed showed signs of a more arid landscape; mesquites dominated, water was scarce, and what small pools existed hosted a variety of reptiles. The night of June 14 was cloudy; dawn again brought moisture to the air and ground. They passed a camp of Americans hunting buffalo; Berlandier thought them a great deal more savage than the Indians with whom he traveled. June 15, they reached the cool, clear waters of the San Marcos River. Soldiers told Berlandier that the feeder river of the San Marcos, the Blanco River, called by the Comanche the Pavococue, rose far to the west in land dominated by the Comanche. The landscape was moist, hosting pecan and plum trees, and a wide variety of wildflowers. From the San Marcos to San Antonio required two days' travel on the Camino de Arriba, during which they forded the Guadalupe River, its banks lined with trees typical of a moist landscape, such as pecan, cedar, and willow. The path to San Antonio was delightful, as spring bloomed by means of flowers and verdure trees amid the hills and valleys of this part of Texas.[10]

When Jean Louis Berlandier and the other members of the Comisión de Límites arrived at San Antonio on June 18, after a fatiguing journey of over two months among prairies, through oak and pine forests, and across the rivers and streams of Texas, the scientist from Geneva was still recovering from the malarial ague with which he had been sickened in mid-May. General Terán had ordered a rendezvous at Matamoros for late summer, which gave Berlandier time to rest and recover at San Antonio; besides, it was rainy and the road to Laredo would be difficult, the rivers impassable. He spent his time organizing his collection of flora and fauna, examining sketches he had made along the way, and employing his brush and palette to record more permanently interesting plants he had observed. He executed, during his stay at San Antonio, an exact and striking portrait of the mountain laurel, called by natives and locals *frijolilla* (by the Comanche, *aincapu*), in flower. In early spring the shrub blooms with wonderful lavender and blue flowers. Berlandier's portrait recreates the delicate beauty of the Texas mountain laurel. Berlandier discovered that the frijolilla held an important role in the religious life and materia medica of the southern plains Indians. He learned from native correspondents that the "pulverized seeds" of the laurel, which are hard and bright red in autumn, "sprinkled on the head will destroy lice." Some tribes used a concoction of the seeds and water to treat eye and ear diseases. Tribes such as the Comanche, Caddo, Tawakoni, and Taovayas (Tawehash) used the frijolilla in the "firstfruits ceremony" that occurred when the first plant blossoms of late winter heralded the coming of spring and the renewal of life. In "Indigenes nomades," Berlandier described the ceremony, "the *feast of the new fruits*," which he apparently witnessed in person:

> It consists of dedicating the firstfruits of the earth and of purifying the tribe. Everything about this feast, which takes place every year, proves the gratitude of those who keep it to the objects of their veneration. . . . To receive the first gifts of the year from the earth each of them must purge himself so as not to soil the gifts of springtime. As soon as a native comes bringing the news that he has seen

some new fruit, preparations begin for the celebration. The chief of the people orders the crier to spread the news, and to tell everyone the appointed day for eating the new fruits. The women set about sweeping all the streets in the village, and they also clean the council chamber, where they arrange a multitude of seats or mats and strew the floor with field flowers. On the appointed day all the head men gather in this hut, where any virgins and women of good reputation may also enter. These are the women who, in time of drought, pray to the Most High to send them rain. After the usual ceremonies with the pipe, committees are appointed to grind the frijolillo seeds . . . and to throw the resultant paste into a great pot of warm water. When the water is well saturated with the purgative and emetic juice of these seeds, all drink of it several times, sipping it through a reed or straw.

The Tawakoni performed the ceremony in a large lodge, where the "whole nation gathered together . . . to vomit and be purged in order to earn the right to eat of the new fruits."[11]

The weeks at San Antonio were spent recovering from illness and catching up on his scientific work preserving plants and making meteorological observations, as well as preparing for the continuation of the journey to Matamoros. During this time Berlandier became friends with José Francisco Ruíz, a colonel in the Mexican army stationed at the presidio of San Antonio. Ruíz had lived in Texas for many years, had fought for the insurgents against Spain at the Battle of Medina, and had been forced into hiding for eight years, during which time he lived with the Comanche on their lands in west Texas known as the Comancheria. Even though the Comanche had been at war with the Texas presidios and their troops, they had shown generous hospitality to Ruíz. The colonel was short and dark, with a full face and deep-set eyes. He lived in a charming dwelling in San Antonio, where he doubtless received Berlandier and other members of the commission. Berlandier had, since arriving at Texas, desired the opportunity to journey west of San Antonio, perhaps as far as the headwaters of the Guadalupe River; Ruíz offered to accompany him. Peace with the Comanche in the wake of Mexican independence was hard to come by; the shattered remains of the Spanish Empire and poverty and lack of discipline of the Mexican troops were inducements to Comanche warriors to enrich themselves, especially with horses, at the expense of Mexican presidios, haciendas, and ranchos. Peace was, however, orchestrated for a time by the commander of the eastern provinces, Gen. Anastacio Bustamante, beginning in 1827, which provided encouragement to Tejanos, the Mexicans of Texas, that the wilderness of west Texas could be opened up to science. Although Berlandier and other members of the commission felt compelled to follow General Terán's orders to rendezvous at Matamoros, Berlandier hoped to return to San Antonio to pursue the journey to the west with Ruíz unmolested by the Comanche. A visit by the Comanche chief Barbakista in August, after Berlandier had departed for Matamoros via Laredo, further solidified the peace between the Mexicans and Comanche. After learning that General Terán's return to Matamoros would be indefinitely delayed, Berlandier quickly returned to San Antonio in late summer. His traveling companion Raphael Chowell joined, as did his Kickapoo friends. The presidio was bustling with a variety of tribes, especially the Comanche, who had come to trade hides and bear grease to the soldiers in return for ammunition and carbines. Several bands with hundreds of Comanche warriors, women, and children arrived in a short space of time; they camped a short distance from the presidio and awaited a ceremonious visit from the commander, who brought gifts that the Comanche interpreted as tribute. The visitors resided in tents, poles covered with hides, with soft bear blankets for the repose of the warriors. Women were little better than slaves, Berlandier thought; the man hunted and warred, while the women did all of the domestic chores. Men practiced polygamy; Barbakista, for example, had eleven wives. They used their women for their own and their friends' and guests' sexual pleasure. A woman who committed adultery of her own accord, however, could be killed or mutilated by the cuckold. Berlandier empathized with the plight of Comanche women, whom he nevertheless thought filthy, both morally, given to savage violence against defenseless prisoners and all too willing to ply their sexual charms, and physically, their hair greasy and skin dirty, clothes unattractive—merely a skin skirt and blouse and moccasins. Men were likewise dirty and often clad in little more than a breechcloth, leather leggings, and moccasins. If the weather was cool, both sexes would don buffalo robes. Men wore their hair long, often intertwined with horse hair or the hair of slain enemies. Warriors might wear either a buffalo cap (with horns) or a feather headdress. Comanche warriors preferred carbines, of course, and lances with steel points (taken from captured sabers) as well as the traditional bow and arrows. They went into battle with a shield (*chimal*) made of thick buffalo hide decorated with feathers or certain types of "medicine," *pouhahantes*, which were the skins of small animals attached to the shield that could provide magical powers of warding off enemy arrows or spent balls. The shield was no protection against a rifle or musket ball, however. Warriors went into battle with their faces and bodies decorated with various earthy paints. Berlandier found the Comanche to be a dignified people in physique and stature, with many men who were tall and strong. He was astonished by their apparent strength and health even though they ate very sparingly. They could endure lack of food, cold, and fatigue. The men plucked out all of their hair, including their eyebrows and eyelashes; white captives who had completely adopted their ways also plucked out their hair, which made for a singular appearance.[12]

As Berlandier, Chowell, and Ruíz planned their western excursion, the arrival of another Comanche chief, Keiuna (Quelluna), along with several score of warriors, altered the plans. Ruíz convinced Berlandier and Chowell that they should join the Comanche on a hunting expedition up the Guadalupe.

Figure 7. The military plaza at San Antonio, Texas. In: "United States and Mexican Boundary Survey. Report of William H. Emory. . . ." Washington. 1857. Volume I. Frontispiece. 1857. NOAA Library Collection.

November was a good time for the hunt, as the buffalo's hide would be thick, and bears would be fat. Ruíz, having lived among the Comanche for years, trusted them and was trusted by the Indians in return. Berlandier's interest in exploration and science overcame his doubts, and he agreed. The only negative was that the two Kickapoo warriors, his companions of the preceding months, refused to go, being inveterate enemies of the Comanche. The jilted Quicapú set forth on his own hunting expedition, joined by his loyal friend, the disloyal runaway wife, and the duplicitous friend; the latter two, the Quicapú claimed, had been granted forgiveness. The four set out south-southwest for the Rio Grande, upstream from Laredo. When Berlandier met the Quicapú later, upon their mutual return to San Antonio, he found out from another source that the Quicapú and his traveling ally had killed the onetime friend and the runaway wife. Shocked by this uncivilized behavior, Berlandier explained it to himself that the Quicapú felt a personal moral and spiritual duty (according to his own values and beliefs) to avenge any wrong committed against himself.[13]

It was with an odd feeling of fascination mixed with foreboding that Berlandier, along with Chowell and Ruíz—and accompanied by thirty dragoons, some serving as an escort, others aiming to supply their family's needs for meat, skins, and bear fat—set out in the company of twice as many Comanche. Although Berlandier had hitherto had some contact with the different Indians of Texas and Mexico, this was the first time that he put himself in the hands of a group of people so wholly unlike himself and his kind, a people reputed to be savages, who had only recently been at war with Mexicans, who had a reputation for duplicity, vengeance, and the most frightful tortures and homicides perpetrated against their enemies. Ruíz had learned that the Comanche were not all that rumor made them out to be. His reassurances, as well as Berlandier's natural curiosity and desire for adventure, bade him to throw aside trepidation and to trust in himself, his friends, and human nature.[14]

The motley group of men, women, children, soldiers, and scientists set out on November 19, 1828. They journeyed northwest of San Antonio into a region of higher elevation, where rugged hills and valleys promised the presence of black bear and deer. Berlandier was surprised, this first day of the journey, by the silence with which the Comanche traveled. The silence, he discovered, was not due to sullenness, inhibition, gloom, or suspicion; rather, the people appeared more joyful and happy in the wilderness away from the presidio. The people and their hundreds of horses were spread out over a broad distance, with a few warriors going ahead as scouts. They camped at the Arroyo de los Olmos, a tributary of the San Antonio River. The women erected the tepees while the men relaxed; after the meal and under the cover of night the men joined together to smoke the pipe. Ceremony and tradition guided tribal smoking: as the pipe passed from man to man, wisdom was uttered, advice given, accusations made, wrongs admitted. This first night, Berlandier met several whites who had been kidnapped long ago and adopted into the tribe. They could still speak Spanish fluently, and did so loquaciously, with the Mexicans and Frenchman in their midst, telling tales of the Comanche. The night was cold but clear; a full moon shone upon the people. Constellations dotted the night sky. The Comanche knew the stars and recognized the patterns of the constellations, even if they were not cognizant of European names. Before dawn, one of the chiefs went from tepee to tepee announcing the day's path and events; again at dawn he repeated the same message. He called upon the tribe to treat their guests with the hospitality owed them. Sunrise elicited a pious response from the tribe. The rays entered the eastern-facing tepees at first light. The people bowed to the sun and offered the celestial body the firstfruits of the pipe bowl, and such prayers as were uttered. After this sun rite, they also bent knee toward the earth and the holy things of the tribe, the pouhahantes.[15]

November 20, they traveled west through a series of gorges and hills that brought Berlandier back in time to the foothills of the Alps. The morning air was cold, as was the water rushing through the valleys. They traced their way from gorge to gorge, a natural path that the people of the Alps called a thalweg. The rushing waters of past months and years had carved a channel on a path of greatest descent and least resistance. Incessant and irrevocable hydraulic power dug at the banks that forced the water in a new direction; when the water receded in dry months the banks of the gorge bore signs of disaster, of past floods, frost and ice, and constant erosion from rain and wind. The naked soil of the bank revealed layers of earth and rock, of organic and clayey sedimentary soil mixed with fossils, sandstone, limestone, quartz, and iron. The disordered creek bed was strewn with tangled branches that accumulated into dams, especially around windfalls that had tumbled from the banks; in some places the roots of trees protruded from the bank, a natural prophesy of a windfall to come. The distant hills were partially covered with oaks and desert evergreens. The journeyers wound their way from the watershed of the San Antonio River to the Medina through old passes in the mountains that had been used by animals and humans for eons. They crossed the Arroyo del León, named for the many panthers that inhabited these wilds, then the Ojo de Agua, which provided a campsite secured by trees and hills from the north wind. They feasted on venison killed by a Comanche who was liberal in his sharing. That night, as on the previous two nights, one of the white Comanches stuck to the Mexicans like a glove, either because of loneliness for his old way of life or through subterfuge. He warned that the mules were restless, which suggested trouble, an accurate prediction, as within minutes there was a stampede of the hundreds of horses through the camp. Tents, tepees, fires, and meals succumbed to the mad onslaught. The Comanches panicked. Women armed themselves to protect their children; others hurried to the Mexican camp that was well guarded by the dragoons. Warriors mounted horses that had been secured and galloped off in pursuit of the stampeding animals; others armed themselves to see what had caused the trouble. They asked to borrow the soldiers' lances and were given them; they rode on patrol and discovered nothing unusual. Throughout the night they awaited an attack, which never materialized. The episode impressed Berlandier with the fear and credulity of the Comanche, as well as their utter ill-preparedness for an attack. The few sentinels were insufficient to protect the tribe, and there were no temporary fortifications or arrangement of tepees to provide for the most security.[16]

After a relatively sleepless night, they set forth from the Ojo de Agua to the Arroyo del Cibolo, "creek of the bison." They continued traveling through a rough terrain of hills and gorges. The botanist learned from the Comanche their preference for such plants as the smooth sumac (*Rhus glabra*), which they called *temaichia*, a shrub with thick, impenetrable branches and reddish leaves and berries in autumn. The Comanche used the leaves as an ingredient in their pipes; leaf tea had a variety of medicinal uses. The Comanche also showed Berlandier the *puip*, called Indian grass by locals, the root of which was a reputed cure-all for wounds. "No indigene exists who does not carry some pieces with him," Berlandier wrote. "When one of them is wounded, they pound the root, which is very long, and squeeze the sap (or saliva) into the wound. . . . I have often heard it said that serious wounds have often been radically cured by that means in a very short time." They camped at a beautiful spot near a stream with fresh, cool water. Hunters among the dragoons and Indians brought in deer and bear. The Comanche were particularly adept at hunting the bear. They eschewed carbines for the lance; the former rarely brought down a bear after a few shots, but the latter could be expertly and lethally thrust through the bear's body. During the night, a particularly indolent and boisterous Comanche who had gone to the stream for water claimed to have seen an enemy warrior, a Lipan. Again the camp was in an uproar, and patrols went out searching for a nonexistent enemy, both during the night and at dawn.[17]

November 22, they continued following the irregular guide of the thalweg (*ouiar* in Comanche, *Puerto Viejo* to the local Tejanos) throughout this hilly region. The day's travel was slow due to the difficult terrain of the rocky gorges; walls of limestone hemmed in the travelers; the wilderness was alive with wild animals, deer and bear. Not fearing hunger, the Comanche still wondered where were the Lipan; the dragoons meanwhile hoped not to be startled by a hungry black bear. Berlandier, protected by armed men, believing the Lipan threat was merely a Comanche fantasy, realizing that in the dry season there was little chance of the sudden flash flood, set to observing all around him. The gorges zigzagged in a northerly direction. The men reached the Guadalupe, crossed it, and made camp early enough for hunters to search the surrounding gorges and forests for game. Bear resources in the area were perhaps limited, as hunters had preceded them and killed with great success. Nevertheless the acorns, which littered the ground, would attract more bears, who especially liked the nuts. The post oak (*Quercus stellata*), a relatively small hardwood, was the dominant tree. The red leaves and berries of the smooth sumac were also widespread, as was western mugwort (*Artemisia ludoviciana*), which Indian healers used to alleviate the symptoms of stomachache, headache, skin irritations, fever, and, when used in the steam bath, so ubiquitous among American Indians, asthma and joint aches. After a very cold night, made colder by the early-morning mists of the Guadalupe, they struggled to acquire sufficient warmth to leave their fires and pursue the journey. Eventually they departed from the river, following gorges and ascending some steep hills, crossing a buffalo trace, and struggling among hills and valleys to a place where they halted for the night. Here a Comanche had triumphantly killed a white wolf, which the Comanche highly esteemed for its ferocious character and inherent magical properties. Berlandier eagerly examined the carcass, though it had already been skinned and butchered. From what Berlandier could tell, the wolf's fur was white with some gray, but it did not appear to be an albino. He wished to see the eyes, to see whether or not they were albino, but they had been removed. The killer would use the pelt for important purposes such as a quiver, in which he would keep arrows that had been doused in the smoke of the burning white fur. Perhaps it was here that a Comanche showed Berlandier the skin of an indigenous dog of the region, which the *dog eaters*, or Chariticas, maintained to supplement their diet. After a night spent alongside the small Arroyo del Lobo Blanco, named for the wolf, they broke camp and went in separate directions. Berlandier, Chowell, Ruíz, and the dragoons were to proceed west, south, east, and north in a roundabout path back to San Antonio, while the Comanche continued northwest toward their homes in the expansive Comancheria of what are today Texas, Oklahoma, Kansas, and Colorado. They parted amiably, trading goods and compliments, the Comanche pressing in a friendly way for their companions to continue to their village, the Mexicans begging forgiveness for their decision to finish the hunt and return to the presidio.[18]

Although it was the last week of November, the twenty-fourth was a warm day, made warmer by the toil of following the winding path through gorges of so many different directions that it appeared a natural maze. They followed animal traces, normally a good technique to find the best path through an unknown wilderness, but in this case resulting in more confusion. The compass and the position of the sun kept them from becoming completely lost. They spied smoke to the northwest, Comanche signals to one another, though unintelligible to the Mexicans and Frenchman. Berlandier discovered, besides the typical oaks and sumac, a species of aster (*Aster argenteus*) for the first and only time on his many journeys in and about the valley of the Rio Grande. Notwithstanding the opportunities for venison and bear meat, that evening the soldiers presented the Frenchman with roasted *zorillo*, that is, skunk. Like other European explorers unused to the customs of hunters on the frontier, Berlandier was disgusted by the prospect of dining on this creature until, to his surprise, upon trying it he found it quite palatable, like "suckling pig," and without the horrible aroma he anticipated. He learned that the cooks skinned the animal, removed the odor-causing glands, then seared the flesh well over coals, and the meal was made. They camped by an unknown tributary of the Guadalupe, next to daunting hills that reminded Berlandier of home. Mustangs roamed nearby in the moonless night; the horses and pack animals of the soldiers were restless. In the morning, surrounded by wooded peaks and stony valleys and myriad animal traces, but no game, they wearily traveled on the halting ad hoc trail toward the south. Finally they came to a makeshift road carved out of the oak forest years earlier by Spanish dragoons;

they followed the path, though it offered little of interest or nourishment, as wildfire had swept through the dry grasses, bushes, and timber, and all was black and bare. Generally they paralleled the Guadalupe, which was mostly like a shallow mountain stream but in places formed itself into wide, lakelike expanses. Berlandier, who had learned from such maps as that of Zebulon Pike of a large lake in the region called the Laguna de las Yuntas, Lake of the Comanches, was told by Ruíz, and confirmed by the Comanches themselves, that no such lake existed. Berlandier concluded that the story of the imaginary lake derived from these lakelike expanses of the Guadalupe. Buffalo traces having hinted that the animals could be nearby, the afternoon of November 25 they spied a herd in a distant valley. The dragoons went in pursuit, but the wily animals heard the sounds of riders, whiffed the scent of men and horses, and fled. For successive nights it was cloudy and cold; at dawn the men greeted another day during which they labored over the steep and edgy ground. Ruíz led them along the Guadalupe and tributaries amid forests of oak and pecan. Signs of recent wildfires were everywhere, as were signs of the past.[19]

Memories of past events surrounded them as they traveled, hunted, and camped amid successive gorges where even the best guides could easily become lost. Ruíz called the region Labor de los Lipanes. Here, Ruíz told Berlandier, the Lipans, seeking protection from the rough terrain and uncertain paths, had once tried to hide and escape from Spanish troops. In 1813, General Joaquín de Arredondo tried to rid the province, at that time called Nuevo Santander, of rebels, warring Indians, and American filibusters. The Lipans, weakened by constant war with other tribes and presidial troops, used this region of the upper Guadalupe as a base to make incursions against the Spanish presidios. Lipan farmers coaxed maize and melons from the reluctant land; they hunted deer and bear, and bartered for other necessities with American traders. Berlandier and his escort bivouacked the evening of November 27 at one beautiful stretch of fertile land along the Guadalupe, where Ruíz told Berlandier that General Arredondo had sent two hundred dragoons to destroy the Lipans but had succeeded only in killing a blind man; Berlandier and Ruíz found a man's skull in the forest, which they thought must be the hapless *indigene*. Succeeding days they made camp at two different locations in the same vicinity by a region called Los Pedernales or, according to a Comanche chief they happened upon, Pasinono. Hunters and soldiers went in pursuit of bison among the limestone and flint hills that surrounded the Guadalupe on both sides. The days and nights alternated between freezing cold, with northerly breezes, and springlike weather courtesy of southerly breezes. Ruíz, who knew the woods better than most Mexicans and Texans, spied signs of a hunter armed with a rifle that had recently come through the forest. Soon buffalo were cited, and the colonel brought down a young one. One hunter in their group, a young man on his first adventure away from home, became lost; the others searched for him for almost two days. When he was discovered, both he and his horse were hungry and thirsty, the horse particularly fatigued because it carried the carcass of a bear that the hunter had the wherewithal to kill with only a lance, like the Comanche. In the buffalo hunt, white and Comanche hunters had different styles. The Comanche had the singular ability to ride along a bison, shooting dart after dart into the animal before it fell, exhausted. White hunters preferred to sneak up on the herd, hiding behind a horse; when in range if the hunter succeeded in killing an animal by a long-range shot without being spied, the other animals stood around stupidly smelling the downed buffalo; they became easy prey for the marksman. The buffalo were still plentiful in this region, but not as much as in years past. Once they roamed down to Mexico, now rarely. Instead, herds evaded the increasing population of Texas and moved west toward the plains and mountains of New Mexico; tribes such as the Comanche, who so heavily relied upon them, followed.[20]

The first week in December, the journeyers moved closer to what they supposed were the headwaters of the Guadalupe River. The many streams collecting the spare waters of these highlands formed into several small tributaries of the Guadalupe. The land continued a rough pattern of rocky hills and chasms of varying depth. Aridity and winter had vanquished most vegetation, though hardy junipers (*Juniperus*) and oaks, the fruits of which attracted bear, were plentiful, as were grasses upon which the buffalo fed. These animals they saw frequently, though killing them was a different story. The ragged savagery of the land combined with the sight of these distant herds of wild beasts, bellowing, hairy, and unexpectedly fast, repeatedly astonished, even frightened, Berlandier. The men camped next to the Guadalupe for several days during the first week of December. The skies were cloudy, but the weather mild. Berlandier joined a hunt on horseback led by Ruíz in which they cornered, then pursued a black bear; it took countless bullets to kill the large creature, the fat of which would bring plentiful grease for cooking. At this time of year, locals considered the thick pelt of black or reddish-black fur also valuable. The Comanche, according to Ruíz, claimed that farther west, in New Mexico, the bears were fierce and not as apt to run when pursued, but to turn and fight aggressively. The bears of Texas would usually not attack humans, unlike their counterparts in New Mexico. Journeying to the southwest on December 8, they passed over the watershed that separates the Guadalupe from the Frio River. The land was dry, though the sky was cloudy and the morning foggy; the ride was punishing and fatiguing, yet the rugged beauty wonderful. After a thirsty night without water, they descended toward a massive canyon, the Cañon de don Juan de Ugalde (Frio Canyon). The canyon had been formed over time by waters that flowed into the Frio. Ruíz informed Berlandier that it extended for miles and widened considerably as one penetrated its length. There were only two entrances to the canyon, both of them difficult to negotiate. The one from the northeast, which they used, was easier, though one could hardly tell because of the angle of descent, treacherous path, and unknown depth. The canyon was a wonderful place for stealth in war, either to hide from enemies or to launch attacks. Berlandier learned that soldiers from San Antonio pursuing Lipan Apache raiding parties were sometimes led to this place. The christening of the canyon occurred in 1790, when General Juan de Ugalde, leading a force of Spanish, Comanche, and Wichita, pursued the Lipan Apaches to the canyon, whence there was no escape, and massacred them. The dramatic, rocky cliffs, shifting, low-lying clouds, and gorges through which narrow, shallow streams flowed, sometimes descending into subterranean beds, other times emerging from the same, brought Berlandier back to the Savoy Alps near the foot of Mont Blanc. The differences were the lack of snow, talk of Indians, oak forests and accompanying black bears feeding on acorns, hardy junipers and prickly cacti, little walnut (*Juglans microcarpa* Berl.) and pecan trees, flowers and trees such as the redbud (*Cercis canadensis* var. *texensis*) in bloom in December, and the frijolillo, prized by the Indians for use in firstfruits ceremonies. The canyon and surrounding gorges attracted animals of all types, herds of wild horses for fresh grass and clear water, and buffalo and wild cattle seeking the same. Hunters and soldiers accommodated Berlandier and his frequent questions and search for specimens. Some helped in collecting; others showed him the different tracks of animals, and how the form and depth indicated size, rate of travel, and type. Berlandier learned to distinguish between the hoof mark of a bison and a wild steer; of the many animal traces in fields and forests, and how to differentiate a deer spoor from a horse path, a buffalo from a cattle trace; when and why herds tended to congregate in meadows

and next to streams; and when hunting was easiest. Tejano hunters reminded him of his Kickapoo friends, whose intuitive awareness of their surroundings and heightened senses of sight, smell, and hearing were beyond
anything Berlandier had ever experienced in himself or among others of
his ilk.[21]

The journeyers made their way out of the deep, practically waterless
Cañon de don Juan de Ugalde and pursued a path to the northeast, returning to San Antonio. The dry arroyos that they forded showed signs of massive
torrents during the rainy season of the spring. Even now, during the typically dry months of late fall, as they approached and followed the Medina
River and its tributaries, recent rains had swollen the torrents and threatened to flood. Hunters showed Berlandier where they had often found flocks
of turkeys perched in trees easy to catch. Also prevalent at such times were
bobcats, who delighted in turkey flesh, and who, the hunters claimed, were
often quicker than their human counterparts in retrieving turkeys felled
by bullets. Berlandier and his companions arrived at San Antonio on the
night of December 18 after a journey of a month in the Texas hill country.[22]

CHAPTER SIX

Father of Waters

⚘

✦ AMONG THE MANY SIMILARITIES BETWEEN DARIUS NASH COUCH AND Jean Louis Berlandier—their interest in botany, their willingness to brave dangers in search of discoveries, their journeys throughout the Mexican frontier—was one keen difference: their respective views toward the indigenous peoples of the Rio Grande valley and parts west. Soldiers associated with the United States and Mexican Boundary Survey, of which Couch was an indirect part, viewed the Indians of Texas and Mexico as savages. In his "Notes on Travel," Couch referred to the indigenous peoples as "wandering hordes" and "devils," and regretted that the United States had not occupied at least northern Mexico so that these people could be civilized. His counterpart William Emory was more to the point, arguing in his *Report on the United States and Mexican Boundary Survey* that the reason the Spanish Empire in America had declined was the creation of an "inferior and syphilitic race," a mixture of whites, blacks, and indigenous peoples. Emory argued that along with the decline of Spanish America was a commensurate rise of Indian savagery, "tenfold more ferocious than ever." Berlandier heard similar attitudes from the settlers he met in Texas who were recurrently afraid of attacks from Waco, Tawakoni, Apache, and Comanche. His own experience was to the contrary. With only a very few exceptions, Berlandier found the indigenous peoples of Texas and northern Mexico to be not so much aggressive as wanting to appear so, to be as savage as any people living off the land in a forbidding environment, to be, in short, not a little like himself.[1]

Berlandier's expanding experiences of living, hunting, and journeying with indigenous peoples caused him to reflect on their supposed savagery. He considered the Comanches with whom he had hunted, the Kickapoos he had come to know as friends, and the other tribes with which he had become acquainted by means of brief visits or interviews. Europeans and Caucasians typically viewed Indians as savage, a social and moral condition of humans who lack self-control, who pursue the immediate needs of pleasure and survival with little reflection on the future or the past, who live in a society of private justice and disorderly chaos where the strong and arrogant dominate the weak and meek. In contrast to savage Indians, Anglo- and European Americans held up their civilized society, one of imposed order and self-control, of established institutions, structured government, and public responsibility. "The difference" between the savage and civilized ways of life, wrote Jeremy Belknap, a missionary and sympathetic observer of indigenous peoples who lived a generation before Berlandier's time, "is so great that it is impossible for either the body or the mind to accommodate itself to the change with any degree of rapidity." Berlandier's writings, based on his experiences, reveal that he doubted the degree of difference between the savage and the civilized.[2]

It is unclear how deeply Berlandier had investigated French literature; perhaps at some point in his life he perused the *Essays* of Michel de Montaigne. One of Montaigne's essays, "Of Cannibals," reflects the thoughts and feelings that Berlandier came to hold about the American Indians. The discovery of the New World and its peoples fascinated the sixteenth-century French aristocrat Montaigne, who tried to find out as much as he could about the customs and institutions of the Indians. He learned that their way of life was completely different from the "civilized" Europeans. The Indians wore the skins of animals—if they wore clothes at all. They sometimes practiced cannibalism. They did not know the techniques of metalworking. They did not practice Christianity. They lived in huts and skin dwellings, hunted and gathered for at least part of the year, practiced brutality against their enemies, had no use for money, were not concerned with private ownership of land, and painted and tattooed their bodies with all sorts of strange images and colors. But more, Montaigne learned that they lived and fought by codes of valor and honor; they lived in accommodation to the natural environment rather than tried to mold it artificially; they practiced a simple lifestyle accepting what nature and fate had given them. At the conclusion of his essay, Montaigne implicitly argued that the Indians were more civilized and less savage than the Europeans, whose constant greed required them endlessly to acquire everything and build as many artificial structures and institutions as they could. Europeans could not accept and be content with what they owned and experienced; hence, they were the true savages and barbarians.[3]

Berlandier's studies and experiences informed him that the American Indians had a limited economy, technology, legal system, and judicial system compared to Anglo-Americans, Mexicans, and Europeans. Yet in other ways the *indigenes*, as he preferred to call the Indians, had a society that was preferable to their so-called civilized counterparts. "Even in the depths of the forest," he wrote in "Indigenes nomades," "even in the heart of the desert, man lives in society. Those beings upon whom we have pinned the badge of 'savages' because they fled from what they did not know are often more closely united with each other than those who live in our cities and villages. In the solitudes of the New World, where one can ride for hundreds of leagues without discerning a single trace of human creatures, live great peoples, distant from one another, but speaking the same language. Though subdivided into tribes of a hundred or so families, they lend aid to each other. Though they must hunt for food in the forests and lead a nomadic existence, they never separate." Though their society was limited by a relatively nonexistent legal and judicial system, relying on blood vengeance and the rule of might, it nevertheless possessed characteristics, such as their tribal councils, that impressed Berlandier. Anglo, European, and Mexican commentators condemned the indigenes for their weakness. The American scientist and Protestant missionary Jedidiah Morse, for example, in *A Report to the Secretary of War of the United States on Indian Affairs* (1822), wrote with avowed scientific authority of the Indian: "In bodily strength they are inferior to the whites; as is true of all savages; civilized man being always superior in strength to savage man." Berlandier, however, had never seen a people so strong and adaptable to the harsh environment in which they lived. Speaking in particular of the Comanche, Berlandier wondered: "Could one possibly say that men who are ceaselessly fighting with their fellows, who love to make war, who go hunting every day, who willingly expose themselves to a thousand hazards, are weak men? Their constitutions, in the land of their ancestors, are as strong as ours, and nature has endowed them with a great advantage over us in the virtue of sobriety, which we do not possess." Most of the nomadic tribes that Berlandier had contact with eschewed alcohol; the Comanche called it "stupid water." When they came to the presidios, they traded skins and meat not for whiskey but for "little loaves of brown sugar, corn, blackberries, sword blades, ammunition, and sometimes mules and horses." The presence of Indians at presidios, he wrote, reminded him of a market-day or bazaar that he recalled from the towns of Europe. Berlandier was also struck by the intelligence of indigenes such as the Comanche. European commentators claimed that Indian intelligence was limited to instinctual mechanisms for survival, rather like animals. The Spanish justified their conquest of Mexico by convincing themselves that the native inhabitants were without reason, and therefore not human. Berlandier had seen too many of the thoughts and actions of the indigenes to doubt their ability to conceptualize, deduce, conclude from observations, and communicate abstract ideas. Not devoted to the sciences or mathematics, because their society was still dependent on the day-to-day requirements of food and shelter, these people nevertheless used "careful observation of natural phenomena" with which to find food, adapt to the climate, and preserve themselves against natural and human enemies. Comanche warriors were as intelligent as any men, especially in the art of survival. The Lipans and Comanches could count to a thousand, and used abstract thinking to conceptualize such sums. They kept track of the passing of the seasons and could estimate how many years had occurred since important tribal or personal events. They understood the concept of time, and when necessary tried to accommodate the Anglo and Mexican obsession with it. The Europeans could engage in advanced mathematics because of the requirements of a more sophisticated society, Berlandier concluded, not because of a greater inherent intelligence. Observation informed Comanche sky-watchers not only that the moon was inhabited, with which Europeans agreed, but that its surface was mountainous, which required inductive reasoning. The Comanche used the stars to keep track of the passing of the night, and to find their way even in utter darkness or when off the trail. Indigenes used smoke signals as well to communicate abstract ideas. Berlandier was once present when such a visible telegram was sent from the Karankawa tribe to communicate their intention to visit in two days' time. The Comanche, he wrote, use "the smoke of a fire, allowed to escape in puffs by removing the burning brands and then suddenly dropping them, its direction, and so on, [to] communicate to other Comanche groups the news of victory or defeat in pursuit of an enemy, the direction an expedition is taking, its progress, etc."[4]

Berlandier heard, perhaps from his friend the soldado, about the various antidotes that locals used. Berlandier was in a long line of European immigrants to America who for centuries had learned from the American Indians how to treat snakebite by using the snake's own organs. The Abenaki of New England had informed seventeenth-century colonists that the best remedy to counter the poison of the venom was to eat the snake's heart, and to counter snakebite by applying the liver directly to the wound. Remedies of the Indians of the Rio Grande included using a plant called the snake herb, which Mexicans, following the practice of the Comanche and Lipan Apaches, carried on the trail. The victim chewed the root of the snake herb and applied the resulting herb-and-saliva mixture directly on the wound. Another, more traditional, remedy required the victim to kill the serpent and remove the liver, mixing the bile of the liver with water and consuming it. Indian hunters and travelers in rattlesnake country carried dried bile to mix with water in case the attacker could not be killed. One's credulity was challenged further with techniques used by locals when traveling to ward off snakes. Berlandier learned that tobacco was an intoxicant to snakes; if spread around the perimeter of the camp, it would attract the rattlesnake and intoxicate it so to immobilize it. Another more absurd idea was to put a black cord around the camp perimeter; the approaching rattlesnake would perceive the cord as its enemy, the blacksnake, and turn away from the camp. More believable information, imparted by the soldado to Berlandier, involved how local soldiers practiced the same celestial observations as their Indian counterparts to keep track of time during the course of the night. They paid particular attention to the Big and Little Dippers, Ursa Major and Ursa Minor, and humorously called the four rectangular stars of the latter the four guards, imagining that they guarded the North Star from the predatory stars of Ursa Major.[5]

Berlandier was not a religious recluse, yet in some ways his character and experiences were like those of St. Anthony, the patron saint of hermits and monks, who spent years in solitude in the deserts of ancient Egypt. Likewise, Berlandier voluntarily left the cultured life of Geneva to travel to the barren wastes of northern Mexico and southern Texas where he lived a reclusive existence, at least for a scientist, for the remainder of his life, such that upon his death few people outside of the Rio Grande valley had ever heard of the savant of Matamoros. Berlandier found personal and spiritual solitude in the vast, arid plains of the Mexican Plateau and in the hill country of Texas, in the swamps and estuaries of the Texas and Mexican Gulf Coast, in the cordilleras of Mexico, and in the rivers and arroyos of Texas. Once he experienced such sublime solitude, he never wished to give it up and thus returned again and again to reexperience it in the extremes of climate and geography of his adopted home.

After the hunting expedition with the Comanches along the Guadalupe River, in late autumn 1828, Berlandier stayed in San Antonio for the next six weeks, examining the materials collected, the sketches made, the notes taken, on his recent journey. He compared his experiences and the knowledge he had acquired with the accounts of others, especially maps that purported to detail the geography of the headwaters of the Guadalupe. The great cartographic works of Arrowsmith, Humboldt, Pike, and Tanner were disappointing in this respect. Aaron Arrowsmith's *Map Exhibiting All the New Discoveries in the Interior Parts of North America* (1795) revealed the ignorance of both the mapmaker and his sources of information about the interior landscape of Mexican Texas. Alexander Humboldt's 1804 *Map of the Kingdom of New Spain* showed the nonexistent Lac de las Yuntas Vado de S. Xavier as the source of the Guadalupe River. *Yuntas* was an incorrect rendering of *Yutas*, the Lipan Apache word for Comanches. Arrowsmith was an armchair cartographer, and Humboldt never traveled through Texas. One might reasonably expect the work of an explorer of Zebulon Pike's caliber to reveal a clearer picture of the region. Pike had explored Texas briefly on his way from Mexico, where he had been brought by Mexican authorities after having been detained in New Mexico in 1807. He journeyed from the Presidio Grande to Nacogdoches during June. Pike's *A map of the Internal Provinces of New Spain*, published in 1810, was based on such travels. Yet Pike also relied on hearsay and legend (and the work of earlier mapmakers, such as Humboldt) in his vague rendering of the region west of San Antonio. He continued the myth of the Lago de las Yuntas, though he made it the source of the San Marcos River, a tributary of the Guadalupe. Henry Tanner's *Map of North America*, published in 1822, was more complete than Pike's, yet still based on inaccurate sources of information. Like his predecessors, Tanner included the Lake of the Comanches as the source of the Guadalupe. He did correctly identify the "Cumanches Indians" west of the Guadalupe in the mountainous lands of west Texas and eastern New Mexico. The cartographic picture of the numerous streams and gorges of the Texas hill country remained a mystery in the wake of Arrowsmith, Humboldt, Pike, and Tanner. Of course, mapmakers rely on the reports of others, and the sources for the region west of San Antonio—the random soldier or foolhardy wanderer—were hardly accurate reporters. Berlandier's many writings corrected mistakes and filled the gap of misinformation with firsthand observations. And there were still many journeys planned in his makeshift itinerary.[6]

In early February 1829, word arrived in San Antonio of a local upris-
ing against Mexican authority at the presidio of Goliad, also known as the
Bay of the Holy Spirit, downriver from San Antonio about ninety miles.
With two new friends, Antonio Elosúa and Ramón Músquiz—the former
the commandant, the latter the civilian head, of San Antonio—Berlandier
set out to the southeast in the company of an escort of dragoons. As often
happens in the Texas winter, a mild day was followed by a frigid day brought
by a cold wind from the northern plains. The men were so uncomfortable
that they hurried on horseback from campfire to campfire, set by a dragoon sent ahead for the purpose. Along the way Elosúa received word from
a courier that General Terán, long delayed in Nacogdoches dealing with
pressures of Indians and Anglo-Americans in eastern Texas, had finally
been ordered to Matamoros in anticipation of disorder resulting from
a growing tempest brewing in Mexico City, where two different parties
disputed the presidential election, and civil war threatened. Terán, who
sought to travel by a route nearer the coast than the way he had come the
year before, planned to pass through Goliad and ordered mules to be ready
for the continuation of his journey.[7]

The road from San Antonio to Goliad, which generally paralleled the
San Antonio River and halted at various campsites (parajes) with grass for
the animals and water for the men, crossed numerous streams that fed the
San Antonio and which, during times of heavy rain, grew into large muddy
torrents that inundated surrounding lands and created swamps everywhere.
The swampy land encouraged the growth of Spanish moss on trees, which
gave an eerie feel to the forest. The presence of warring tribes, the Tawakoni
and Waco, added to the discomfort the men felt in these wooded enclosures.
Because some of the creeks on their route were swollen, even though it was
February, which was drier than most months, the journeyers had at times
to take the high route. From this vantage, Berlandier could see the river's
course, indicated by the long line of pecans, willows, elm, and ash. The surrounding land was less wooded, save where a feeder creek approached from
west or east on its path to join the San Antonio. Such travel, off the road, was
more difficult, yet more secure from ambush.[8]

As Berlandier approached Goliad, from the bluffs of Arroyo de las
Cabezas he could see the presidio sitting atop a hill surrounded by small
white houses among scattered trees and grazing livestock; there appeared
to be little order or design to the town. At the center of this bucolic village was the mission church, surrounded by sporadic huts. At first glance,
the town appeared to Berlandier nicely situated on a rise amid rolling hills

surrounded by groves of trees; the alluvial soil was rich, which promised an expanding, wealthy community. But reality did not mirror his initial image. The problem was the inhabitants, who were indolent and given neither to toil nor trade; they lived on what they could encourage from the soil with the least energy. This was, he discovered on his varied journeys throughout Texas, too often the case with the resident Tejanos, who could not compare with the greater energy and resourcefulness of the immigrating Anglo-Americans, whose power and influence in Texas were consequently growing. The fortress that provided security for the inhabitants and soldiers of Goliad was a simple square affair with moderately thick walls twelve feet high. There were two terrepleins for artillery, but little else in the defensive way; no moat surrounded the fortress, and it did not have a well; such ill planning led, in the Texas Revolution, to the destruction of Goliad by Mexican troops. The Franciscan missions that had served the local populace for two hundred years were on the brink of abandonment. Several tribes of the region, the Aranama, whom Berlandier called the Jaranames, the Cocos, and the Karankawas, had abandoned cannibalistic practices for farming under the supervision of three missions of the lower San Antonio and Guadalupe Rivers: Nuestra Señora del Espíritu Santo de Zuñiga, Nuestra Señora del Rosario, and Nuestra Señora del Refugio. Father José Antonio Díaz de León embraced the Aranama tribe at the mission of Espíritu Santo, located in Goliad. Díaz taught farming to the Indians, joining them in the work of the fields and in the breaking of wild horses. Berlandier met and sketched members of this Christian tribe. The female wears a dress not unlike what Mexican women wore, though she is shoeless; her hair is pulled back into a bun. The man wears a long tunic to his waist, below which he is bare save for a breechcloth. He wields a farming tool. The mission is in the background in the watercolor executed at Matamoros by Lino Sánchez y Tapía after Berlandier's sketch. Father Miguel Muro worked with the Cocos at the Rosario mission, a few miles west of Goliad; he also kept school in Goliad. The Cocos were Christian, though their dress little reflected it, unlike the Aranamas. Berlandier sketched members of this tribe, which formed the basis for Lino Sánchez y Tapia's watercolor portrait. The hunter wears only a breechcloth. He carries a bow and quiver of arrows. The woman has a short leather skirt and blouse; her midriff is bare, as are her legs; unlike the man, she wears moccasins. Both Indians have blue circles tattooed on their faces. The Karankawa tribe (called Caranchueses by Berlandier) hunted and fished downriver at the mouth of the Guadalupe in the environs of Aransas Bay. Father Muro told Berlandier that he had worked with the Karankawas at Mission Refugio until 1826, when he was forced to abandon it and move upriver to Mission Rosario. The baptized Karankawas, in the absence of the missionary, became more nomadic, living on fish and shellfish rather than farming. Karankawa warriors were tall, strong, and of arrogant bearing; they wielded large bows used in fishing. They formed their bows of red cedar; their size required the man to sit and support it for a long-range shot, which could pierce an animal from quite a distance. A portrait by Lino Sánchez y Tapia, executed at Matamoros, perhaps based on Berlandier's observations of a fisher's skill, shows a hunter having just released an arrow; a pile of large fish lies at his feet. The warrior is naked save for a breechcloth; he wears feathers in a headband made of plants, and leg-bands and ankle-bands of the same type. The woman wears a short leather top and skirt, her midriff showing. Both man and woman are barefoot. Berlandier learned that the Karankawas' feet were hard-soled by constant walking and running over discarded oyster shells. They fished from small dug-out canoes of their own manufacture, which were made sufficiently large to hold several people as well as baggage; sometimes the Karankawas salvaged pirogues or rowboats that had drifted ashore from shipwrecks. They scavenged what they could from shipwrecks, often decorating themselves with pieces of glass or mirrors.[9]

Upon arriving at the presidio, Elosúa took control of a disorderly situation where the local civilian leader, the alcalde, was in cahoots with the parish priest and commander of the garrison to resist the planned seizure of their power. The resistance crumbled quickly. Berlandier wrote that this kind of situation was all too common in small Mexican towns and isolated presidios, where there was little communication with outside authorities, which encouraged a decentralized political leadership. After Berlandier, Elosúa, and Músquiz had been at Goliad for a week, joined in the meantime by Col. José Batres of the Comisión de Límites, a courier arrived with news of the approach of General Terán. The men quickly set out east for the small colony of Guadalupe Victoria on the Guadalupe River, a day's journey away. The route traversed a mostly treeless plain beside the valley of the Coleto, a tributary of the Guadalupe. There they surprised the general and his men, who included Lt. José María Sánchez y Tapía, who had been with Terán during their long stay at Nacogdoches. The reunited members of the Comisión had a joyous reunion, including a ball given by the founder of the colony of Guadalupe Victoria, Martín León. A February cold front descended upon the revelers, and for several days they had to stay in a small cabin and fight to keep warm. Berlandier met with the local Tonkawa who were residing along the river. They told him that such cold was rare in Texas. The Tonkawa were suffering from terrible privation. They were weak compared to such tribes as the Comanche, so feared to go on extensive hunts. One old woman, about eighty years old, was so thin, her leathery skin barely covering the outline of her skeleton, that Berlandier thought she appeared more like an Egyptian mummy than a living person. The Tonkawa would do anything for food; when a few horses drowned crossing the Guadalupe, several men braved the frigid waters and struggled with the weight of the dead animals and force of the current to drag the horses to shore, where they butchered and ate them. Berlandier spent some time interviewing the chief, Joaquín, who could speak Spanish. The chief taught Berlandier some Tonkawa words, which the scientist recorded. Berlandier also learned about the colony of Guadalupe Victoria from Martín León. The inhabitants were from varied places—Mexico, Canada, even Ireland, though most were from Tamaulipas. As in most such new colonies, there were few women. León brought prostitutes to the colony, where after a time they married and had children. The fertility of the soil, which promised much wealth, was often washed away or, in the case of livestock, dragged away by the flooding Guadalupe. Terán compared León's Mexican colony with Austin's American colony, observing the differences between the group mentality of the Mexicans and the individualism of the Americans. The Mexicans lived in community, residing in the town, journeying, sometimes infrequently, the several miles to their outlying fields to work the land, whereas the Americans eschewed living in town, rather building cabins on their fields, where they could guard and tend them around the clock. Whereas shopkeepers and artisans lived in American towns, Mexican towns rarely had such specialists, only farmers.[10]

Berlandier accompanied Terán and Sánchez to Goliad, whence the latter two continued on to Matamoros. Terán ordered Berlandier to return to San Antonio, retrieve the specimens he had collected, journey back to Goliad, and from Aransas Bay take passage by water to New Orleans, where he could safely ship the specimens to Mexico. Berlandier set out for San Antonio on February 19 notwithstanding the threat of Tawakoni warriors, who were reportedly harassing travelers. Berlandier refused a military escort, deciding rather to travel with just one dragoon, the soldado, a man he had traveled with for some time, who was an excellent hunter and tracker, and therefore the best person to lead Berlandier through treacherous country. The soldado suggested that they rest by day and travel by night to avoid the Indians. When they crossed Arroyo de las Cabezas under cover of darkness, they could see the Tawakoni campfires in the distance. At dawn they had reached Arroyo San Bartolo, where they bivouacked under cover during the day. Their vista allowed them to observe, without being seen, a Tawakoni war party pass by. After dusk, Berlandier and the soldado continued on in bitter cold, reaching Arroyo las Calaveras during the night; hearing people and horses nearby, they retired to a place where they hid throughout the next day until nightfall, when they finished the journey to San Antonio. Berlandier gathered his collections and set out to return to Goliad on February 25, this time in the company of half a dozen soldiers. Although Berlandier was a civilian, his friendship with General Terán and important role in the Comisión de Límites as well as growing experience gave him the right of command. The Tawakoni threat continued, and the men took every precaution possible. They spent a restless night camping next to a stream with men on guard in shifts. During the night the soldado awakened Berlandier to hear the soft wails of the Eastern Screech-Owl. Berlandier and his companion, knowing that the Tawakoni were excellent imitators of this owl's cry, asked one of the soldiers, a corporal who knew the Tawakoni well, to identify the sound; the corporal agreed it was an owl. But as they heard the wails all night from different directions, Berlandier and the soldado began to suppose that there might be a few Tawakoni owl imitators mixed in after all. At daybreak, Berlandier directed the men to allow their horses and pack animals to graze after having been restrained all night. This was a mistake. Soon the alarm was given, as the Tawakonis had quickly surrounded the animals and driven them off. As there was a rancho nearby, Berlandier sent soldiers to procure mounts. They returned with the melancholy report that the Tawakoni had attacked the rancho in the night, had killed some teamsters bivouacking nearby, as well as their oxen and dogs, and had driven all of the captured horses before them. Berlandier decided on quick action. He ordered the dragoons to stay put on guard while he and the soldado quickly departed for San Antonio, where they reported the Tawakoni attacks. Immediately the commander Elosúa sent out dragoons and armed men in several directions to recapture the stolen animals, raid the Tawakoni village, and gain revenge for their brazen attacks. After several days, Berlandier, accompanied by his friend and fellow traveler Batres as well as the soldado, returned with mounts to the soldiers, who had been bivouacking next to the same stream and guarding

Berlandier's baggage, which included money and specimens. They continued the journey to Goliad in the first week of March. Although it was the
time of the firstfruits, the inhabitants and soldiers of Goliad lacked even
basic foodstuffs after the winter and recent disturbance of travel and trade.[11]

Among those awaiting spring and sufficient cargo and passengers to
sail was Captain Prieto of the American vessel the *Paumone*. Berlandier
joined the captain and an escort journeying south of Goliad toward where
the schooner was anchored at the port of Cópano, named for a band of the
Karankawa tribe. They journeyed in parallel to the San Antonio, then the
Guadalupe after the two rivers merged just above the maze of islands and
shallow bays of the Texas coast at the mouth of the Guadalupe. Departing
southwest from the Guadalupe, they journeyed overland toward Cópano
Bay. Approaching the coast, the landscape changed to one of sandy plains
and dried-up estuaries that would soon, when the spring rains came, become
massive, shallow ocean inlets. In just such an environment, Matamoros on
the Rio Grande, Berlandier would shortly take up residence, spending the
rest of his life among the estuarial shallows, viewing and sketching shore-
birds and watching wily predators, such as foxes and wolves, try to sneak
up on geese, egrets, ducks, herons, sandpipers, and gulls. Cópano was the
Mexican port located on a peninsula jutting into Aransas Bay. The maze of
islands, channels, and shifting winds and tides made for dangerous shipping. The captain of the *Paumone* kept the schooner at anchor for several
days, waiting for the strong southerlies whipping up waves on the bay to
abate. Berlandier spent his time making astronomical observations, trying
to determine the latitude of the place; walking about the tidal basin looking
for interesting new plants; and talking with sailors and soldiers about the
shipping lanes and islands and peoples. The evening of March 10, Berlandier
could see in the distance smoke signals, which sailors told him were between
members of the coastal Karankawa tribe. This once formidable opponent
was declining in numbers and power, and excited little concern among the
sailors compared to the terror these warriors once wrought upon ship's
crews. But warfare with the Spanish, Mexicans, pirates, Tejanos, and other
Indians had severely reduced their numbers.[12]

By March 11, the southerlies had died down sufficiently to allow the
schooner to cast off into the treacherous waters of Aransas Bay. The Gulf
Coast from Galveston Island to Padre Island to Brazos de Santiago is a maze
of shallows alternating with random deep channels, shoals of sand and
shells, contrary currents running west and east, and long and narrow sand

Figure 8. Panorama of the seat of war: bird's-eye view of Texas and part of Mexico, drawn from nature and lithograph by John Bachmann. Library of Congress.

islands built by the waves, winds, and currents. The schooner sailed before a west wind, arriving at shallows south of Aransas Peninsula, where it ran aground on a bar of shells. After an hour the crew freed the boat without damage but anchored to await the tide to add depth for unhindered sailing. After the schooner rode at anchor for hours, the winds and currents allowed it a brief voyage in a deep channel cutting through the shallows. Sailors were busy trimming sails according to the changes in the wind and dropping the lead to check the water's depth. They rode the waves at anchor for the night; with dawn they weighed anchor and tacked into a northeasterly breeze. Approaching the Aransas bar, shallows south of Aransas Peninsula, the captain became cautious and again they anchored, but only briefly; resuming, the surf crashing over shoals again forced them to halt. Here they anchored for almost a week, awaiting good winds and deeper water. Daily, officers and men took the ship's boat to nearby isles for water and to hunt and fish for food. Berlandier accompanied them, examining the tracks of

various animals that came at night to prey upon fowl. He watched the winds
to see if they prognosticated a change in the weather. He found a variety of
shells deposited in the sand and signs of places where the Karankawa had
feasted on turtles and oysters. Berlandier conversed with his informants,
officers and sailors, who told him that even if a good wind (from the west
or northwest) came up, the cautious mariner must examine the shoal water
to see how much spray was produced by the waves, and how loud were the
crashing breakers. If the spray was thick and the breakers noisy, the ship
should stay at anchor even if favorable winds encouraged departure, for the
spray and breakers foretold a strong current coming toward shore, which,
once the ship was freed from the protection of the sandbars, would over-
whelm it and send it crashing back into the mainland. Since experienced
sailors rarely made such a mistake, shipwrecks were few along the bays and
inlets of coastal waters. Not that the refuse from shipwrecks did not frequently wash ashore. Indeed, along the beaches and bars of bays and inlets
within the outer banks, because the current flowed from east to west, waters
flowed from the Mississippi to Texas rivers, and beyond to the Rio Grande.
The Mississippi, a destroyer of shipping, cast the remains of schooners and
barges from its mouth, where the westerly current took the refuse eventually along the Texas coast. The Karankawa tribe was adept at salvaging the
battered remains of boats that had meandered in the coastal currents from
the great river.[13]

Finally, on March 18, the winds changed to the west, which gave the
captain and crew the opportunity to hoist the anchor and carefully follow
the channel of deeper water between islands and bars. The men christened
one island of sand that they left behind the Islet of the Birds, because of
the incredible number of fowl that made it their refuge from predators. The
wind drove the ship forward, away from the dangers of the coast into the
equally dangerous Gulf, which threatened with high waves and contrary
winds. "Violent tempests" battered the *Paumone* at the spring equinox;
Berlandier, as before when he crossed the Atlantic, experienced not the
slightest sea-sickness. On May 25, a gusty easterly forced Captain Prieto to
tack to the south, where they could pick up the Gulf current flowing east.
Once they gained the current, the captain ordered the crew to "hove to"
all sails; they drifted with the current. Unbroken clouds for days prevented
the mariners from knowing their position. After three days of suspense,
a strong storm from the southwest allowed them to unfurl the sails and

ride the wind. When the storm abated, they were in turbid waters and still unsure of their position. The lookout spotted land before dark on the twenty-eighth, which compelled the captain to drop anchor in seven fathoms of water and wait for dawn. During the night they spied a lighthouse; in the clear weather of the morning they could clearly see the coast. They found themselves opposite the old French port of Balise, which stood at the end of the delta jutting into the Gulf of Mexico. Tall ships under sail going north heralded the mouth of the Mississippi. Berlandier was thrilled by the sight, yet sobered by looking upon the Louisiana shore, littered with the remains of countless shipwrecks. They rode at anchor near Balise, where sailors and river pilots lived in the moist environment of spongy, wet soil covered with tall reeds. After a time, a pilot from Balise guided the *Paumone* into the mouth of the river. This was a moment for which Berlandier had long waited. He had read much about the Mississippi, or the Meschacebé, according to the romance of Viscount de Chateaubriand. As a boy growing up in France, Berlandier read Chateaubriand's *Atala*, the story of "savage love" in America. Chauteaubriand described the Meschacebé as a river that

through a course of more than a thousand leagues, waters a delightful country, which the inhabitants of the United States call New Eden, and to which the French have left the soft name of Louisiana. A thousand other rivers, tributary to the Meschaceba, the Missouri, the Illinois, the Akanza, the Ohio, the Wabash, the Tennassee, &c. enrich it with their slime, and fertilize it with their waters. When all these rivers are swelled by the rains and the melting of the snows; when the tempests have swept over the whole face of the country, TIME collects, from every source, the trees torn from their roots. He fastens them together with vines; he cements them with rich soil; he plants upon them young shrubs, and launches his work upon the waters. Transported by the swelling flood, these rafts descend from all parts into the Meschaceba. The old river takes possession of them, and pushes them forward to his mouth, in order there to form with them a new branch. Sometimes he raises his mighty voice in passing between the mountains; expanding his waters; overflowing the loftiest trees, those colonnades of the forest; and deluging the pyramids of the Indian tombs. This is the Nile of the deserts.[14]

Berlandier knew that New Orleans had been founded and built on dreams. Robert Cavelier, Sieur de La Salle, descended the Mississippi in 1682, sailing past the future sites of Baton Rouge and New Orleans, claiming the lands to the west for France, christening them Louisiana. Looking for an adequate place to establish a fort to protect French interests, and not finding it in the Mississippi delta, La Salle followed the current west to Texas and planted a colony at Matagorda Bay, but was killed soon after, in 1689. The French knew that if they could control the Mississippi, they could control the trade of the interior of North America. Their initial attempt at founding a port that would be easily defensible was at Baton Rouge, which offered several routes to the Gulf of Mexico that evaded the hazards along the Mississippi delta. Jean-Baptiste Le Moyne, Sieur de Bienville, however, believed that the route from Baton Rouge through Lake Maurepas, Lake Pontchartrain, and the Rigolets, to Lake Borgne and the Mississippi Sound, was too cumbersome. He preferred the location between Lake Pontchartrain and the Mississippi that was rather like an island, where the river jogged south, west, then north in a horseshoe. Bienville's site of New Orleans was a good place for a port, not so much for a town. The surrounding lands were swampy and easily flooded. Heat and humidity in summer were staggering, and such diseases as malaria thrived. The French also had a difficult time holding on to New Orleans and Louisiana, and lost it to the Spanish in 1763 at the end of the French and Indian War, in which England defeated France and forced the French from North America. Two score years passed, and another Frenchman dreamed of another great empire in America, centered again on control of the Mississippi. Napoleon Bonaparte in 1800 forced the Spanish to return Louisiana to the French, where Napoleon could realize his dream of an American empire. Napoleon's vision was short-lived, however, and he sold Louisiana, and control of the Mississippi, to the United States in 1803.[15]

Dreams of conquest and empire, accounts of travelers both real and imagined, could hardly prepare Berlandier for the reality of the muddy brown water filled with the refuse of thousands of miles of runoff descending from the Rocky Mountains of the west and the Appalachian Mountains of the east. The river deposited along its shores the remnants of ash, pine, birch, oak, and maple from the Ohio and Missouri valleys, and cottonwoods and sycamores from the Arkansas and Red valleys. Planks and cargo from destroyed flatboats, which had been casualties of tree trunks, called planters, hidden just beneath the brown water, and logs swept by the current, called sawyers, had become part of levees and dams of mangled trunks and branches that lined the banks. Inland, in the massive floodplain, were impoverished, dirty towns of a wretched coastal people. Literary romance failed to capture the degree of misery that Berlandier found at and near the mouth of the Mississippi. After looking forward for so long to seeing the Mississippi, the disillusioning sights of the delta brought an attack of melancholy upon Berlandier, who felt sick at heart for the suffering of immigrants like himself who sought a new life, only to be foiled by the harsh environment of the American South. The *Paumone* ascended from Balise past an old French fort, Plaquemines, the namesake of the peninsula through which the river flowed, followed by another, Fort Philippe. Wishing to see firsthand the contrast between fiction and fact, when the ship rode at anchor at dusk during its journey upriver, Berlandier went ashore and visited a small fisher hamlet in which the huts were bare, decorated by absolute necessity, the residents impoverished if hardworking. The land was so frequently inundated that some farmers planted rice. The poor lived on isolated stretches of land in the delta surrounded by the many fingers of the river. As the *Paumone* progressed upriver, tugged by a steamboat, Berlandier noted that the delta land was drier, firmer, supporting the mansions of rich sugar planters. Slave communities, which adjoined the plantations, appeared tidy and well ordered, not so bad a place to live, Berlandier thought, if one was not a slave! Continuing the journey upriver, the *Paumone* approached Lake Pontchartrain, where the Mississippi made a dramatic change in direction, which sailors called the English Turn. Before the age of steam, and the numerous steamboats that towed sailboats up the river, the contrary winds of the Mississippi forced long delays for ships attempting to navigate the English Turn. Near here the British had, fourteen years earlier, lost the closing battle of the War of 1812 to American general Andrew Jackson.[16]

The voyage of one hundred miles up the river, which used to take ships weeks because of contrary winds, took the *Paumone*, thanks to the steam tugboat, just over a day to accomplish. Berlandier spied the masts of tall ships in the distance, heralding New Orleans. The countless tugboats, steamships, flatboats, scows, and sailboats of all sizes and burdens, which made the mouth of the Mississippi the busiest river Berlandier had ever seen, could not compare with the hundreds of ships that crowded into the port of New Orleans. The ships were from the ports of North and South America, Europe, Asia, and Africa; a great babel of tongues greeted the visitor of the streets near the customhouse. Berlandier heard some French, but by and large English was the dominant language, which visitors were required to use if they were to buy and sell goods and make their way about the city. From what he had read and heard from informants, Berlandier knew that the city was expanding in trade and population. As the United States expanded west from the Appalachians to the Mississippi, and after the purchase of Louisiana, from the Mississippi to the Rocky Mountains, the number of products shipped by flatboat and steamboat down the dozens of rivers that fed the Mississippi were multiplying at a staggering rate. No matter if a farmer or merchant lived as far to the north and east as Pittsburgh or as far to the north and west as the upper Missouri River— shipping and business had to go through New Orleans.[17]

During Berlandier's six-week stay in New Orleans, he traveled about the city and environs seeing the sights, investigating the geological, botanical, and hydrological marvels, studying American culture, looking in vain for signs of Spanish culture, and enjoying, whenever he could, French culture.

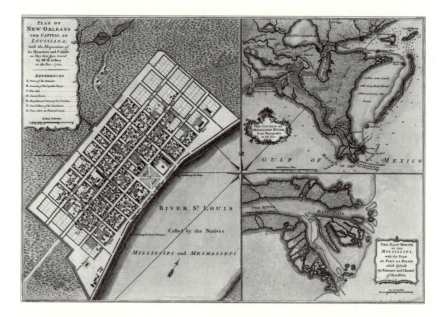

Figure 9. Plan of New Orleans the capital of Louisiana;
with the disposition of its quarters and canals as they have been traced by
Mr. de la Tour in the year 1720 by Thomas Jefferys. Library of Congress.

Berlandier visited the various suburbs and population centers of the city, such as Sainte Marie, the busy American community, where the houses were built of imported brick; Berlandier disliked the sameness and plainness of the American neighborhoods. Americans had neither manners nor sophistication, but they were hard workers and excelled at buying and selling, with the result that New Orleans was a thriving port. The French of the old city were being outpaced by the Americans in money, power, and numbers, which compelled the former to isolate themselves more and more from the latter, whom they greatly disliked. The geography of the city encouraged the segregation of ethnic communities; the cityscape was formed by layer upon layer of silt, surrounded by and interspersed with cypress swamps, and divided by levees, the only solid geologic structures. The levees were artificial and natural, the former built of crushed shells and earth to prevent the river, the surface of which was higher than the city, from inundating New Orleans; the latter were formed by the deposit of silt and organic matter by the river. Levees formed the thoroughfares of the city and surrounding suburbs. In between were the low-lying basins in which neighborhoods were built, constantly threatened with flooding should the river rise and the levees break.[18]

The ever-changing Mississippi delta fascinated Berlandier, and he spent much of his time gathering information about this phenomenon. The Mississippi is unique among North American rivers in the creation of its delta. Berlandier read about contemporary studies of the Nile and Yangtze deltas and the volume of silt to water measured by English scientists. He had neither the tools nor the expertise to perform the same measurements on the Mississippi but could nevertheless reach conclusions by observation and anecdote. Research informed him that the banks of the Mississippi were constantly rising because of annual silt deposits. Likewise, he discovered that the Mississippi delta grows outward at about three miles per century; old forts, originally built at the mouth, now lay several miles inland. After an acquaintance presented Berlandier with a figwort attached to a shell unearthed at a depth of one hundred feet near Lake Pontchartrain, he calculated that it had been five to six thousand years since the plant grew next to a much different Mississippi River.[19]

The French community of New Orleans was a blessing and a curse to Berlandier. On the one hand, he experienced great joy at being around people of his own kind, with the same language, customs, and assumptions about life. The French were so much more cultured than their American counterparts. They enjoyed life and expressed their happiness in a way that was foreign to the Americans. At the same time, Berlandier's experience of the French culture of New Orleans brought back memories of his youth, of the Rhône, the Alps, and Geneva, places he had yet to see equaled in America. Indeed, New Orleans brought melancholy feelings of what he was missing, living a "semisavage life in the vast wilds of Texas." And yet this life pulled him as well. Perhaps he was not too disappointed, then, when on May 8 he rejoined the captain and crew of the *Paumone* on the return voyage. Upon taking in the river air filling the sails of the *Paumone*, bringing her downstream, Berlandier quickly noticed the absence of mosquitoes, a lessening of humidity, and the thrill of adventure that travel brought. The voyage downstream was not as quick as it could have been, as the captain decided to stop along the way taking in a load of wood to bring back to San Antonio. On several occasions Berlandier disembarked to hunt, walk (gingerly, as the spongy soil would sometimes give way and suck like quicksand), observe nature (such as spring clover, blooming trees, eerie swamps, and hoary Spanish moss hanging from trees), and talk with the inhabitants. They told him that the spring was retarded because of a fierce winter; hence, the Mississippi had not yet risen. Those who planted rice were anxiously awaiting the flooding waters; every day a new prognostication of the river's rising was told. Steamboats filled the river, but there were fewer flatboats coming from upriver. They would come with the rising water. Upon reaching Plaquemines, the *Paumone* took aboard a pilot to bring the ship to sea. The pilot told Berlandier that recently a boat with a pilot and sailors was lost at sea. Sometimes the winds prevented their return; often a pilot brought provisions in case he had to bivouac on an island or a shipwreck until a passing ship could return him to shore.[20]

The return voyage was quick and easy, unlike the voyage out. An easterly propelled them forward along with the westward-flowing current. Porpoises accompanied the ship, sometimes taking the lead, sometimes in its wake. Sailors informed Berlandier that porpoises, like dolphins, swim in the direction of a coming headwind, and the easterly was sure to change; they were perplexed but still credulous after the wind failed to accommodate their expectations. It took only four days to reach Aransas Bay; Captain Prieto gingerly guided the ship in, looking for the treacherous bar that in low water barricaded the entrance. Berlandier helped the captain determine the precise latitude with the sextant, and they came near the bar accordingly, passing it safely. Unfortunately, they raced into the bay under full sail, entered some shallows, and ran aground in mud, causing no damage. The next morning, May 14, the water level rose, and the ship got off easily. The next challenge was to guide the schooner into Cópano, the port from which they had departed two months earlier. The navigation was tricky, requiring the gentle winds from the north. Although they could see the port, they could not risk approaching with an east wind; they anchored and waited. Impatient to disembark, Berlandier and another traveler requested the ship's boat to row to shore; two sailors performed the duty. Upon arriving at Cópano, however, they found the place deserted. Berlandier in his journal described Cópano as a "wilderness port," which was an overstatement; it was an anchorage to embark and disembark, where sometimes a small detachment of troops guarded the coast against smugglers. Berlandier and his companions searched about the place in vain and spent an uncomfortable night in humid, rainy conditions. A diversion from their dismal situation were the sights of tall, graceful wading birds, such as white herons, egrets, and the rarely seen roseate spoonbill, hunting for fish and crustaceans; the spoonbill was both beautiful and odd, with pink feathers like a flamingo and a flat, awkward bill. The next morning, while the first mate and a few others decided to journey toward Goliad; Berlandier returned to the *Paumone* to wait. About four miles from Cópano, the journeyers came upon a small troop of soldiers waging war against mosquitoes. They had evacuated Cópano because of the swarms, hoping to find respite inland, but to no avail. It was May, the air was hot and sultry, the ground wet and swampy, and the mosquitoes ruled. Berlandier, disembarking again, had rarely seen the enemy so powerful. Forced to journey on horseback from Cópano to Goliad back and forth for several days, carting his baggage because no muleteers could be found for the purpose, he and his companions of the moment could not escape from the relentless foe. At night the insects' sound was deafening, their bites preventing sleep. By day they formed clouds obscuring vision, hovering around horses and mules and humans. After some of his experiences along the swamps of Tampico and the inundated forests of the Brazos, where heat, moisture, mosquitoes, and fatigue had caused such memorable suffering, Berlandier was unpleasantly surprised to find these few days in May 1829, on the wilderness road from Aransas Bay to Goliad, to be even worse. The swampy land hosted few trees to escape the daytime sun, which glared on the surrounding water, half-blinding him. When clouds hid the sun, rain fell— not a refreshing, cool rain, but a sweltering, humid rain. Berlandier was constantly wet. Mosquitoes were not bothered by sun, rain, wetness, or darkness—they were sleepless, unrelenting, torturing, ubiquitous. There was no wood in the marshy land to build a fire to cook food and bathe in smoke, which even the mosquitoes disliked. There were no trees to tie one's horse to at night; the locals taught Berlandier how to bundle up some grass, tie a rope around it, bury it in the sand about two feet deep, and tie the rope to the horse, which could not extricate the grass no matter how hard it tried. The route from Cópano to Goliad covered about forty-five miles. From the coast to Arroyo de los Alamitos, a known camping spot on the route, was nine miles of treeless, grassy, moist and swampy land. Flora on the route from Cópano to Goliad included a species of *Lantana*, a small hardy plant with red and yellow flowers in bloom. Berlandier also saw herbal plants from the Chenopodiaceae family that thrived in saline conditions. The eighteen miles that separated Los Alamitos from San Nicolás, a grove where travelers halted for the night, featured a strange phenomenon of the soil, which appeared like waves at sea and could fool the newcomer into thinking that a bay was in the distance. This passage had no trees, only grass, in which hid rattlesnakes. It was along this path that Berlandier's horse reared, perhaps because of a snake, which caused his saber to fall to the ground. After calming the horse, Berlandier dismounted to look for the lost sword. Nearby he saw an Indian, probably a Karankawa, who with bow and arrow appeared to be lying in wait for him. Discovered, the Indian departed. Two others from the same tribe sought to surprise teamsters driving a wagon on the same route. The teamsters were, however, well armed. Later on the road Berlandier again met the Indian who he believed wished to kill him, skinning a deer which he had just killed; the Indian demanded tobacco, which Berlandier traded for venison. After finally retrieving his supplies from Cópano, he received word at Goliad to journey to San Antonio to rejoin the Comisión; from there they were to proceed to Matamoros to join General Terán.[21]

CHAPTER SEVEN

Waters of the High Sierra

✿

✣ THE TWO TIMES THAT JEAN LOUIS BERLANDIER MADE THE JOURNEY
from San Antonio to the Rio Grande, he and his companions watched for
attacks from the Comanches, particularly in 1834, when Berlandier and
Raphael Chowell took the same way that Couch would in 1846 to the presidio of San Juan Bautista. The trail in 1834 was inordinately dry. But in
the early summer of 1829, the weather in south-central Texas was unusually wet; it had rained enough to make travel almost impossible because of
the flooding streams and rivers. Nevertheless, members of the Comisión
de Límites set out in mid-July on their way to Matamoros near the mouth
of the Rio Grande by way of Laredo, to reunite with their leader, Gen.
Manuel Mier y Terán. Joining Jean Louis Berlandier were soldiers, officers,
and friends who had been with him for a year or more, including the two
Kickapoo warriors who had adopted the transplanted Frenchman. As there
was no safe and direct trail from San Antonio to Matamoros, the expedition had to first take the road to Laredo, from where they could pick up
another trail on the Mexican side of the Rio Grande that led to Matamoros.
Berlandier had journeyed from Laredo to San Antonio by the same road in
February 1828. The general aridity of the climate, despite the recent rains,
was quite the same then as presently, in July; otherwise, the journey was
more of a challenge because of the unrelenting heat, penetrating rays of the
sun, and hordes of insects. For Berlandier, there were more opportunities
to collect botanical specimens than during the previous winter.[1]

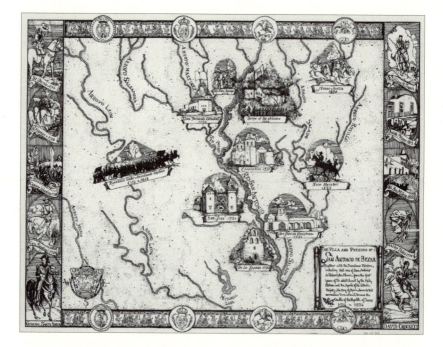

Figure 10. The villa and presidio of San Antonio de Bexar : together with the
Franciscan Missions, including that one of San Antonio de Valero, the Alamo,
from the first years of its establishment by the holy fathers and the agents of his
Catholic Majesty, the King of Spain, down to that momentous time when it became
the cradle of the republic of Texas, 1716–1836 by Fanita Lanier. Library of Congress.

The first night on the road, they stayed at one of the several missions surrounding San Antonio, the Franciscan mission of San José. The Franciscans
had long since abandoned the mission, and the structure was generally in ruin.
Hints of its past beauty suggested an extensive complex, an arched walkway, a
domed nave, and a simple bell tower. Utterly impoverished farmers worked the
land thereabouts. The second night out the party camped next to the Medina,
which was quite a different river than a year before in March. The river was
flooding, bringing along trees that had hitherto perched perilously on the
bank. The usual fords were unavailable, which required the dragoons to build
a makeshift raft large enough to cross baggage, horses, and men. Terán's major-
domo, or secretary, Col. José María Díaz Noriega, whom Berlandier had known
since they had departed Mexico City almost two years before, was swept away
by the current while bathing; notwithstanding repeated attempts, they never
found the body.[2]

The plants of summer were in full bloom. Where available, oaks and hickories provided shade to escape the midsummer sun. A species of *Cassia*, brightly colored red and yellow, as well as various species of cactus and mesquite, covered the plains; less inviting was the presence of poison ivy and bur grass (*Cenchrus echinatus*); the oil of the former clung to the skin, the seeds of the latter to the clothes. As they marched closer to the Nueces, the landscape was more forbidding, shade trees a luxury, potable water hot and cathartic. General Terán's impractical carriage, which still accompanied them, was a nuisance, breaking down time and again. The heat of midday was suffocating and brought almost total silence to the natural world, as all creatures awaited sundown and the gentle easterly zephyrs of night. Water was sufficiently scarce that the men took to eating the prickly pear; some of them had a violent reaction to ingesting the cactus, including fever, vomiting, and diarrhea. Berlandier was unaffected. He noted, however, that over a course of days, as a man ate the cactus his system tolerated it better each time, eventually experiencing no adverse reactions. Another cathartic Berlandier discovered was *Jatropha cathartica*, which he published in *Memorias de la Comision de Limites* in 1832. If the heat and lack of good water were not enough, every night the men were plagued by large, smelly black bugs and mosquitoes. Even so, by day there was plenty to engage the observant traveler. Berlandier came upon a fascinating phenomenon when he was exploring the environs of their camp; as he entered a gully where there were plentiful mimosa shrubs, the leaves of the shrubs closed as he approached, but not close enough to touch. He correctly assumed that these plants must be extremely sensitive to any disturbance in the habitat. A host of trees grew on the banks of the Nueces, and the water was deep and cool. They crossed the river on rafts that the dragoons fashioned from skins and wood. They were still four days out from Laredo, and the days were growing hotter, and the land more parched; water and food were scarce. The night of July 26, soldiers captured one of the many wild mustangs in the area, this one a colt; they killed it, cut it up, and cooked it. Berlandier and some soldiers ate, but others refused, including the two Kickapoo Indians who traveled with Berlandier. The Kickapoo had rarely missed the opportunity to feed the men and show off their hunting skill; that the band had to resort to horsemeat was absurd. So, while others ate, they quickly rode off, returning later, before the horseflesh feast was concluded, with two deer to feed themselves and everyone else. The last few days of the journey, approaching Laredo, the land became increasingly hilly and broken by periodic ravines. Berlandier collected and studied desert plants that the land reluctantly offered. July 27, one day out of Laredo, a courier arrived with letters for the men of the Comisión, including a few for Berlandier from his "family and friends" in Europe. Feelings of joy in reading letters from home helped to counter the privations of a two-week journey in a land sterilized by heat and lack of water, where not a single human habitation was encountered, where the emptiness of the landscape mirrored the barrenness and loneliness of Berlandier's "vexed soul."[3]

The Rio Grande, which Berlandier saw again July 28, appeared far different from what he remembered when he first encountered it in February 1828. Then, the water level was low if the current was rapid; now, the river was unexpectedly full, charged with energy, its waters a deep brown, filled with the silt gathered from its long journey from the Rocky Mountains. The local inhabitants used the river water for drinking, cooking, and washing; women had a variety of ways to remove its sediment. Some used ground seeds such as almonds, others a grilled prickly pear. Berlandier discovered that the sediment formed 5 percent of the river water. Dust filled even the air, carried by the east wind. In such uninviting circumstances the men of the Comisión stayed for a fortnight while General Terán's carriage was repaired. On August 11, after crossing the river by flatboat, they continued the journey on the southern side of the river east toward Matamoros. The land was generally uninhabited save for the random ranchero; in previous years the Lipan Apaches and Comanches had crossed the Rio Grande in this area south of Laredo and north of the confluence with the Salado to commit their depredations on isolated ranches. A feeder stream of the Rio Grande flowing from the south, the Saladito, was deep and rapid, challenging to ford. Vegetation was limited to mesquite, *tasajillo*, a desert plant, part of the cactus family, and the creosote bush. Continuing east, they came to the town of Guerrero, nicely situated near the confluence of the Salado and Rio Grande. The Salado was broad and powerful, with hints of its source in the mountains, the Sierra de Santa Rosa, found west of Laredo in Coahuila. Sandstone ledges punctuated the current, forming frequent rapids and falls, and making navigation by anything bigger than a canoe impossible. Cypress lined the clear, potable waters of the Salado. Guerrero, once named Revilla, was a colony, like Laredo, founded in the mid-eighteenth century by José de Escandón, the colonizer who organized the Spanish colony of Nuevo Santander north of the Pánuco. Escandón, the Count of Sierra Gorda, had reconnoitered the region of Tamaulipas in the late 1740s and received the charge of settling the region with soldiers, colonists and their families, and Franciscan missionaries from the College of Guadalupe de Zacatecas.

At a time when France was expanding its colony of New France into the vast Louisiana Territory, and the British controlled the eastern coast of North America and were seeking to expand their power, Escandón and the Spanish determined to do what they could to hold on to, indeed to expand, their colony of Nueva España. Escandón's Nuevo Santander would also provide a buffer against the growing strength of Plains Indian tribes north of the Rio Grande. The new settlers displaced the local Indians, who in coming years sought to avenge their loss and extricate the squatters with attacks from the cordilleras to the west.[4]

Berlandier and companions bivouacked at Guerrero for a day, during which time Berlandier explored the town and an abandoned coal mine. The inhabitants of the town and surrounding ranchos successfully raised all varieties of livestock; they used sheep's wool to make beautiful quilts and cloaks. The journeyers crossed the river on the evening of August 14 to prepare to continue on in the morning; their horses and mules, however, stayed behind to graze in the rich grass of Guerrero. The morning of the fifteenth, the soldier in charge of the animals crossed them where the current was strong and the river deep; a dozen unfortunate horses drowned. Even so, there were enough remaining mounts to continue the journey toward Mier, which they reached on the seventeenth. Like Guerrero, Mier was founded by Escandón, thrived on livestock more than farming, and produced excellent woven goods. A small stream surrounded the town on three sides. The Garzas tribe coexisted with the Mexicans at Mier, living in huts resembling the Mexicans,' though they dressed differently—the men wearing only breechcloths—and relied on hunting and fishing. They spoke Spanish so well that Berlandier conversed with them, particularly the chief, who provided the Frenchman with a host of details about his tribe, including samples of their unique language. Berlandier noted that Mexicans often associated the Garzas with another tribe, the Carrizos, who lived nearby. Indeed, they dressed the same and had the same reliance on the hunt; but their language was quite different, and the two tribes could communicate only, Berlandier wrote, "by signs or in Spanish." Berlandier had experienced the Carrizos once before, on the journey through Nuevo León on the way to the Rio Grande in January of the previous year. The Garzos and Carrizos were friends and allies, sharing, for example, their hatred of the Comanches.[5]

The road continued east from Mier toward Camargo. The journeyers came upon more people, inhabitants of a number of ranchos that thrived in the ongoing peace that existed between the Mexicans and Comanches. Before

Camargo they had to cross, by raft, the Río de San Juan, a wide, deep river that at Camargo was about to empty into the Rio Grande. Berlandier had never seen the San Juan, though in Nuevo León in January 1828, he had journeyed along several of the river's tributaries that descended from the Sierra Madre. Camargo was a town similar in size and industry to Mier and Guerrero, founded about the same time. A Franciscan mission served by three monks served local Indians—the Carrizos—and others at Camargo. The last town before Matamoros was Reynosa, also the beneficiary of Escandón when he founded Nuevo Santander. Reynosa lay near the banks of the Rio Grande and sometimes suffered from floods. Indeed, the landscape between Camargo and Matamoros was more subject to floods, hence hosted more vegetation, even forests of mimosa and mesquite.[6]

Berlandier had first entered Matamoros on August 21, 1828, when he was still recovering from the bout with malaria that he had experienced the previous spring along the rivers of Texas. Matamoros was a growing port city adjacent to the Rio Grande, built on the site of an old Franciscan mission, Congregación del Refugio. Opened by decree in 1826, Matamoros was an attempt by the Republic of Mexico to garner and control the trade of the Rio Grande valley and Texas Gulf Coast. The city occupied the land opening of a great horseshoe bend in the Rio Grande; indeed the river, as it neared the Gulf, was winding, creating snakelike patterns, and subject to recurrent floods. The remains of the old mission of Refugio had vanished in floodwaters, which often inundated Matamoros as well. Lakes and swamps surrounded the city, which was neatly planned like a checkerboard. When Berlandier first entered from the Reynosa Road, he was struck by the plainness, filth, and poverty of the city. The few nice dwellings were foreign, built mostly by American merchants. Impoverished Mexicans, drawn from the inhabitants of villages upstream (such as Camargo and Reynosa), who had relocated to Matamoros because of the opportunity for wealth through trade, lived in reed or baked-mud hovels. The population had grown to nearly ten thousand. Although crowded and dirty, with no public buildings of beauty; a half-finished cathedral without a plan of completion; a cosmopolitan populace from the United States of America, Mexico, islands of the Caribbean, and Europe; and disgusting smells from the market squares and open sewers, Matamoros became Berlandier's home. He chose Matamoros mostly by default, as there the Comisión, while it lasted, was headquartered, and Terán, while he lived, was stationed. When the men of the Comisión arrived in August, however, General Terán was absent, having led troops south to Tampico because of the Spanish invasion to recapture their former colony.[7]

The surviving record is silent regarding Berlandier's activities from August to December 1829. Over the course of his long residence at Matamoros, Berlandier made numerous journeys down the Rio Grande to its mouth either by boat or on horseback along both the north and south sides of the river, exploring particularly Boca Chica, the Brazos de Santiago (Arms of St. James), and Point Isabel. On December 14 he set out on what appears to have been the first of many journeys. The road from Matamoros to La Burrita was about thirty miles over a low-lying land frequently inundated by the river, dotted with numerous *esteros*, swamps. Few trees grew in the marine environment. Berlandier used the sextant to take frequent measurements of latitude; he also kept accurate records of temperature. La Burrita was one of the few habitable locations along the southern bank of the river; it lay ten miles from the mouth. Enterprising boatmen at La Burrita offered ferry services, to which Berlandier agreed whenever the weather and winds allowed. The ferrymen brought the traveler across the river to Boca Chica on its northern shores. Boca Chica was a small port, the population of which was limited to ferrymen, customs agents, and a few soldiers assigned as a coast guard. When he arrived at Boca Chica on August 13, locals informed him of the high surf of early summer, the result, they suspected, of a hurricane in the Gulf. The large waves damaged houses and came close to inundating, hence sweeping away, the town; just a few feet higher would have done it. The region between the mouth of the Rio Grande and Brazos de Santiago was waterlogged, filled with brackish ponds of saltwater and freshwater; at high tide, or when the waves of the Gulf ran high, seawater spilled over the sand dunes into tidal ponds and waterways that sometimes connected the Rio Grande to the Laguna Madre, west of Padre Island. During this visit or some other (for Berlandier made this same journey a number of times), he observed that in the wake of great storms the waves "discarded dead fish on the shore in great quantities." The road from Boca Chica to Brazos de Santiago was good at low tide. The small port of Brazos de Santiago was at the northern extreme of the peninsula opposite Padre Island; sometimes at high tide or when the Rio Grande was overflowing its banks, the peninsula became an island. The inhabitants of Brazos de Santiago were, as at Boca Chica, customs agents, mariners, and soldiers. The few houses built at these coastal towns were made of imported wood, as few trees grew along the coast. Tropical storms and hurricanes frequently hit the area, damaging the ports and destroying most of the homes. Berlandier investigated the strait separating the arms of St. James, making observations and collecting specimens. Strangely, the sandbar, usually covered by a few feet of water, was dry in places. What phenomenon could cause this? He was not sure, though he could rule out the tide, which was barely noticeable here. Conversing with the locals about the shore and depths of water in the strait, Berlandier discovered that people still talked about the strange lights of 1788, over forty years earlier. These lights, Berlandier surmised, were an extremely rare sighting of the aurora borealis. This phenomenon, he wrote, "struck the inhabitants of Texas with wonder, who at its end believed they had seen light coming from great flames."[8]

Berlandier returned to Brazos de Santiago the following summer, in August 1830, upon General Terán's orders that the scientist descend the Rio Grande to La Burrita, ford the river, and proceed to Boca Chica, to investigate sightings (reported to the general by an anonymous source) of an abnormally large tortoise caught in the waters of Laguna Madre. Berlandier duly journeyed from Matamoros to Brazos de Santiago and back from early August to September 13, 1830. Whether or not Berlandier ever found the giant tortoise is unclear, as that part of his manuscript has been lost. In the collections that Darius Couch purchased from Berlandier's widow in 1853, and which ended up in the Smithsonian, are tortoise specimens—not the large ones Berlandier sought at Brazos de Santiago, but rather small tortoises that Louis Agassiz in 1857 named after Berlandier (*Gopherus berlandieri*).[9]

Berlandier observed on his journeys along the Rio Grande extending from San Juan Bautista downriver to La Burrita near the mouth that the river grew large and lazy beyond Mier, with great curves that frequently led to new channels, washing away all in its path, trees as well as houses. Nevertheless, the river was generally navigable for steamboats that drew less than six feet of water up to Mier, and for small boats further upstream; even so, trade was limited along the Rio Grande as well as Brazos de Santiago; few ships carrying cargo arrived from Europe or the United States. Settlement along the Rio Grande was too sporadic, and the roads extending inland from Brazos de Santiago to Matamoros, and from Matamoros to other larger settlements, were too inadequate to sustain a healthy trade; besides, the waters off the coast were treacherous, and shipwreck was all too common. Brazos de Santiago and the mouth of the Rio Grande were hazardous and dependent upon the wind, waves, and tide. The bar at the entrance of the former was particularly dangerous, being unyielding sand; the Rio Grande, however, was muddy and inconvenient but generally not dangerous for ships. The Mexican government was too corrupt, inefficient, and poor to curb graft among customs agents, to regulate trade and curtail smuggling, to build adequate roads, and to maintain secure shipping canals.[10]

Jean Louis Berlandier's raison d'être for his sojourn in Mexico was the Comisión de Límites, under the authority of General Terán, himself a scientist; his orders for Berlandier were of a scientific nature, requiring journeys of exploration and collection. General Terán made frequent use of Berlandier's energy, willingness to travel, and ability to make and record excellent observations of the countryside through which he journeyed. On April 1, 1830, Terán ordered Berlandier to travel to Monterrey to obtain smallpox vaccine for the inhabitants of the Rio Grande valley. Terán, still in charge of the Comisión de Límites but promoted to commander of the Eastern Interior Provinces (during the summer of 1829), feared the spread of smallpox, which was ravaging habitations in Mexico to the south. Vaccine had already been acquired, and inhabitants vaccinated; but for unclear reasons the vaccine was not preventing the spread of disease. Berlandier's job was to go quickly to Monterrey to acquire a new batch. He and his escort of three dragoons, one of whom was the soldado who had been Berlandier's companion and escort for over two years, chose the more-traveled, though longer route to Monterrey that paralleled the southern bank of the river through Reynosa toward Camargo. Berlandier, under commission from General Terán, in command of the small group, could have chosen the less-traveled route, which departed the river route to go through arid lands that had few inhabitants and few watering holes. But Berlandier, having grown up at Fort l'Ecluse, France, on the Rhône River, had a special relationship with soldiers, knowing their ways and empathizing with the demands on their lives; when the soldado told Berlandier that his parents lived in Reynosa, and that he had (apparently) not seen them for a long time, Berlandier decided to take the longer route and allow a reunion of parents and son. This accomplished, the small band set out overland for Monterrey.[11]

On the road to Monterrey, April 3, they decided to bivouac for the night at one of the few wet environments along this route, where pools of water stood, the product of old floodwaters of the Rio Grande as well as sporadic rainfall. The mosquitoes, however, were torturous, which forced them to move on to a more arid campsite where the lack of water complemented the lack of mosquitoes. As they journeyed west, the number of ranchos, and therefore inhabitants, declined; not only were there few sources of water, but even wells were dry. When they came to a rancho, they found it to be a place of despair, an oasis mostly in name, where warm and brackish well water was sold to travelers and muleteers, where there were no crops grown and few trees, a waterless desert. Berlandier had to decide when to travel based on reports of where water might be found. On the road to China, only two arroyos were encountered, both of which were practically waterless mud-holes during the driest seasons; on this occasion, April 5, 1830, the Arroyo de las Tunas had a few inches of water. It was fortunate that there was even that slight amount, because the next, Arroyo del Coronel, was impregnated with minerals and therefore not potable. The lack of water could have been a blessing in disguise, because the way they traveled was known to be frequented by bands of thieves rarely pursued by Mexican authorities, who therefore were free to come and go and attack at will. April 6, they passed through China, a town that Berlandier decried as "grotesquely named." It was an impoverished hamlet built at the joining of two tributaries of the Río de San Juan: the Río de la Purísma de Ramos and the Río de Pilón, two minor rivers that possessed enough water to allow the inhabitants to irrigate fields of crops if they chose to—but indolence reigned. China did offer Berlandier one appeal: from the town he could spy the foothills of the Sierra Madre, which he had not seen since 1828, when he had last spied the mountains on the road to Laredo. Upon passing a small hill known as Cerro del Capadero, the entire prospect of the grand cordillera came into view, which again engendered in the French immigrant recollections of his mountain home near the Alps of Savoy. China was the halfway point in the route from Reynosa to Monterrey. The immediate goal was the Cerro de la Silla, near the small town of Cadereyta, toward which they marched. The stairlike cordillera stretched out before them; upon reaching it they would be near Monterrey. The Cerro de la Silla was like the other peaks of the cordillera, a craggy, barren summit of rock. After a night spent next to the mountain, Berlandier and his men passed through the small town of Guadalupe and entered Monterrey on April 9. Berlandier believed that, compared to Texas and Tamaulipas, the inhabitants of Nuevo León lived in more orderly, peaceful, pastoral communities, the product of their focus on agriculture and avoidance of political conflict. Monterrey, surrounded on three sides by the Sierra Madre, was blessed with plentiful mountain streams that allowed the inhabitants to grow a variety of crops for consumption and sale—the most important and lucrative was sugarcane. Berlandier spent a week at Monterrey, ordering his collection of plants gathered there and along the way, as well as procuring the vaccine for the inhabitants of the Lower Rio Grande.[12]

Berlandier and his escort set out for Matamoros on April 16. The land was drier than on the journey out, and they saw livestock dying of thirst. Berlandier collected samples of desert plants, such as guayacán (soapbush,

Porlieria angustifolia), a small shrub the roots of which the people of Nuevo León and Tamaulipas used to make soap. *Retama* (horse bean, *Parkinsonia aculeata*) was a small tree with yellow flowers in bloom. The *ébano* (*Ebenopsis ebano* Berl.) was a small tree that produced seeds that shepherds and other inhabitants of northern Mexico roasted and considered nutritious, sometimes using them as a substitute for coffee; in large amounts the seeds acted as a purgative. They passed Cerro del Capadero again, where they could spy the fires of shepherds burning in the night. They crossed the Río de San Juan, then came upon one of the tributaries of the San Juan, Río de Pilón, before arriving at China. Hearing of a shorter, northerly route to the road from Camargo to Matamoros, they hired a guide to lead them. They had to leave behind their spent horses at China, where they borrowed fresh horses and a mule to get them to Matamoros. The arroyos they crossed on their way had become dry, even though a build-up of clouds heralded a coming rainstorm. The guide told them of two routes they could take to the Rio Grande; the one they took was longer than the alternative, which was called the *viborero*, a place of vipers, in particular rattlesnakes. The guide told Berlandier that rattlesnakes were plentiful in the region between eastern Nuevo León and western Tamaulipas. The following autumn Berlandier experienced firsthand that the serpents were prevalent in eastern Tamaulipas as well. Berlandier noted as they approached Matamoros that spring came earlier to the coastal regions compared to Monterrey, the higher elevation of which made the climate slightly cooler.[13]

In October 1830, Berlandier joined another member of the Comisión de Límites, Lt. Col. Constantino Tarnava, on a journey to Tamaulipas. In the wake of the failed Spanish attempt to reconquer Mexico during the invasion of the Pánuco valley in the summer of 1829, Terán, commander of the Eastern Interior Provinces, decided upon the necessity of a scientific reconnaissance of Tamaulipas; knowledge gained could prove useful in case the Spanish made a second attempt. Lieutenant Colonel Tarnava, an engineer with whom Berlandier had traveled before (in January 1828 they were reconnoitering a path to Monterrey when they became lost), headed the small expedition, which included cavalry major José Manuel Micheltorena in charge of the escort and muleteers and their pack animals. Terán charged them with investigating the landscape, topography, natural productions, and natural and human history of the province, as well as with making charts and maps that would be helpful in mounting a defense of the country. Berlandier began making discoveries as

Figure 11. General chart of the kingdom of New Spain betn. parallels of 16 & 38° N.
from materials in Mexico at commencement of year of 1804
by Alexander von Humboldt. Library of Congress.

soon as the expedition departed Matamoros. They journeyed south into largely flat land that during the rainy periods of the year hosted small, temporary lakes and ponds that dissipated only through evaporation. The atmospheric pressure and humidity were both high, which explained why these rain-produced lakes took a long time to evaporate. Berlandier used the hygrometer invented by the Swiss scientist Saussure to measure the amount of moisture in the air. He and his companions took frequent baro-metric readings to obtain an understanding of the relative elevation by which to draw topographic maps. Berlandier's observations contributed to several sketches that he executed in which he mapped the salt marshes and estuaries of Tamaulipas south of Matamoros, the routes from Matamoros to San Fernando, and the forested environs south of the town. The land-scape and climate apparently attracted insects not typically seen along the Rio Grande, as Berlandier discovered a dozen unique species of butterfly on the road between Matamoros and Moquete. The air was sultry and the rain frequent; for a day and a half they camped next to a temporary lake, where they dried their gear that had become drenched by a violent rain the first night out. The vegetation along the way was sparse, fit only for ani-mals to graze upon, and even that was insufficient, for they had to employ mules to carry fodder for their horses and pack animals. Sporadic forests of mesquite presented opportunities for camp and hiding places for bandits. There were several routes that took the traveler south from Matamoros. Berlandier and companions chose one bearing to the south-southeast. They paralleled a stream, the Arroyo del Tigre, descending from the highlands south of Matamoros; just west of the stream was an arid valley, Llanos de la Venada. There were several ranchos along the way, though none directly on the trail. The first settlement they came to was the hamlet of Moquete, situated on the southern banks of the Arroyo del Tigre, which was named after a hamlet upstream from the village of Moquete. The stream took the name of Moquete after passing by the village on its descent to the south-east. The Moquete was swollen and rapid due to recent rains. The only way to cross it was by flatboat or pirogue. The stream, Berlandier observed, drained the flat, clayey region south of Matamoros, gathering waters of the surrounding plains as well as the excess of the Rio Grande. Although on this first journey into the region, Berlandier did not pursue the route of the descending Moquete, later, during the summer of 1838, he made a precise study of this region.[14]

Having traveled six leagues from Matamoros to Moquete, the journeyers continued south the five leagues to Laguna de Quijano. The trail traversed
a flat landscape littered with seashells, which reminded Berlandier of a sea-
scape. The soil was sandy and salty, hosting few plants; one, called *sangre de
drago* (dragon's blood, *Jatropha dioica*), possessed edible roots that the men had
with their dinner; the plant also had reputed healing properties. Berlandier
also saw a plant of the goosefoot family, Chenopodiaceae, as well as the tornilla
(*Prosopis reptans*), with its star-shaped, spiraling fruit. There were no settlements or ranchos along the way. They passed the Laguna de Quijano without
halting. Rattlesnakes were plentiful, which required extreme caution from
the men when dismounting and setting up camp. Berlandier either witnessed
or heard that local Mexicans and Indians handled rattlesnakes with ease and
used its fat as a salve on wounds.[15]

During the next few days before they arrived at San Fernando, Berlandier
and his companions traveled on ancient trails that wound through an arid
land hosting mesquite bushes and shallow, temporary lakes that reluctantly
evaporated; the rays of the sun dipped more to the south as autumn progressed. From Laguna de Quijano to Rancho de Saint Teresa was nine leagues;
on the way they passed by a few small ranchos, such as El Baradusal. Coming
to the hills of Saint Teresa, they found a stream of freshwater; descending,
they reached the rancho of the same name. The people of the rancho suggested that they take the western fork in the trail to get to their destination,
to which the travelers agreed, spending the night on the hills of Saint Olaya.
Regaining the main trail the next morning, they journeyed into another
highland, named after the badger, *tejón*. From Lomas del Tejón, they continued south over a plain to another set of hills, Lomas del Maguey, named for
a local rancho. This land of small peaks hosted scattered forests, whereas the
surrounding flat land was largely barren of trees, hosting desert plants such
as the yucca, one species (*Yucca treculeana*) of which was locally known as
"Spanish dagger," as well as pretty plants of the pea family—indeed, plants
in this part of Tamaulipas were generally Leguminosae. Though the land was
variably clay and limestone, and the waters often salty to the taste, the plants
were not of the saline variety found along the Texas Gulf Coast or inland at
places in the Mexican Plateau. The rainy seasons in this region were spring
and fall; an autumn rainstorm on October 20 caught animals by surprise,
forcing ants to form into balls for their preservation and tarantulas to perch
on sturdy stalks of plants. Berlandier found several tortoises, one of which
was the *Gopherus berlandieri*.[16]

On October 21, they passed by one more rancho, Las Adrias, amid the Lomas del Maguey, before arriving at San Fernando, after a journey of thirty-five leagues. The village lay on a flat plain nestled in a forest; from the north the observer could see beyond the town the bluffs formed by the river. The town was picturesque and pastoral, at least according to a sketch Berlandier made during one of his many journeys to this part of Tamaulipas. The river of the same name flowing from the Sierra Madre to the Gulf was high, bringing a salty-tasting water to the town's inhabitants, who during dry times had to rely on well water. San Fernando was known for its limestone, and Berlandier spent time investigating a quarry. The limestone was cut in rectangular blocks, allowed to dry and grow hard in the air and sun, then used for buildings both in the town and, as an export, in other towns.[17]

Berlandier, Tarnava, and the others stayed at San Fernando for a week, investigating the town and environs, resting, and waiting for the water of the Río San Fernando to drop so to cross safely. They set out on October 29, forded the river (how, Berlandier did not record), and went a dozen miles before they halted for the night at a stream (Arroyo Carrizo) lined with reeds. The next morning they set out for the Rancho Encinal. They journeyed southwest on the route to Santander and Victoria. The Sierra Madre formed a beautiful background to the scenery before them. "Often on the march," Berlandier wrote in "Voyage pour reconnoitre les principaux points de l'Etat de Tamaulipas," "we observed a great irregularity in the distant heights of the mountains: so much so that one of the great beauties of these mountains is the forming of buttresses running from East to the West; formerly it seemed parallel to the chain and finished often very far from where it originated." Five miles out of San Fernando, traversing a pretty, verdant country, they came to a largely dry creek that clearly showed signs of dangerous flooding at other seasons of the year. Near Rancho de Encinal, Berlandier studied the arboreal and floral offerings of the land, such as species of mimosa, willow, nightshade (*Solanum*), and lupine. Proceeding southwest on October 31, Berlandier and Tarnava arrived at Santander, also called Jiménez, a small village surrounded by the foothills of the Sierra Madre. Santander was founded almost a century before as the capital of the province of Nuevo Santander, named after the Spanish homeland of the organizer and founder of that province, José de Escandón. Santander had recently (1827) received a name change in honor of a fallen citizen, Juan Nepomuceno Jiménez, executed by order of Gen. Joaquín de Arredondo about fifteen years earlier. Notable hills surrounding the town included the Cerro de Sán Cárlos, lying southwest; Cerro de la Misión del Forlón standing to the east-northeast; and Cerro del Aire and Cerro de las Jardinas, also seen to the east. These peaks were frequently shrouded in clouds; on a clear day Berlandier observed them with a theodolite sold by the Blunt Company of New York. Santander Jiménez was a poor town. The inhabitants grew a paltry number of crops for their own use and raised few livestock. The mortality rate was high among all ages. Inhabitants succumbed to dysentery, putrid fevers, and measles. Infantile tetanus, or *mocezuelo*, was prevalent, as throughout all of Tamaulipas, though not so much as in Matamoros. Berlandier and his companions departed Santander Jiménez for Padilla on the first day of November. The trail ascended to a plateau known as Mesa de Solís, where Berlandier saw a number of parrots squawking from their perches in palm trees. At the Rancho de San Antonio, they forded the Río del Pilon, which originated in Nuevo León, merging with the Río Purificación (Río Soto La Marina) east of Padilla. These rivers had deep banks that made them difficult to ford during times of flooding. At such times, lacking ferries or boats of any kind, travelers crossed the floods over trees swept by the current from above, lodged between the high banks. San Antonio de Padilla, Berlandier found, was a miserable settlement of impoverished peasants. Padilla, once the capital of Nuevo Santander, replaced by Ciudad Victoria, was a place of "sadness and misery," where the houses and public buildings lay in a state of decay and ruin. Locals informed Berlandier that deposed emperor Agustín de Iturbide was buried at Padilla; he had been exiled from Mexico on pain of death and had been foolhardy enough to return, unaware of the consequences. Captured on the Gulf Coast of Tamaulipas, Iturbide had been brought to Padilla for execution. Padilla was surrounded by hills, and hardly defensible. Leaving Padilla, they forded the Río Purificación and marched through a well-watered valley of numerous rivers descending from the Sierra Madre, which stood a little over twenty miles to the west. East of San Fernando de Güemez, a hamlet founded in 1749 under the authority of Joseph de Escandón, the Victoria and Croix (Corena) rivers flowed into the Río de Santa Engracia. Examining trees such as cedars, nut trees, and willows on its banks, Berlandier saw evidence of mighty floods in these rivers. Away from the rivers grew mesquites, the seeds of which the inhabitants of Güemez had once relied on for food. Down the road from Güemez, at the Hacienda de Santa Engracia, the well-watered soil produced delightful citrus fruits that locals avidly consumed. As they approached Ciudad Victoria, situated next to the Sierra Madre, Berlandier could detect a chill in the night air that hinted of a mountainous environment.[18]

Berlandier and companions arrived at the capital of Tamaulipas, Ciudad Victoria, the evening of November 6, 1830. Originally founded in 1750 as Santa Maria de Aguayo, for the first half century of its existence the town had been subject to frequent incursions by the local Janambre tribe. The Janambre threat had forced traders to avoid Santa Maria de Aguayo; trade caravans during the eighteenth century had followed a circuitous path from Tampico across the eastern slopes of the Sierra Madre to Tula, then north paralleling the cordillera to Padilla and Santander. In the early nineteenth century, however, Spanish troops and settlers had turned back the Indian resistance; the Janambre had retreated to an insignificant nearby hamlet, San Pedro, built on the ruins of an old Franciscan mission known as the Three Palaces. Disease was quickly reducing the numbers of the once fierce tribe. Ciudad Victoria was a small town. Berlandier was surprised to hear from locals that inhabitants succumbed to the same diseases, especially fevers, of the seacoast. The townspeople quarried limestone for buildings, and cedar was plentiful as well, but as yet the town had no significant buildings or monuments. Nevertheless, the population was growing, as people of surrounding villages relocated to Ciudad Victoria. And the fertile soil promised good crops and expanding trade. Berlandier stayed at Ciudad Victoria for eight days, resting and enjoying the climate of late autumn.[19]

On November 12, Berlandier, Tarnava, and the escort of dragoons set out for Tula, guided by muleteers who traveled this way frequently, bringing trade goods and supplies over the high sierra. The muleteers, rather than journeying southwest from Victoria directly into the cordillera, led them south along the valley, the mountains just to their right. They forded, again and again, mountain streams descending into the plain. The route was lined with such trees as sycamore, ash, and oak. They bivouacked for a day at the foot of the cordillera, at a place called La Alba; the muleteers wished to start at dawn on the next day because of the strain of the ascent. The morning of November 15 they began the day's journey early, and indeed the climb was rugged. The trail wound amid the flanks of the peaks of the Sierra. Berlandier estimated a thirty-degree slope to the mountains that they skirted through narrow thalwegs. Oaks dominated a forest that included palms and willows. Upon reaching a high point on the trail that afforded a view to the east, they could spy some of the towns through which they had journeyed, though Victoria was largely hidden from view. Continuing on, the trail grew more rugged, the thalwegs deeper amid the rising peaks. The men gingerly threaded through a pass called Voladeros, which had a treacherous drop where the muleteers claimed they had lost mules on previous journeys. The trail descended to the valley, through which flowed a crystal mountain stream. If the banks of the stream had been crusted in ice, and slopes of the peaks covered with snow, and clouds hovering about the summits threatening more, Berlandier would have thought himself making his way through the Alps of Savoy. Several species of oak dominated the forest, which also included drooping willows, the cenizilla (cenizo—*Leucophyllum frutescens* [Berl.]), and a species of nightshade. The trail led to isolated ranchos, founded fairly recently, the owners having fled the political difficulties of more populous states to the solitude and peace of the Sierra. The morning of the sixteenth they pursued a stony, difficult trail toward the town of Jaumave. As the elevation decreased, the prevalence of oaks lessened. Spying the desert valley and Jaumave from the perspective of the cordillera to the east, Berlandier thought the scene picturesque, if forbidding. Desert plants such as the Spanish dagger and other varieties of yucca, the pincerlike leaves emerging from the top of a short or tall trunk, as well as the ground plant agave, with similar-looking leaves, dominated. Jaumave, situated in a valley surrounded by the peaks of the Sierra Madre, was an old Franciscan mission reinvigorated by the colonizer Escandón in the 1740s. The valley was sufficiently watered by streams coming off the surrounding mountains—and particularly by the Río de Yera, flowing from the west, in the vicinity of the town of Bustamante—that maize grew plentifully. Even so, Berlandier found that the farmers lived in utter poverty. Beautiful ebony trees thrived in this environment, indeed throughout most of Tamaulipas.[20]

After bivouacking at Jaumave for a night, on the morning of November 17 they picked up the trail west out of the valley into the Sierra toward Palmillas. The route from Jaumave to Palmillas was over another range of the arid peaks; they traveled through thalwegs, entering one sterile gorge after another. Vegetation was limited. A poor band of indigenous people offered pulque, the fermented beverage made from the agave, which the Mexicans declined. Along the way there were a few poor ranchos that featured some fields of maize, species of the yucca tree, ebony, and sugar cane. The journeyers descended into a very pretty valley with several streams and the town of palms, Palmillas, which, Berlandier found to his surprise, was a "beautiful villa." The town was well planned, by Escandón in 1755, after he had founded the mission of Divisadero ten years earlier. Besides Mexicans, descendants of the original indigenous inhabitants lived in the town, holding on to their customs and culture, continuing to speak in their native tongue. Having spent the night at Palmillas, on November 18, Berlandier and his companions continued on the road, heading west-southwest, toward Tula. Ascending again into the Sierra, they kept to a thalweg amid rounded, sterile mountains; pines and oaks crowded to the slopes, along with palm trees and cedars; Berlandier observed flora such as horehound, the Mexican (yellow prickly) poppy, a species of puccoon (*Lithospermum*), and the beautiful frijolillo. The first place of habitation they came to was the Ranchos del Chapulin (Capulin), owned by residents of Tula, who employed Indians in the manufacture of maguey. They descended quickly from the ranchos, located next to a mountain of the same name, and entered a thalweg through which they arrived at Rancho de la Presa, where a dammed stream and resulting pool of water invited muleteers and other travelers to bivouac. Berlandier and his group pressed on another five miles to Rancho de las Norias, where they camped.[21]

On the road to Tula, November 19, the men exited the cordillera into an arid plateau surrounded on the east, north, and west by mountains. Their path traversed a waterless environment with little vegetation. Tula lay at the southern end of the valley. It was surrounded by heights save to the north. "The land on which Tula is founded," Berlandier wrote in *Diario de viage*, "is one of the worst that nature has presented to man." Houses and buildings of Tula were constructed of adobe, clay being dominant on the surface of the valley. The erosive action of streams descending from surrounding hills resulted in extensive, irregular gorges, miniature canyons that cut through the soil paralleling the angle of descent. The town itself was subject to such erosion, which periodically made streets uncrossable and dwellings uninhabitable. The climate was wonderful, high elevation and dry air bringing delightful evenings and clear skies; people rarely suffered from the epidemics of the lower river valleys brought on by heat and humidity. Even so, the inhabitants acted as if they lived in a villa of oppressive climate. Berlandier heard from his companions that the people of Tula were called *pelados*, loafers. Perhaps this derisive term resulted from bigotry, as many of the original indigenous inhabitants, Mascorres and Pisones, still lived in Tula. Or perhaps it was because the people of Tula extensively practiced neither agriculture nor trade, although the town was perfectly situated on a network of road crossings that should have guaranteed fruitful trade. Tula was one of the oldest towns of the region, founded at the beginning of the eighteenth century near an older Indian town. Berlandier wondered about the wisdom of the founders of Spanish Tula.

They clearly took little care to guarantee the town's security from attack, as they chose a site nestled among hills from which an enemy could easily surround and lay siege to it. Having grown up at Fort l'Ecluse, Berlandier knew something about defensive fortifications, such as forts made of stone hugging the side of a mountain, looking down upon a valley, dominating it by vision of distant paths and by commanding the high ground. Tula lacked such defenses, and was open to attack by the Spanish (or other hostile nations) that landed on the coast near the Río Soto La Marina or Río Pánuco and marched inland unopposed. Berlandier recommended to General Terán that only a rear guard should be stationed at Tula, to provide the last, desperate defense if the vanguard defenses failed. By fortifying a nearby hill to the west of the town, Cerro de la Cruz, or perhaps a peak to the northeast, Cerro de las Cebollas, with artillery, troops could bombard the town should it be taken over by the enemy, and attack advancing enemy troops arriving from Tampico or Ciudad Victoria. It was best, he argued, to place the most experienced troops not at Tula, but rather along the mountain roads from Victoria to Tula and from Santa Bárbara to Tula. In the mountain passes of the Sierra, skilled defenders could ambush the invaders and halt their advance.[22]

Departing Tula on the road to Tampico on November 25, Berlandier and Tarnava halted, per the orders of General Terán, at the abandoned site of the old Indian town of Tula. There the explorers found ancient fortifications that reminded Berlandier of Xochicalco, south of Mexico City, which he had explored in October 1827. The old town of Tula lay next to the salty Laguna de Salitre; the two fortifications were massive, partially walled hills from which defenders could survey the routes into their town and take action if need be. On the other hand, attackers who occupied the fortifications could also dominate the town. Berlandier concluded that the military planners of ancient and modern Tula left something to be desired. At the ruins of old Tula, known as *cuisillos*, Berlandier saw numerous monuments and artifacts that he painstakingly sketched as a record for himself, General Terán, and posterity. As Terán had particularly ordered that Tarnava and Berlandier reconnoiter the route between Tula and Tampico, they were careful to make extensive descriptions, and to map out literally and cartographically the terrain, points of interest, and ranchos and parajes at which to halt for food, water, and rest. Berlandier made sketches of the route, which he later turned into precise drawings of the road from Tula to Santa Bárbara through the Sierra Madre. After departing the old town of Tula, they journeyed along the path just south of the Laguna del Salitre that had formed in a depression between peaks. Soon they began an ascent through a mountainous plateau by means of a narrow pass, the Puerto de Boquillas. Ever on the lookout for flora, Berlandier spied a species of butterfly bush (*Buddleja*). Oak trees grew everywhere, both in the foothills and atop the broad summit, where Berlandier also found a species of polygala (*Polygala*) and a species of the sedge family (Cyperaceae). The scenery and vegetation reminded Berlandier of the foothills of the Alps of his youth. The road was appropriate only for hikers and pack animals; wagoneers would find the ascent impossible and the limestone path forbidding. They camped the evening of November 25 next to a small village called Acahuales. At a similar height in the Alps, Berlandier would have felt a distinct chill even on an otherwise temperate day; here in the Sierra Madre, the temperature was pleasant, even during the night. A barometric measurement the morning of November 26 gave an approximate height of 4,700 feet. This day they ascended, Berlandier reckoned, another three thousand feet to the divide in the Sierra Madre Oriental. As they made the descent toward Santa Bárbara (Ocampo), the road turned out to be steep and hazardous. Although the locals galloped horses and nonchalantly rode mules (at least according to report) along this narrow defile, Berlandier and his companions made no such attempt. Even the muleteers were extremely cautious. Berlandier noted that the path as it stood provided an excellent defense against an enemy invasion, which could hardly be mounted with more than a few troops on foot and horseback; even these small numbers could be halted with some obstructions placed along the way. They reached a plateau amid the mountains where they stopped at Rancho de Los Gallitos, situated next to a mountain stream in a verdant valley. Here, Berlandier found plane (sycamore—*Platanus*) trees growing next to the stream. The valley and town of Santa Bárbara lay before them. Their muleteer guide wished to make a quick detour to a place called the Chapel of the Cliff, where there was a mass of rock that appeared to the faithful to be an image of the Virgin Mary. Berlandier scoffed at the credulity of the muleteer and other locals who frequented the place, especially on All Saints Day, when they littered the shrine with marigolds in commemoration of the dead.[23]

At the end of the day on November 26, the men entered the Valle de Tamasaqual, where poor farmers grew fruits typical of the *tierra caliente*. The typical north-south mountains of the Sierra Madre surrounded Santa Bárbara; small chains of cordilleras split the valley into varied parts of badlands and more lush counterparts. These last days of November were calm and pretty. When night fell Berlandier and companions slept in the valley on the road to Santa Bárbara, sheltered by a species of the hardwood hackberry tree (*Celtis*). The hackberry likes a moist soil, which the Valle de Tamasaqual had aplenty. The townspeople of Santa Bárbara had wonderful gardens of bananas, avocados, and oranges that invited a person's many senses to partake of. The valley was dotted with cuisillos, the small stone monuments that were remnants of the Janambres, Pisones, and Panis tribes. Locals informed Berlandier that the Indians had put up a fierce resistance against the first colonists, sent by José de Escandón in the mid-eighteenth century. Retreating to the surrounding cordilleras, they swept down on the unsuspecting, raiding farms and travelers. Eventually defeated and broken, a few score still lived in the area, served by surviving Franciscan missions. It surprised Berlandier to find that the inhabitants of these mountain valleys lived by farming rather than ranching, which was so dominant in the valley of the Rio Grande. The inhabitants of the cordilleras were apparently very healthy; the diseases of the coast, such as yellow fever, were rarely found in towns such as Santa Bárbara.[24]

Berlandier had a natural interest in the Earth's geologic history, dating from his time in Geneva, studying under Candolle, and earlier when growing up at Fort l'Ecluse on the Rhône, when the shapes and formations of the Jura Mountains and Alps attracted his admiration and fascination. During his journey to Mexico, Berlandier did not make a systematic study of geology, but rather made observations and constructed basic hypotheses according to the occasions of time and chance offered during his many excursions. Surface formations and their apparent causes, such as wind and water, fascinated him, as did lithology, the study of rocks and minerals, in particular sedimentary and igneous rocks. Few scientists of his time had a clear understanding of stratification under the Earth's surface, or the vast distances in time that had resulted in the geologic present. Berlandier was one of many ad hoc geologists who contributed to the slow progress in human understanding that results from collective observation and study. When he heard from the local inhabitants of Santa Bárbara of an ancient volcano several miles to the southwest of the town, he decided to take time from his journey to Tampico for a geologic excursion in the company of Constantino Tarnava. The volcano, known to the locals as Volcán del Chaburro, better known today as Cerro Partido, was a small mount that except for its igneous nature would hardly inspire interest from the explorer and geologist.

Berlandier and Tarnava hired a local pilot from Santa Bárbara to lead them on horseback. They traveled in an environment of scattered trees toward a range of hills (Cerrito) of which the volcano was a part. Berlandier's well-executed drawing of the volcano, based no doubt on a sketch that he made on the spot and drawn at an unknown later time, is a precise illustration of the small yet fascinating volcano. Berlandier and Tarnava noticed little evidence of catastrophe among the flora—no ancient tree trunks distorted by the heat of flowing lava; they assumed that the vegetation postdated the most recent eruption of the volcano, which must have been a long time ago. The igneous land, covered with volcanic ash and long-cooled lava, extended along the arm of the Cerrito to the volcano, yet the Cerrito was of a higher elevation; Berlandier deduced that the entire range had over the eons produced active volcanoes that spewed lava and ash, covering the surrounding land. The guide and scientists sought the opening of these volcanoes with little success. Berlandier was reminded of a past experience in which he had explored the volcanic remains of the Auvergne range in central France in a futile search for the elusive craters. The local pilot led the explorers up the slope of the Cerro Partido, which appeared like a plume over a helmet; the emission of lava time and again, Berlandier thought, had created this strange extension above the crater. The rock at the crater's mouth was unstable, and they approached it gingerly. They could not see the bottom of the hole; the guide told the scientists that only a few times a year could the bottom be seen, when the sun was directly overhead at the time of the summer solstice. The scientists inspected another, smaller crater nearby, which likewise appeared to be a prime source of volcanic ash and lava, as well as the source for the fault that appeared to split the volcano into parts, giving the entire area fascinating geometric shapes and angles that mirrored ancient geologic activity. Berlandier theorized that the action of volcanoes, heating, erupting, spewing, and cooling, again and again over the years, led to a gradual buildup of the ridges of craters and awkward cones, which were split, expanded and contracted, time after time. Such observations were similar to those made by Constant Prévost in the 1820s and Charles Lyell in the 1830s, based on their study of such volcanoes as at Auvergne. This theory of the uniformity of natural change over an immensely long period of time was growing in popularity among European scientists at the time that Berlandier made his journey and, a decade later, penned his *Journey to Mexico*. Berlandier in joining ranks with Prévost and Lyell was departing from his mentor Candolle, who followed the theory of periodic catastrophes causing dramatic changes in natural history, which had been advanced by his teacher Georges Cuvier. European naturalists such as Prévost and Lyell were pushing back natural history to a distant time hitherto unsuspected. Berlandier likewise examined the volcanoes of Tamaulipas in search of an approximate date of past eruptions. Berlandier collected records and traditions of the Mexican inhabitants, the Spanish, and the indigenous people before them, and discovered there was no recollection of volcanic activity. European scientists knew of the dates of the last eruptions of Mt. Etna and Mt. Vesuvius, and sought to correlate the dates with the depth of soil covering the igneous rock on the mountain slopes. Berlandier recalled that the slopes of Auvergne were, however, barren, and its last eruption millennia before; he reasoned therefore that the depth of soil did not unfailingly suggest dates of past natural events. What is more, on Berlandier's journey he discovered evidence to confirm the theory advanced by Baron Humboldt that volcanoes tend to appear along a fault line at a similar latitude or longitude, and perpendicular to the north-south range of the Sierra Madre. The French geologist Jean François D'Aubuisson de Voisins made this observation about the volcanoes in the Auvergne range. Berlandier discovered later in his journey through Tamaulipas that Cerro Partido was on the same latitude as a volcano close to the coast of the Gulf of Mexico, Cerro del Maíz; likewise, volcano Jorullo, to the west of Cerro Partido, near the Pacific Ocean, was on the same latitude.[25]

In early December, Berlandier and companions pursued the journey east from Santa Bárbara to Ciudad de Horcasitas (González) over plains interspersed with small mountain ranges. The most significant of these ranges was difficult to ascend, because of the massive limestone slabs that broke the path. But upon reaching the watershed, they enjoyed an extensive view of the valleys of Santa Bárbara and Ciudad de Horcasitas. By the extent of his description in *Journey to Mexico*, Berlandier clearly enjoyed the sublime vision before him of the valley of Santa Bárbara that gave way to the distant Sierra; the Volcán del Chaburro was visible because of its singularity compared to the rest of the landscape. To the east, the view extended to the sea; Berlandier could see streams and rivers flowing from the cordillera toward the Gulf; he spied again the dramatic Bernal de Horcasitas, which he first saw upon arriving to the coast of Mexico from France in December 1826. This ancient rock arising from the barrenness of the surrounding plain was surrounded by mist at its base; it could have been any rocky Alpine summit rising above the surrounding clouds. Berlandier took time to sketch the distant valley that lay before the dramatic peak of Bernal.[26]

The way to their ultimate destination of Tampico lay vaguely before the men as they descended from the mountainous divide into the plain that was part of the valley of the Pánuco River. The descent to the plain was steep and winding; with proper defensive measures, an enemy force attempting to cross the cordillera could be repelled along this route. They camped at one of the ranchos of the plain, surrounded by flora, such as palms and huisache, typical of the low-lying valleys near the coast. One more small range of hills blocked their path, which they ascended and descended on December 3. Before him, as Berlandier gazed from the summit of a small hill, lay the immense valley shielded by the Sierra Madre to the west and the Sierra de Maratines to the north. Berlandier realized, after the extensive travel of the past few weeks, the stages in the rise of elevation from the coast to the Sierra Madre. The small ranges of cordilleras from east to west grow in height, ending in the Sierra Madre Oriental. The valleys on the western side of each range are higher than valleys to the east. Those to the east of low elevation host the humid, tropical forests and swamps of the tierra caliente. Those to the west of higher elevation are cooler, dryer, the flora sparse and sparing. As they approached Ciudad de Horcasitas, they came upon the Tamesí River, which had been generally paralleling their route since they left Tula. The Tamesí, which rose in the highlands near Jaumave, descended through the valleys of the eastern slopes of the Sierra Madre. The river changed names along the way—Berlandier referred to it as the Río de Limón—and picked up numerous tributaries descending from the mountains until it merged with the Pánuco above Tampico. At Ciudad de Horcasitas the river was broad, deep, and rapid enough to require a ferry to cross it. The water, cool and clear from the mountains, was good to drink. The large number of muleteers and their loaded pack animals—which Berlandier guessed numbered up to 1,500—on their way from Tampico to the interior crowded the road. Many of the mule drivers were ill, having picked up a late autumn fever along the Pánuco. Berlandier saw them lying in the shade of trees along the road, seeking to escape the burning fever; many were delirious or otherwise too sick to continue, their pack animals roaming freely. Some of the muleteers would make it to Santa Bárbara, only to succumb to the illness there.[27]

Ciudad de Horcasitas was another of the towns planned by José de Escandón for the colony of Nuevo Santander during the mid-1700s. The town was not, in Berlandier's opinion, well situated in the flood plain of the Tamesí River. The poorer inhabitants lived across the river from the main town, where they and their homes were particularly susceptible to floods.

The population of the town was small, though it possessed the ostentatious name of *ciudad*. For the first half century of its existence, the local Indian tribes raided the town from their hideouts in the mountains to the west and north. These tribes were now long defeated, and partially integrated into society, forming part of the lower class. Horcasitas had a central plaza, like most Mexican towns; from it Tarnava and Berlandier took the base and angles of the distant Bernal in an attempt to ascertain its height; they estimated that it rose almost three thousand feet. Sensing that the estimate was inaccurate, their interest and excitement to explore increasing, upon leaving the town on December 6 the men journeyed to the foot of Bernal to obtain an on-site measurement of its height. Eighteenth-century Swiss scientist Jean-André de Luc first suggested using the barometer to assess altitude. Berlandier's scientific heroes Saussure and Humboldt used the barometer to measure such mountains as Vesuvius. American scientific explorers were using the glass tube barometer (into which the scientist had to pour manually the mercury to gain a reading) as early as 1784. By the time of Berlandier's journey, he was perhaps using the more recently invented "banjo" barometer that already contained the mercury. Arriving at Rancho de San Juan on a plain approaching the mountain, Berlandier and Tarnava, upon questioning the locals, heard contrary reports of successful and unsuccessful ascents of Bernal. Meanwhile, Berlandier took the time to sketch the peak so seemingly nearby. His formal drawing of the Bernal shows a craggy mass of rocks rising abruptly from the arid plain. Undeterred by the obvious primitiveness of the peak and its approach, the two explorers moved on foot toward the mountain. The ground was littered with large granite stones. Despite their attempt, night came upon them before they had reached the foot of the mountain, so they returned. Berlandier was still intrigued and continued to examine the hill from afar whenever he had occasion, in the future, to observe it. He concluded that Bernal was a surviving core of a much greater mountain that had been eroded or destroyed in some calamity.[28]

Returning to Horcasitas to spend the night, they awoke the next morning, December 7, to pursue the journey toward Tampico. The road led southeast from Horcasitas, passing by Bernal, crossing a descending brook on its way to Tamesí; later they forded the Arroyo del Bernal, a mountain stream descending from its namesake. Arriving at the Rancho del Carrizo, south of Bernal, Berlandier achieved the best look yet at the mountain; its strange shape, more tall than wide, confirmed his theory that it was the remaining core of an ancient mountain. At the rancho, the travelers came upon a feverish mule driver who had been abandoned by everyone and left to suffer and die. Tarnava and Berlandier gave him some coins, to which Berlandier added some quinine to relieve the effects of malaria, and tried to get the locals to help the ill man. The last few days of the journey to Tampico were over difficult land for travel, part of the time a spongy clay, part of the time sandy soil. The route skirted salt- and freshwater lagoons formed by the Tamesí, Pánuco, and tidal water. They journeyed by Altamira on December 10, arriving at Tampico. Berlandier made note of some of the places where Mexicans engaged Spanish forces in the recently failed attempt by Spain to reconquer its former colony.[29]

Berlandier rested at Tampico for a week before proceeding south to Tantoyuca, retracing the route he had taken in the spring of 1827. From this town he journeyed east, then north and west, visiting various ranchos and describing the land in the region east of Tantoyuca that he had never seen. Returning to Tantoyuca on December 22, he stayed for several days, observing the customs and society of the local Huasteco Indians. The Huastecos had converted to Catholicism; Berlandier joined a local, señor Micheltorena, to visit the parish church for Christmas Eve services. As he had before during his journey to Mexico, Berlandier criticized the superstition and gaudiness of the Catholic mass. The Huastecos had their own self-government within the overall authority of the Mexican state of Veracruz. They grew maize and sugarcane, and manufactured the intoxicating maguey, to which they were very devoted.[30]

On January 29, 1831, Berlandier and his companions set out from Tampico north along the coast of Tamaulipas on a journey back to Matamoros. The first town they came to, Altamira, was, like Ciudad Horcasitas, founded by José de Escandón in the 1740s and was during the late eighteenth century subject to repeated attacks by the local indigenes. After 1800 these attacks ceased as the tribes fled to the Sierra de Tamaulipas to the northwest. Berlandier found Altamira to have a more pleasant climate than Tampico, as it stood at a slightly higher elevation that allowed the sea breeze to reach the town. Some of the places that he recently visited along the coast south of Tampico had the same pleasant and refreshing breezes. Several hills dominated Altamira, which was a small and impoverished town. Altamira was noteworthy for Berlandier and Tarnava as the place where General Terán made a valiant and successful defense and orderly retreat against overwhelming odds when, in 1829, the Spanish invaded the Pánuco valley. Upon considering the location of Altamira respecting the lakes, hills, rivers, and coast, Berlandier believed that the town was not of prime importance to defend from an enemy invasion. An invader of more skill than the Spanish could easily outflank a force holding Altamira. The town lay on the northwestern shores of the Laguna de Altamira near the Río Tamesí.[31]

After spending several days in the dense forests surrounding Altamira and its neighboring lagoons (Laguna de Altamira, Laguna de Chairel, Laguna de San Andrés), they journeyed north-northwest paralleling the coast along a sandy, hot (even in February) route. Estuaries and saltwater lagoons typified the Mexican Gulf coast here as elsewhere. They came to the Rancho de Chocolate and Rancho de Barco. A species of oak hitherto unseen by Berlandier, which he called *Quercus tropicae*, dominated the forest. One inlet from the sea, Estera del Barco, actually had to be crossed like a river; ferrymen stood awaiting customers. On the route beyond the estuary was prairie. The grasses of the prairie were dry and on fire; Berlandier and companions had to wind their way through the flames to reach a safe haven. Flocks of vultures awaited the mammalian and reptilian victims of the fire. With the estuary to the right, and small limestone and igneous mountains to the left, they proceeded north during the first few days of February. The most notable mount was the remains of an ancient volcano, Cerro del Maíz. The small town of Aldama, or Presas, to which they arrived on February 3, lay at the foothills of the Sierra de Tamaulipas to the northwest and the smaller Sierra de los Maratines to the northeast. The Maratines were a local Indian tribe that had largely died out when Berlandier visited Aldama in 1831. Other local tribes included the Olives, the Panguayes, the Pajaritos, and the Caramiguayes. The people were impoverished because of the lack of good water, dry conditions, and indolence. Harvesting salt was their primary occupation, notwithstanding the nearby forests that had plentiful timber, and the iron-rich mountains of the Sierra de Tamaulipas to the west. For the next few days the journeyers traveled through badlands that had little to offer the botanist but more to excite the geologist. The action of the wind over time had carved unique formations into sandstone, which from a distance resembled the ruins of ancient towns. After traversing the gap between the Sierra de Tamaulipas and Sierra de Maratines, they passed through two hamlets, first La Sacrosa, then Santa Maria. Both lay in the valley between hills wherein small streams flowed: the Ciénega and the Tigre. The latter was larger, in part because water from a small hill, El Gato, flowed into it. They followed El Tigre north toward Bejarano.[32]

The north wind was harsh in this region of the eastern extreme of the Sierra Madre, bringing intense, unexpected cold. The journeyers were forced to bivouac for five days in a barn belonging to a landowner; they suffered from cold and slept on recently shorn sheep's wool. Restless, Berlandier braved the cold on one occasion to journey amid the surrounding hills of Bejarano. These hills were smaller counterparts to other ranges, the Sierra de la Marina, the Sierra de los Maratines, and the Sierra de Tamaulipas. The peripatetic Berlandier explored the Arroyo de Bejarano, which flowed east toward the gulf; the water collected near the coast in the Laguna del Tordo. The people of this part of Tamaulipas were terribly impoverished, often almost enslaved (economically) to large landowners who owned the sporadic ranchos. February 12, they continued the journey through a well-watered valley formed between hills to east and west. Scant vegetation along the way included mesquite, huisache, ebony, and buddleja. They forded numerous arroyos, first the Realito, then the Palitos and the Carrizal, which in the rainy season were unfordable and dangerous. These streams flowed from the Sierra to the east. Many streams washed the valley north of Bejarano, which gave rise to forests of mesquite and huisache trees. Journeying north past ranchos named Encarnación and Cruces, they repeatedly crossed the Río Lavadore, which generally flowed north, where it was called Palmas, toward the Río Soto La Marina, entering downstream from Soto La Marina. The Sierra de Tamaulipas was less distinct here, nor could they spy many hills to the east and northeast. Even so, they followed the Palmas north through a gap between highlands to east and west. They could see Cerro del Bernal Forlón to the northwest.[33]

The Río Soto La Marina, Berlandier thought, was as broad as the Rio Grande, gathering the waters of more rivers than the great river to the north. The sources of Río Soto were in Nuevo León, where the Río de la Purificación rose on the eastern slopes of the Sierra Madre Oriental in the southern part of the state. Flowing east, the Río de la Purificación was augmented by the Río del Pilón, then the Río de Santa Engracia east of Padilla; the Santa Engracia was quite a large river, having gathered the waters of the Güemez, Croix, and Victoria Rivers. By the time that the Río de la Purificación approached the town of Soto la Marina, it was broad and powerful, especially during the rainy season. At Soto la Marina the river was called Río Soto la Marina for the rest of its journey to the sea. Soto la Marina served the region of central Tamaulipas as a port, though the mouth of the Río Soto La Marina made navigation tricky, as it was often obstructed by a sandbar, was littered with islands, and, having broadened to the size of a bay, narrowed considerably where river met sea; during high tide and the flood season the level of the Laguna de Morales, south of the river, rose.[34]

Leaving Soto La Marina, they followed the descending Río de la Purificación upstream; the trail skirted the river a short distance to the east. They passed an old, abandoned mission shortly after leaving Soto la Marina. The river was deep and rapid, and difficult to ford because of high banks. The surrounding landscape was arid and sterile; only plants that could adapt to such an environment grew: grasses, mesquite, ebony, and huisache. The drier the land, the more cacti grew. Small hills lay to the east by the coast; the larger Sierra Madre continued to loom to the west from north to south. Berlandier could see the Cerro del Aire to the southwest and the Cerro de Sán Cárlos to the northwest. As they traveled north, mesas dotted the land; local ranchers devoted themselves to horse breeding and goat raising. There were two paths to choose from: the westerly went to Santander; the easterly, which the men followed, went due north to Encinal. In this region, near the Mesa del Encinal, palm trees flourished. On February 20, they passed by an old mission called Palmitos, named for the neighboring plant that provided sweet, nutritious food for the inhabitants. At the height of the dry season in midwinter, there was scant vegetation and little verdure to greet the eye. Travelers rarely came this way, and sometimes the trail was nonexistent. The land hosted small limestone cavities or caves that rattlesnakes used for dens. Indeed, limestone caverns were plentiful in the region around Santander and to the west. These caverns reminded Berlandier of similar caverns found in the mountains of Europe. While crossing the broad Mesa del Encinal, a prized horse that someone in his troop bought two months before near Horcasitas became lost; they searched with no luck. Eventually it was decided that the men should continue on their journey while one man, probably the soldado, retraced their steps in pursuit of the horse. The soldado knew the skills of white and indigenous hunters in the tracking of animals. When a few days later the soldado rejoined them with the errant horse, he described his technique of trapping; knowing that the horse was grain-fed, unlike the vast numbers of wild horses of the prairies, he was able to trace the horse by its singular manure. Berlandier, fascinated, believed that such wilderness skills revealed a different kind of intelligence rarely recognized by the academics of the world.[35]

The path from Encinal to San Fernando was a wilderness cut by water-starved arroyos. The first significant stream, the Three Forks, flowed east, soon to join the Arroyo de las Chorreras; this combined stream added to the growing volume of the San Fernando River farther downstream. The land from Chorreras to San Fernando was dry and sterile; the soil hosted gypsum and clay, which made the neighboring waters almost undrinkable. Even the livestock refused to drink from the streams. Fortunately, mule-teers camping nearby directed Berlandier and companions to a hollow with runoff water, from which man and beast quenched their thirst. The men skirted the lonely "black hill," Loma Prieto, standing above to the east of the trail. The journeyers arrived at San Fernando on February 24; three days later they came to Matamoros.[36]

Berlandier made repeated trips into Tamaulipas from Matamoros during the ensuing months and years. These were natural history expeditions, pursued either alone or with others, typically for the sake of accumulating information and samples of flora useful for medicine or other applications. In November 1831, for example, Berlandier set out from Matamoros on a journey to the Pánuco valley to discover arborescent dyes. Upon reaching San Fernando, however, he heard that an unexpectedly harsh beginning to winter had deprived the trees of most of their foliage. He therefore altered his plans and headed west to explore the Sierra de Tampaulipas. The jour-ney, undertaken during the dry season, was over particularly arid lands that provided scant water for the traveler and his beasts. Even so, Berlandier discovered and collected various useful plants and trees, such as a species of acacia useful for dyeing buckskin, as well as the purgative frijolillo. The road west took Berlandier through Cruillas and Burgos, two small towns that lacked available water—at least for the traveler, as residents could over time acquire the ability to swallow the stuff from their wells. Both of these towns were the product of Escandón's plan to create a thriving colony that would exploit the natural resources of the Sierra and protect villages against Indian attacks. The inhabitants built houses out of limestone, which was prolific throughout the region. From Burgos, Berlandier followed the road—well maintained by local authorities—to San Nicholás. Near this town the landscape became more hilly, and consequently more wooded. Although water remained scarce for the traveler, there were small oak forests, and sudden storms could slake the thirst of the resourceful outdoorsman. When at night outside of San Nicolás a storm descended upon Berlandier and his companions, they gathered water in the large, flat leaves of the maguey. The mining town of San Nicholás, when Berlandier visited in 1831, was impoverished, so much so that the town appeared to be abandoned—though here and there an old, crumbled adobe dwelling had walls or ceiling covered with maguey leaves. The inhabitants of the region pursued little agriculture, devoting most of their activities to distilling pulque. The town of San Carlos, down the road close to twenty miles from San Nicholás, presented a very different picture. Unlike San Nicholás, San Carlos had thrived over the years since its founding in 1766 under the auspices of Escandón. A mining town situated in the valley of the Río del Pilón, surrounded on all sides by tall to moderate mountains, the river valley being the only way out, San Carlos reminded Berlandier of the Alps and the many towns of Switzerland lying within a small valley surrounded by peaks, their summits obscured in the clouds. The summits of Cerro del Diente and Cerro de San José were akin to craggy summits of the Alps of Savoy without the snow. These small peaks sometimes had snow during winter, when the weather was rainy, foggy, and cool. The Sierra's winter rainy season enabled a host of flora to take root on these mountainsides, making it a veritable winter garden. Berlandier saw oak, sycamore, buckeye, and a species of Cycadaceae. Berlandier, who had originally set out on his journey to Tamaulipas to find tree bark and roots with which to dye skins and clothing, discovered a species of Mahonia that he christened *Chrysodendron tinctoria* (now known as *Mahonia tinctoria*), which was useful to color cloth and skins yellow. A plant called locally *yerba amarilla* was also useful for yellow dye.[37]

Berlandier and guides set out at the end of the first week of December, heading southeast toward Padilla, winding through passes amid the eastern slopes of the Sierra de Tamaulipas. The path took them along varied mountain streams that required constant crossing from one side to the other according to which side of the canyon was easiest for mule travel. Along the way he climbed a small mesa that stood alone, from which he could spy the flat summit of Cerro de la Malinche. They continued to follow descending streams to their confluence with the Río del Pilón, traveling through a mesquite forest before entering Padilla. Río del Pilón was typically deep in the rainy season, but relatively shallow with steep banks when Berlandier saw it on December 8. Padilla had shown improvement in food and appearance since Berlandier had seen it the preceding year; the inhabitants seemed more cheerful and, as a result, hopeful of the future. Not so the inhabitants of Güemez, who seemed as impoverished and desperate as before. Arriving at Ciudad Victoria on December 10, Berlandier stayed for week, studying the surrounding countryside, making astronomical and meteorological observations. Snow fell on nearby hills if not in the city, though the temperature did reach freezing. December 18, he left Victoria for Matamoros, at which he arrived on Christmas Eve.[38]

CHAPTER EIGHT

Río Bravo del Norte

⚘

☙ CHANCE, KNOWLEDGE, AND AVAILABILITY RATHER THAN EDUCATION
and career ambition turned the immigrant naturalist Jean Louis Berlandier
into the apothecary and physician of the town of Matamoros. Berlandier's
botanical collections and extensive notes gathered over the course of several years journeying in Mexico and Texas made him an apothecary by
default. General Terán wrote in his journal of the Comisión de Límites that
the towns of the Americans in Texas were more apt than Mexican towns to
have shopkeepers such as "carpenters, locksmiths, blacksmiths, and blood-
letters." This latter craftsman, bloodletter, was also called a surgeon, chirur-
gist, apothecary, and, at times, physician. To be sure, the presence of a person
skilled in materia medica in the Rio Grande valley of the 1830s and 1840s was
quite an anomaly.[1]

Precisely when Berlandier settled permanently in Matamoros is not
clear from the sources. His ongoing desire to be on the move suggests that
he could never feel permanently settled anywhere. Yet with the dissolution of
the Comisión de Límites upon the death of General Terán in 1832, he might
have felt that he had few options and fewer alternatives to Matamoros. The
sick and suffering of Matamoros, as during the cholera epidemic of 1833,
required someone who knew about the methods and materials of medicine.
The role of Matamoros healer fit the young Frenchman perfectly. Assuming
that Berlandier set up his apothecary business in the wake of the cholera
epidemic, his 1834 journey into Texas was to replenish his stores of materia
medica. Berlandier planned an extensive excursion during which he would

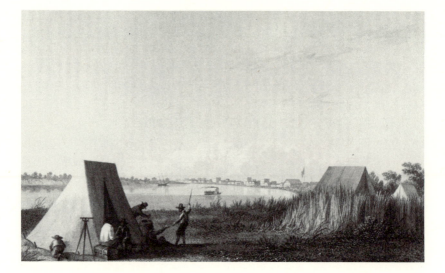

Figure 12. Brownsville, Texas. In "United States and
Mexican Boundary Survey. Report of William H. Emory. . . ."
Washington. 1857. Volume I. P. 60. NOAA Library Collection.

be gone for months, traveling all the way to Santa Fe. When he and Chowell
returned to Matamoros in July 1834, after a shortened three-month journey,
Berlandier was planning to pack up and go forth again, but an extensive illness forced him to remain at Matamoros.

The primary objective of Berlandier's final extensive journey into Texas,
which began in April 1834, was to augment his knowledge and specimens of
particularly the flora of Texas. Much of the collection he had gathered during
the spring and summer of 1828 had been destroyed by rains and floods, especially along the Colorado River on June 12, 1828. Now, six years later, he set
forth accompanied by his military friend the soldado as well as four "domes-
tics"; they crossed the Rio Grande at Matamoros on April 18. The three paths
Berlandier could take were the easternmost to Brazos de Santiago, a path that
he had taken numerous times; the westernmost to the Rancho de Santa Rita;
and the middle route to Goliad. The men followed the road to Goliad, where
by prearrangement Raphael Chowell was to join his old friend and traveling companion. Berlandier and Chowell planned to journey farther than in
previous years, traveling across west Texas into New Mexico. Berlandier's
initial route from Matamoros to Goliad was not well-traveled, and he hoped
to make precise measurements, record his exact itinerary, and illustrate with
maps the way, providing a visual and literary map for others to follow.[2]

Although ostensibly at peace with the Mexicans and Texans, the Lipan Apaches and Comanches had been busy in recent years raiding settlements along the route from Matamoros to Goliad, stealing livestock, particularly horses. As a result, along with the aridity of the environment, few Tejanos settled along the Gulf Coast from Matamoros to Goliad. Berlandier and companions passed by a few "miserable" ranchos called Viejo, Pina, and Anacuas, before reaching the Arroyo Colorado on April 19. This arroyo was not in reality a creek with a freshwater origin, but rather an inlet from the Laguna Madre. Small trees and plants grew along the banks of the arroyo, which compelled Berlandier to bivouac for a full day as he collected flora; besides, he wished to ascertain the latitude and climate of the place, a desire hampered by clouds and the extreme humidity of the environment, which obscured the faces of his thermometer and barometer. By and large the landscape was treeless, though wildflowers were blooming. The landscape was similar to that of northern Tamaulipas, flat and filled with small pools of water that had collected in infrequent rainstorms, waiting to dry under the hot sun. Wading birds, such as the blue heron, hunted for snakes and frogs in the brackish ponds; larger predators, such as the bobcat, preyed upon the birds. So too did the men, who tried to supplement their meager diet with roasted fowl. Success required hunters who were excellent marksmen, as the heron is a skittish creature that upon hearing the slightest noise or seeing movement will launch from its perch, using its broad, powerful wings to gracefully soar to another, reclusive location. From the Arroyo Colorado to the Nueces River, the land continued largely barren, suitable for grazing; the numbers of wild horses, called by the locals *mesteños*, astonished the travelers. Indian warriors posed a threat to the shepherds and ranchers and hindered any pioneers who might be courageous or foolhardy enough to settle here. The few ranchers were mixed-blood Tejanos called *mesteñeros* who lived in the vastness of the region south of the Nueces River, competing with the Apaches and Comanches for horses.[3]

After passing through the lands of the mesteñeros, Berlandier and company reached the Nueces River, which was unexpectedly high, almost unfordable. Yet Berlandier decided to cross the swollen river anyway, losing a horse in the process, and becoming briefly marooned on an island in the middle of the river. On the northern bank of the Nueces was an Irish colony, San Patricio, four years old and desperately poor. The colonists informed Berlandier that the Nueces descended another twenty-seven miles to the Gulf and the Barra de Corpus Christi. The Nueces, which the Mexicans, like the Spanish before them, believed formed the southern boundary of Texas, was a river that rose deep in the interior of the country; Berlandier would have liked nothing better than to have ascended the river to its source, but this was not the time. The route from the Nueces to the town of Goliad was hardly more settled than the region south of the Nueces, but the climate provided more moisture to the land; hence, there were forests not just of mesquite but of oak. Berlandier reached Goliad on the San Antonio River on May 5.[4]

Raphael Chowell, the onetime mineralogist of the Comisión de Límites and a resident of Goliad for an unspecified number of years, had made a thorough examination of and journeys in and about the San Antonio valley, which had convinced him that the sandy soil of Texas had a maritime origin; many of the small inland Texas hills reminded him of ancient sand dunes. Chowell had discovered a few remains of a mastodon in a creek bed and convinced Berlandier that they could find many more such antediluvian remains in the sandstone of the beds of streams in this region. Chowell had also taken extensive readings with the sextant to determine the latitude of the region of Goliad and the nearby mission, Espíritu Santo; Berlandier likewise took a measurement while at Goliad and found his estimate was similar to Chowell's (at 28°38'23"). From the perspective of Espíritu Santo, Berlandier sketched Goliad, which was later rendered into a watercolor by his artistic collaborator Lino Sánchez y Tapía. Berlandier quickly drew his sketch in the early morning hours of May 26, after having spent the night encamped with a few Mexican troops going north to San Antonio; they had invited Berlandier and Chowell to accompany them and had ferried their gear and the two scientists across the San Antonio River the night before. The sketch made, the men ready, they set off for San Antonio on the west side of the river; when they arrived at Arroyo de las Cabezas at midday, the heat was sufficient to cause an extended siesta. During the journey, Chowell and Berlandier spent their time examining the geology of the river valley, taking samples of limestone, gypsum, and sandstone. Along streams, however, the scientists and their escort trod more carefully, as Indian warriors often hid along the forested shores to ambush unsuspecting travelers.[5]

In June 1834, after a stay of a few weeks in San Antonio, Berlandier, Chowell, the soldado, and their servants set out for San Juan Bautista on the Rio Grande. Joining them was a Mexican officer on his way to Monclova in the state of Coahuila. There continued to be a threat from the Tawakoni tribe, but not enough of one to prevent travel; at night they took proper precautions to avoid being surprised by aggressive visitors. The landscape of early June was relatively well watered; flora responded in kind. Arriving at the Arroyo de el Sauz, they were forced to camp as the steep banks completely filled with rushing water. Berlandier availed himself of the opportunity to collect medicinal plants such as *toronjil*, and a species of Artemisia. Chowell took evening measurements to estimate latitude. After finding a ford and crossing El Sauz, they journeyed west to the Medina River, where high water again forced them to halt. They feasted on turkey and honey, the latter of which was intoxicating and a purgative in large quantities for those who were not used to it. Across the river two other travelers were similarly bivouacked, waiting for the water to recede. The late spring forest along the Medina was thick with pecan, oak, cedar, and hickory trees; sycamores exuded their perfume; mulberries drooped with fruit; and hazardous plants such as poison ivy and bull nettle threatened he who would veer from the path. Berlandier collected samples of more beneficial plants, such as *encinilla* (*Croton fruticulosus*) and *yerba del Cancer* (*California loosestrife—Lythrum californicum*), the latter of which had reputed qualities of combating cancerous growth; locals also used a root tea to combat fever. Upriver from their camp, Chowell and Berlandier noted that the land was hilly, the Medina piercing the small cordillera rather like the Rhône piercing the Jura Mountains. The high river did not recede, however; Berlandier hurried back to San Antonio for provisions to guarantee that once the waters receded, they would be able to finish the journey to San Juan Bautista. Returned and reprovisioned, he set out again for the Medina, notwithstanding reports of Tawakonis nearby. This journey to and from San Antonio was no mean achievement; it required crossing and recrossing seven streams both ways! Perhaps after such a journey, the Medina, though still high, did not seem like as much of a challenge; Berlandier decided to risk a crossing. The men were thus engaged when a storm broke, drenching them and threatening an even more impassable stream. The men set to work building skin rafts, which when accomplished, they crossed the river without incident. The two travelers on the western banks turned out to be a Frenchman traveling with a Koasati Indian. The former had heard from the latter that the Koasati tribe was growing stronger in the area of the Trinity River, even enjoying success against the Comanches in recent battles. In "Indigenes nomades," Berlandier wrote that the Koasati resembled whites in dress and industry. Setting forth from the Medina on June 18, they rode over a flat plain dominated by sunflowers so high they engulfed horse and rider; the flowers released a sappy substance onto the men's clothing. The path soon exited from the field to a hilly, stony country, after which they descended into a notch between hills where they crossed the Arroyo del Chacón and the Arroyo de Francisco Pérez. The next day, the nineteenth, they reached and crossed the Arroyo Hondo in a fertile, forested valley; indeed, the growth was dense enough to support winding vines about the branches of the elms and oaks, which made the forest seem more primitive and pro-vided much-needed shade. Shortly after crossing the Hondo, they arrived at a stream named for the Tawakoni tribe; fortunately, several soldiers had joined their group, making the Indian threat less of a concern. Crossing this stream, they traveled toward the Frio River, ascending a small mountainous rock, Tierritas Blancas, along the way. Berlandier discovered diverse plants along the banks of the Frio, such as blackbrush acacia (*Acacia rigidula*), a hardy desert shrub that resembled the mesquite, which was more dominant in the area. Also found was the Texas persimmon tree (*Diospyros texana*), and the beautiful red-leafed lacey oak (*Quercus glaucoides*). Berlandier, wishing to collect a specimen, wandered from the rest of the men. Before coming to the Frio, they had to traverse a swampy landscape called by locals Cañada Verde. That evening the men camped along the Frio, having crossed the deep and rapid river during the late afternoon. Berlandier and Chowell hoped to see a lunar eclipse that evening, but clouds mostly obscured the sky.[6]

Preparing for the stretch from the Frio River to the Rio Grande, Berlandier and Chowell worked to preserve their floral and mineral col-lections; of the latter, Chowell had found specimens of petrified trees and ferruginous clay in the soil that reminded Berlandier of the *greube* of Switzerland. This part of the Frio, upriver from where Berlandier had jour-neyed before, had deeper banks and evidence of violent flooding; refuse from floods was scattered among the trees. Berlandier estimated that floods had risen up to fifty feet above normal. West of the Frio the trail took them across a plain with a few small arroyos and sporadic forests of mesquites and oaks. Along the way they ascended a slight incline that gave them a view of the surrounding plains; the guides informed Berlandier that Indian scouts often came here to spy on their enemies. The landscape thereabouts had floral specimens such as a pink-flowered species of cenizilla, the Texas per-simmon, the white-flowered rose of San Juan (*Macrosiphonia macrosiphon*), saw greenbriar (*Smilax bona-nox*), and a species of *Euphorbia* used by locals for medicinal purposes. June 24, they reached the Nueces, which was broad and deep enough to take hours to cross; trees gouged from banks by the current encumbered the stream; entwined with branches were carcasses of horses that had drowned attempting to ford the river. Around the environs of the Nueces were willows, elms, and the bush retama (*Parkinsonia aculeata*), which thrive in wet valleys; Berlandier found this tree throughout northern Mexico and Texas. The journey from the Nueces to the Rio Grande was much of the same; rattlesnakes were more prevalent the farther south the men journeyed. Just as horrid, at least according to legend, were the eerie inhabitants of the Laguna Espantosa. Berlandier knew that caimans inhabited the lake; legend indicated that once upon a time a monstrous reptile lived in it and killed some hapless Indians. Berlandier believed that there was once such an animal, which was killed in 1813; he even roamed about the place looking for signs of its former existence.[7]

The final leg of their journey to San Juan Bautista was over a rocky, almost lifeless plain of limestone and sandstone, dotted with rounded hills; water was scarce. Exceptions were the parajes of La Peña and Palo Blanco, where there were oases of freshwater. These places were well known among travelers, soldiers, and indigenous peoples. On June 27, they continued toward the Rio Grande, hoping to cross the river and reach San Juan Bautista by the end of the day, but lack of water slowed the march. At expected watering places, La Rosita and San Ambrosio, the men found only dry pond and stream beds. The first indication that they were near the Rio Grande came when they ascended the small hill of El Cuervo and saw the river valley. The route from El Cuervo to the river continued barren; infrequent rushing water had carved ravines in the land. They were surprised by the river's breadth when they arrived at the Rio Grande; it was much wider here than at Matamoros. The water was about three feet deep; they forded it by loading their baggage on mules and leading the animals across. Upon reaching the other side, it was dusk; they bivouacked along the river among willows and mulberry trees next to an old fortification or parapet guarding the ford. The next morning, after a brief journey west, they came to the presidio, formerly mission, of San Juan Bautista (recently renamed Villa de Guerrero). The presidio was distant from the river and its inundations by about five miles; at the eastern outskirts of the town was the old mission of San Bernardo, founded by Franciscans in the early 1700s; at the western outskirts were the ruins of the mission of San Juan Bautista, founded even earlier. Both missions had been abandoned years before Berlandier saw them in 1834. Small hills surrounded the town; Berlandier knew that not too far distant to the west was the Sierra Madre.[8]

San Juan Bautista was a pretty town, well built, with a lot of potential for growth, in Berlandier's opinion, though as yet it was very small, with fewer than one thousand inhabitants. Someone, perhaps the local priest, kept track of demographics and told the scientist that the birthrate outpaced the mortality rate 2 to 1. The population would have been higher in 1834 save for an outbreak of cholera the year before, which killed 120 people who tempted fate by remaining in town amid tainted water and refuse. Indeed, Berlandier found the town's water almost undrinkable, as surrounding ranchos diverted the freshwater spring for their own uses, leaving the townspeople with disgusting water from nearby limestone hills. A small reservoir near the old mission of San Bernardo hosted frogs and fish, which Berlandier tried to preserve in brandy for the return journey to Matamoros—a journey that he began presently, and unexpectedly. Berlandier and his friend Chowell were planning to continue up the Rio Grande, taking astronomical measurements all the way to fix accurate latitudes so to execute exact maps of Coahuila. But political events intervened. The long-standing rivalry between liberal reformers and conservative reactionaries in Mexico, which had spilled over into a conflict between President Santa Anna and the congress in Mexico City beginning in May 1834, came to a head in the department of Coahuila y Texas in July, and two opposing governors claimed authority from two separate capitols. Berlandier and Chowell decided it would be best to return to the security of Matamoros. Besides, alarming reports reached them that a new outbreak of cholera was spreading through coastal and inland communities in Texas and Tamaulipas.[9]

The road south from San Juan Bautista toward Laredo, which paralleled the Rio Grande, was dry and almost unbearably hot. Fortunately, there were plentiful small tributaries of the river by which they could camp, refresh themselves, and obtain water. As the road was a good mile distant from the river, the only diversions from the barren landscape were periodic arroyos, small limestone hills, and desert vegetation such as mesquite and huisache. At Arroyo el Amole, which provided the traveler with freshwater, there was a hint of an oasis, with willows, cedars, and the rose of San Juan. A little farther along, they stopped at a remarkable natural production caused by erosion of sandstone hills, which over time had created a series of formations that resembled a lost city dotted with cathedrals. Berlandier sketched the place, known locally as Las Iglesias, "the churches" (from which he later made a detailed drawing), notwithstanding that he was worried about their location, where the Lipans and Comanches reputedly made frequent incursions.

The heat of the day between freshwater sources caused such a thirst that Chowell thought to quench it with the juice of the cactus. Berlandier had heard of travelers lost in the desert who lived off cactus fluid; he had also learned, however, that one must grow accustomed to the juice. Nevertheless, Chowell greedily consumed the cactus juice, which made him violently, if temporarily, ill. July 10, they reached the abandoned hacienda of Pan, which was across the river from the abandoned presidio of Palafox; both places had experienced attacks from the Lipans and Comanches. Berlandier ascended to the roof of a hacienda so that he could examine the ruins of the presidio to the north; he delayed there long enough to sketch the environs. From Pan to the region near Laredo, the road continued through the hot, tedious landscape of small hills, desert conditions, and scattered plants overwhelmed by the heat of the sun. They halted on July 12 opposite Laredo, at a small hovel called Monterrey; Berlandier forded the river on horseback to obtain supplies at the presidio.[10]

The journey from Laredo to Matamoros took ten days of traveling in a hot, dry, desert landscape that rarely provided diversion for the eyes. The waterless path from Laredo paralleled the Rio Grande south to Palo Blanco, a stream that flowed into the Rio Grande, at the confluence of which shepherds camped, enjoying the cool night air. July 14, Berlandier and Chowell journeyed over wastelands to the rivulet Saladito, near which were ranchos that Berlandier did not recall seeing on his journey six years before; this was proof, he thought, that the Lipans and Comanches were leaving the Mexican herders alone. Flora along the way included mesquite, creosote, ebony, and cenizilla. Before arriving at the mouth of the Saladito, they passed by a ford, literally "horse crossing," of the Rio Grande, where Berlandier saw numerous remains of wrecked pirogues, perhaps because just upstream was a series of rocks impeding navigation in the river. Continuing south, they passed through Revilla (Guerrero), at the confluence of the Río Salado and Rio Grande. Spectacular bald cypresses grew along the banks of the former stream, which also featured beautiful waterfalls along its course. Chowell and Berlandier spent some time analyzing the bank of the Salado, where the action of water had cut into a ledge, exposing a series of different strata of sandstone, limestone, and clay. Coal was mined in the environs of the Salado valley; inhabitants extracted the element for personal use. Berlandier condemned the local authorities for generally forbidding the burning of coal because it polluted the air. The road south from Revilla took them to the Rancho de Salinillas, where the owner showed the scientists the bones of a

Figure 13. General D. Antonio Lopez de Santa-Anna,
president of the Republic of Mexico. Library of Congress.

mastodon found nearby. Berlandier examined them carefully, noting how the
sandstone had operated on the interior of the bones, displacing the marrow
and solidifying them. Berlandier believed, following the work of such geologists as Charles Lyell, that the mastodon was an antediluvian beast of the
Tertiary period, during a still unclear distant past. Further on, at the Arroyo
de Noche Buena, the scientists discovered heart-shaped shells exposed from
limestone of the family Cardiaceae (Cardioidea). At the town of Mier, the
fallout from the conflict between Santa Anna and the congress had led to
the displacement of one party and a revolutionary fervor that Berlandier and
Chowell wanted to avoid; they camped with little fanfare on the edge of the
town, which was very small and poor. The road from Mier to Camargo was

due east over a dry, hot landscape. Camargo was built on the eastern banks of the San Juan River, floods of which had sometimes damaged the town. From Camargo, the road continued south of the Rio Grande, passing by small ranchos and dried-up ponds. As they approached Reynosa, the road entered a rocky highland where Berlandier found samples of peyotl, or peyote plant (*Lophophora williamsii*), which, he wrote, "is still highly esteemed by the indigenes along the banks of the Río Bravo." Berlandier correctly ascertained that the plant was part of the cactus family. The tribes of the region, poor and few in number, subsisted on farming supplemented by hunting of small game and gathering of wild plant food such as water lilies and mesquite pods. The last two dozen leagues from Reynosa to Matamoros traversed a region that was, according to the season, insufferably dry or flooded but, Berlandier thought, still promised future prosperity. Berlandier and Chowell arrived at Matamoros in the middle of the night; local Indians living on the outskirts of town were awake still, singing and dancing.[11]

Upon his return to Matamoros, Berlandier examined his specimens, making sure that they were adequately preserved, and he prepared itineraries for other journeys. He became ill, however, in July 1834, and was laid up convalescing for several months, which interfered with his plans to journey west of Laredo into Coahuila. By the time he recovered, in late fall, the restless man decided on a lesser journey, repeating the ascent of the Rio Grande to Laredo, then journeying east to San Antonio. He made a detailed map of the route to San Antonio and kept scant notes of his journey. The trip was significant for him, because he was able to make the journey between San Antonio and Laredo during late fall and early winter, whereas his previous trips along this way had been during late winter and summer. The notes he made on the journey were, therefore, significant notations to add to his earlier, more complete journals. When, for example, he saw the line of trees along the Nueces River, particularly healthy and green willows and ashes after a wet autumn, it struck him that the Nueces was the clear, logical boundary between Tamaulipas and Texas.[12]

Berlandier was rarely satisfied with his collections, and was constantly making plans for new excursions and writing detailed itineraries by which he could accomplish the most scientific activities in the least amount of time. Short-term plans included further journeys into Mexico and Texas to supplement collections, and to make scientific and artistic observations. Political events sometimes intervened, such as in 1836 and after Texas independence, when Mexicans did not feel comfortable traveling north of the Nueces River.

Berlandier was also interested in traveling farther west beyond Nuevo León into Coahuila; he wished to journey east toward the Laguna Madre, exploring the varied rivers and streams flowing east, such as the Moquete and San Fernando. Indeed, during the autumn of 1835, the itinerant scientist journeyed south of Matamoros to the region between the Moquete and San Fernando Rivers. Three years later, in the summer and autumn of 1838, he made a more extensive journey south, this time following the descending Moquete to the Gulf of Mexico. He executed several drawings based on his journeys and observations, which are preserved at the Beinecke Library. These maps, along with measurements that he also recorded of compass and sextant readings (found at the Smithsonian Institution Archives), suggest that Berlandier was surveying the region in an official capacity. He painstakingly journeyed from rancho to rancho, noting the tremendous wealth of these landowners compared to the rest of the population. His journey encompassed a region that is even today relatively unsettled, a land of aridity mixed with estuaries and lagoons, of highlands of the eastern extreme of the Sierra Madre and lowlands, dominated by the Laguna Madre along the Gulf Coast. His itinerary included small villages such as Moquete and Caracal to the southeast and Barreales to the southwest, and large ranchos such as Sacramento, Anacahuitas, and Garza, the latter two near the Laguna de Morales. Berlandier was able to envision the extent of the Gulf Coast north and south of the mouth of the Rio Grande based on limited information, and hypothesized that the Moquete's unexpectedly deep and broad bed suggested that it was once one of several mouths of the Rio Grande.[13]

The resident scientist of Matamoros, when not traveling and exploring, must have been considered quite a novelty by the inhabitants of the Rio Grande valley. The home and business of the savant was the sanctuary of the cartographer, artist, journalist, historian, ethnologist, preservationist, chemist, meteorologist, astronomer, zoologist, mineralogist, botanist, apothecary, physician, and surgeon. Berlandier made a study of everything that came within his reach. He learned science from a variety of sources. During his early years in Geneva, under the influence of Candolle, who was himself a product of postrevolutionary French science, Berlandier learned that physicians of his time were adding to the traditional knowledge of the past. French physician René Théophile Hyacinthe Laennec, for example, invented the stethoscope in 1816. Early-nineteenth-century French medicine was highly organized by the state, as it had been in the eighteenth century before and after the Revolution. Each of the three fields of medical practitioners, physicians, surgeons, and apothecaries, used apprenticeship as the means to train young scientists in the received traditions. Organizations such as the Société de Médecine de Paris and the Académie Nationale de Médecine mandated separate training for physicians, surgeons, and apothecaries. Surgeons and apothecaries were, savants of the French medical establishment believed, practical technicians of a specific medical art, whereas physicians were great thinkers, speculative and meditative, able to observe and know intuitively what were the possible illnesses that fit the specific symptoms and what were the best treatments to achieve a cure. French physicians were beholden to the writings of the fourth-century BCE Greek physician Hippocrates, whose *Air, Water, Places* required the physician to be a feeler as well as a thinker, and to make a study of geography, hydrology, and meteorology, as the forces of climate and landscape had profound impacts on human health.[14]

Berlandier's apprenticeship to an apothecary in Geneva erected an early foundation of knowledge in the botanical, animal, and mineral materials of medicine. His work under Candolle in botany as well as his broader association with the savants of the Société de Physique et d'Histoire Naturelle de Genève exposed him to current ideas in science and medicine. Berlandier's natural openmindedness allowed him to combine the formal study of his years in Geneva with the research of Mexican scientists as well as traditions of presidial soldiers, muleteers, townspeople, hunters and trappers, and indigenous peoples of northern Mexico and southern Texas. Berlandier's isolation in Matamoros forced him to rely on the testimony and narratives of local inhabitants, particularly about the supposed properties of local flora. Berlandier kept a number of memorandum books filled with notes on what he heard from Mexicans, Tejanos, Comanches, Apaches, Kickapoos, and other indigenous peoples, about plant remedies that addressed particular ailments. When possible, he checked the validity of local traditions of plant properties with authorities ranging from contemporaries such as Cervantes, Mociño and Sessé, Humboldt, and La Llave to writers of the Spanish conquest such as Hernández, Oviedo, Clavigero, and Cortés, to ancient authorities such as Pliny the Elder.[15]

Berlandier's American materia medica was a work in progress that began when he sailed into the Pánuco River aboard the *Hannah Elizabeth* in 1826 to begin his lengthy journey into Mexico. By the time he was practicing medicine in Matamoros, he had acquired a collection of plant remedies for many of the ailments that afflicted the inhabitants of that and

surrounding towns of the Rio Grande. In addition to journeying to augment his own collections, Berlandier encouraged suppliers, who were often
Indians, to bring him as much as they could find. Berlandier recorded his
materia medica in a variety of sources, most of which have not been published. Notable are "A estudiar en viajes: Histoire naturelle des plantes
employees dans la matiere medicals les arts, etc. des Mexicains anciens et
modernes," and "Des plantes usuelles chez les Indiens du Mexique," both
found at the Gray Herbarium Archives. Berlandier also provided extensive
descriptions of plants and their medical uses in the journals of his many
trips throughout Texas and Mexico.

Berlandier oriented his worldview as a physician around identifying,
preventing, and treating disease by common sense; using the natural resources commonly available in the environment; and mitigating the conditions in the environment that produced and spread disease. Physicians
were herbalists who knew how to locate, collect, preserve, and prepare medicines from roots, seeds, fruits, and leaves, to be administered either by direct
ingestion or in brewed teas, tinctures, or salves and plasters. Physicians
learned which natural remedy would lessen the symptoms of which disease.
While some of the serums, poultices, and teas that the apothecary and physician prescribed were for specific complaints, many were supposed cure-alls,
effective for almost any illness. Indigenous peoples considered coral bean
(*Erythrina corallodendron*) a cure-all, as well as sweetgum (*Liquidambar
styraciflua*); chewing the gum found in the bark was useful for throat and
stomach ailments. An evergreen that Berlandier frequently encountered
on his travels, the eastern red cedar (*Juniperus virginiana*), yielded berries
that when boiled and made into a tea was a useful treatment for a variety
of ailments such as bronchitis and rheumatism. Also common was the red
mulberry (*Morus rubra*), its fruit maturing in late spring, the root tea of
which indigenous peoples used as a general panacea and especially to treat
the effects of dysentery and worms. Another legendary panacea used by
the inhabitants of Mexico City, *mispacle* (*Buddleja sessiliflora*), Berlandier
discovered when waiting for the Comisión de Límites to depart in the fall
of 1827. Mexicans used the huisache tree, a desert shrub that Berlandier
repeatedly found on his journeys, to treat malaria, skin lesions, and diarrhea. Locals called the castor-oil plant (*Ricinus communis*) *higuerilla* and
employed plant oil for constipation and other digestive complaints. Mexican
tea (*Chenopodium ambrosioides*), a potentially toxic plant, was used daily,
according to Berlandier, as a tonic to treat indigestion. Berlandier had

learned at Geneva that opium was useful for treating digestive problems; he prescribed a potion to muleteers who were guiding him through Mexico in the spring of 1827. At Matamoros, Berlandier developed several recipes for opium concoctions to treat cholera and diarrhea.[16]

Mexico, a land of tropical flora, offered apothecaries and physicians a variety of resinous substances useful in treating diseases and injuries. In "A estudiar en viajes," Berlandier engaged in a long literary discourse on the different opinions regarding *Bursera excelsa* (known to Berlandier as *Elaphrium excelsum*) of the naturalists Clavigero, Mociño and Sessé, and Linnaeus. "In medicine," Berlandier wrote, "this resin" has qualities of a true gum, and is a useful antiseptic. Balsam of Peru (*Myroxylom pereirae*) contained a resin used as a salve by the ancient Mexicans; Berlandier found the tree growing about the Pánuco and thought it had quite an agreeable smell. Berlandier found descriptions of the balsam of Peru in the *Historia medicinal* of Spanish botanist Nicolás Monardes. A resinous plant called by Berlandier *Hymenea candolliana* not only provided ointment for healing but, like myrrh, was used in religious ceremonies by ancient Mexicans.[17]

On Berlandier's travels, and when practicing medicine at Matamoros, he repeatedly treated patients seeking cures and relief for venereal and other diseases of the sexual organs. The oils and seeds of the peanut (*Arachis hypogaea*), Berlandier learned, were used widely in traditional Mexican medicine, especially for treating gonorrhea. Plants such as the sunflower (*Helianthus annus*) from the family Asteraceae were useful in this regard, as were plants of the families Begoniaceae and Bignoniaceae. Indians, according to Berlandier, believed that a species of cineraria (*Cineraria*) was not only a powerful vulnerary but was also good to combat liver and venereal diseases. Berlandier heard about another "antisyphilitic" during his journey west of San Antonio in the company of Comanche Indians in 1828; the plant was a species of the family Compositae, which locals called *yerba de la capitana* (*Verbesina microptera*). Inhabitants of the mountainous region surrounding Mexico City knew that the purple prairie-clover (*Dalea purpurea*) was useful in treating syphilis as well as the skin disease yaws. Inhabitants in the environs of Monterrey used a plant of the spikemoss family, called locally *doradilla* (*Selaginella lepidophylla*) to treat syphilis. The sulfuric baths around Monterrey had a reputation for curing syphilis, and Berlandier sometimes recommended the waters for his patients, though he found over time that the waters worked better for throat ailments than for syphilis. Respecting other sexual concerns, Berlandier wrote, "Doctor Hernandes claims that a decoction of the flowers of Loloxschitl mixed with [*Magnolia mexicana*] stimulates the cure of sterility."[18]

Berlandier used his research and travels to learn how local peoples treated common diseases with available plant remedies. A species of the myrtle family, *Psidium guajava,* Berlandier discovered when reading about the Franciscan missionary Bernardino de Sahagún, was useful to reduce severity of dysentery. Indigenous peoples considered cheeseweed (published as *Malva longifolia* in Sessé and Mociño) to be an excellent emollient for poultices and a good ingredient in "mollifying beverages." Berlandier wrote in "Des plantes usuelles chez les Indiens du Mexique" that "this plant is common in the environs of Mexico at Chapultapec and in the whole valley of Tenochtitlan." A species of leadwort, called by Mexican botanists *Plumbago mexicana,* was useful in tissue healing but also had the reputation of being caustic on the skin. Nineteenth-century medicine was, as in former times, dominated by the use of emetics and purgatives. Berlandier discovered that Mexicans relied on the seeds of the Texas ebony for such purposes. Ancient Mexicans used *Casimiroa edulis,* vulgarly called *cochitzapotl* or *zapote blanco,* as a narcotic and cathartic. It is, Berlandier wrote, "astringent and very bitter." The Carrizo Indians of northern Mexico employed cenizilla, Berlandier learned on his travels, as a fever reducer, especially to combat the ravages of yellow fever. They also used a decoction made from the leaves of the black willow similarly as a febrifuge. Mexican apothecaries typically recommended peppers such as *Piperonia* "as a stimulant," but Berlandier disagreed with the practice.[19]

The connections between natural and human history fascinated Berlandier, who entered into the debate long carried on by other human and natural historians respecting the origins of and use of plants by Mexicans, ancient and modern, for other than medicinal purposes. Berlandier's knowledge was informed by studying the natural histories of the early Spanish naturalists Gonzalo Oviedo and Francisco Hernández, the eighteenth-century Mexican historian Francesco (Abbe) Clavigero, the flora of the early-nineteenth-century botanists Sessé and Mociño, the works of the great eighteenth-century Swedish taxonomist Linnaeus, the natural and human histories of Baron Humboldt, the ongoing *Prodromus* of his mentor de Candolle, and the works of contemporary French botanist Aimé Bonpland. In addition, he relied on the work and discoveries of his former friend and colleague the late "Professor D. Vicente Cervantes, Director of the Mexican garden," and his current friend and acquaintance "Don Pablo de la Llave, distinguished botanist and minister no less skillful." In his memoranda and journals Berlandier entered into such debates as whether or not the plantain, or banana (*Musa paradisiaca*) is native to America. Berlandier wrote about *Verbesina mexicana*, a species of crownbeard, a plant of the family Compositae, which the botanist Vicente Cervantes had published, and which was used to cover the dead to remove the odor of decomposing flesh. Also good, Berlandier discovered, was *Tagetes mexicana*, a species of tarragon. Such herbs might be quickly used as an antidote to the poisonous jimsonweed (*Datura stramonium*); indigenous peoples used it in smaller quantities as a vinegar. Naturalists such as Oviedo praised the sapodilla (*Achras sapota*) as a delicious fruit, though Berlandier merely wrote that this plant has an odor that resembles the pit of a peach and makes a useful paste for washing the hands, and it makes a good perfume. Reading Francisco Hernández, Berlandier came upon mention of a plant that existed at the time of the Spanish conquest. "The grandeur and corpulence of the tree," Berlandier wrote in "A estudiar en viajes," "fixed the attention of the Spanish," who knew it from the Aztec word *pochotl*, since called the shaving brush tree (*Pseudobombax ellipticum*). The Aztecs considered the tree sacred; Christian converts used the flowers to decorate the altar during Lent. Also used in Aztec religious festivals was a species of the family Apocineae, a flowering bush that the "Indians named cacaloxochitl, or flower of the crow or raven" (*Plumeria alba*); Berlandier also noted that the plant was used "by many people in preparing preserves." A plant with the name *Apomea arborescens*, which Berlandier placed in the Convolvulaceae family, was a "parasitic plant extremely common on the Mexican Plateau used as a paint by the Aztec Indians." Indigenous peoples extracted the sap of a plant, *croton*, of the family Euphorbiaceae, for use as a body or war paint; they called the sap "medicine of blood," because it gave a "bloodthirsty color."[20]

During the course of his twenty-year residency in the town of Matamoros, Berlandier wrote extensively on the town, its environment, and the epidemics that plagued the inhabitants. Observation and recording of data were the key tools of diagnosis. The alleviation of symptoms was of prime concern. Physicians in America as well as in Europe were quite in the dark as to how most diseases were spread and hence how to prevent contagion and discover cures. Berlandier's approach to medicine, like most of his contemporaries,' was still very much beholden to a Hippocratic approach in which an imbalance of the four humors—blood, black bile, yellow bile, phlegm—caused illness. If the humoral theory and the practice of venesection (bloodletting) were less common by the time Berlandier practiced medicine, the focuses on observation of the illness, analysis of symptoms, alleviating symptoms, and taking basic steps for prevention were part of the Hippocratic corpus of knowledge handed down for centuries. Theories of cause were so rudimentary that some physicians still believed that illness resulted from the imbalance of the four humors; others thought that illnesses might develop spontaneously, without apparent cause; others looked for the cause of illness in bad air and water and the subsequent creation of miasmas. Tradition and the way things had been done, the old remedies and the age-old diagnoses, were still most important, so that a person could pick up medicine, become a physician, merely by observation, study, and a quick mind able to learn the received tradition.[21]

Berlandier was young and inquisitive, open to new ideas; it is hardly surprising to find that he was very much a part of the public health movement that captivated nineteenth-century European and American scientists. His observations and reflections on the cholera epidemic of the early 1830s revealed his concern for improving sanitary conditions in Mexican cities such as Matamoros. This movement acted upon the awareness of the role of filth in human living environments that contributed to the spread of disease. Contagion as a phenomenon was recognized, if sometimes disputed among physicians and sanitary workers; the mechanism of the spread of disease from one human to another—its epidemiology—was not understood. Naturalists such as Berlandier, who had an appreciation of the beauty and sublimity of the natural environment and its positive impact on health, theorized at the same time that the contrasting natural tendency of decay and death had a comparable impact on human health. The circumstantial connection between the putrid smells arising from the stagnant lagoons in Tamaulipas and the spread of fever during hot summer months was not lost on the young French naturalist. The theory of miasmas, rotting animal and vegetable matter that corrupts air and water, the breathing and drinking of which brings about illness, was an extension of Hippocratic humoral theory: the natural balance of the four humors in the human body is upset by the inhalation of air infused with rotting material. To bring health again is to correct the humoral imbalance: clean the air and water of the community, especially among the poor, which will also purify, restore the healthy balance of, individuals. Humoral imbalance could also affect emotions and behavior; hence, to restore the balance was to advance moral improvement. Berlandier believed that impoverished areas should be addressed first by sanitation advocates.[22]

The Hippocratic physician of Berlandier's time of necessity studied meteorology and geography, knowing that health and disease were closely associated with temperature, winds, moisture, aridity, landscape, latitude, and longitude. Berlandier, for example, blamed many of the fevers and epidemics that afflicted river valley and Gulf Coast towns on the pools of stagnant water that formed in the clayey depressions after river and tidal floods. In the wake of spring floods, the hot rays of the sun evaporated the stagnant water, revealing the muck and decaying animal bodies of the lagoon, which caused sickly miasmic air. Interestingly, Berlandier found after keeping track of the illnesses, climate, and weather of Matamoros over a course of years that the town was relatively healthy compared to those situated nearer the Gulf Coast. Although the Rio Grande periodically flooded the environs of the town, leaving behind stagnant estuaries, and notwithstanding several permanent swamps surrounding the town, the arid landscape, a combination of sporadic rainfall and dry winds, prevented most epidemics from taking hold in Matamoros. There were of course exceptions, such as in 1829 when fevers killed five hundred residents, and 1833, when the cholera epidemic of the Gulf Coast spared few towns—again about five hundred residents of Matamoros succumbed to the disease. Besides the summer heats, when particularly at night the hot, humid air encouraged sickness, the cold north winds of winter sometimes visited illness upon the people of Matamoros. The hot Sirocco winds blowing from the south frequently affected the nervous system of some inhabitants; the physician Berlandier noted a general increase in the pulse rates of his patients. He noted in his journal for February 23, 1842, for example, that "the wind has been very strong & at intervals so violent, that it seemed like a hurricane. Almost every one is affected by it, & its influence is so great that while it lasts the faculties of the mind are almost stupefied, & the individuals who give up to its influences, feel a kind of head ache & a nervous excitement, hard to describe, but very disagreeable. This indisposition appeared to increase with the force of the wind. The South wind has an influence on mental derangement—with strangers it increases in violence." The unusual aridity and warmth of the winter and spring of 1842 presaged "a sickly autumn"; already that spring there were cases of yellow fever and typhus, and the summer was still a month off! Later that year, in July, Berlandier combined the activities of meteorological investigator and physician when a lightning bolt hit a hut in the middle of the afternoon. The hut had a reed roof and walls made of clay and reeds; seven people occupied it, including two children. When the bolt hit, "one of the women who was sick & confined to bed, was lifted up & thrown near the door without other injury than a considerable change in the faculties of her mind"; she became convulsive. The children, though "safe & sound, retained a timorous character, the least noise frightening them." Otherwise the family was unharmed, though the hut was partially destroyed. Berlandier visited the scene several times and interviewed the inhabitants to find out exactly what happened and what were the natural and human physical consequences.[23]

Like any physician and apothecary, Berlandier saw many patients who had a wide range of illnesses. Smallpox was not the scourge that it was in the early 1500s, when the Spaniards first arrived in Mexico and huge numbers of the indigenous inhabitants succumbed. Berlandier, who kept records on the origins, extent, and prevalence of such epidemics, wrote that "the Spanish of the Narvaez Expedition brought this illness to Mexico. A negro of this headman transmitted the scourge to the Indians of which the majority died. Cuetlahuatzin successor to Moctesuma [Montezuma] to the throne of Anahuac died from this sickness within days of the commencement of his reign." The spread of disease helped the Spanish in their conquest of Mexico. Berlandier claimed in *Journey to Mexico* that smallpox made its appearance in Mexico "every sixteen years." In 1830 he journeyed to Monterrey on General Terán's orders to obtain vaccine for the residents of the Rio Grande valley; manuscripts are otherwise silent as to when or if ever Berlandier treated patients with smallpox. Yellow fever never appeared at Matamoros when Berlandier was resident there. In surrounding areas, however, the disease appeared, such as at San Fernando, in January 1842, and at Brazos de Santiago at an unknown date; Berlandier failed to indicate whether or not he was present during these epidemics. Other fevers besides *vomito prieto* appeared frequently at Matamoros and surrounding towns. These fevers, such as those arising (in Berlandier's opinion) from putrid miasmas and humoral imbalances, were often quite lethal. Residents of Matamoros and surrounding towns suffered from various skin ailments; some women experienced symptoms of colored blotches on their skin, which the French physician Alibert called hepatic ephelis. Berlandier thought the cause of the blotches might be the sediment-filled water of the Rio Grande, which people often used for drinking and cooking. Boils and tumors of the skin, such as herpes and anthrax, were common among residents of northern Mexico and southern Texas. Berlandier also treated quite a number of people who suffered from vertigo (*aire*). He eschewed the folk remedy of treating the disease with the penis of a male coyote; Berlandier recommended consuming tea made with western mugwort.[24]

A man and scientist of his time, Berlandier still used, on occasion, venesection, in which he used a lancet or a leech to draw blood from a patient to balance the humors, relieve swelling, or lessen fever. He noted, in the unpublished manuscript "Surgery and Medicine," that "of bloodletting, its origins are obscure in the ancient world nor are they clear in the new." Not only did Hippocrates and Galen establish the practice among European physicians, but ancient Mexicans practiced bloodletting as well. Aztec surgeons used obsidian blades to open a vein. Berlandier witnessed bleeding using obsidian blades in the mountains of Mexico and saw a Comanche north of the Rio Grande bleeding a companion with the tip of an arrow. His friend the Quicapú, with whom he traveled and lived, once tried to bleed a Cherokee with "a piece of glass." Berlandier came to his assistance and bled the Indian with his lancet.[25]

At his apothecary office Berlandier saw many people with illnesses for which there were few if any remedies. The most horrible included rabies, which was astonishingly prevalent in the valley of the Rio Grande. Not only dogs but wolves, coyotes, and foxes became rabid, attacking livestock and shepherds. Tetanus was another killer that Berlandier frequently saw but could hardly treat. Mocezuelo, infantile tetanus, which was caused by an inflammation at the cut umbilical cord, was seen "every day in Matamoros," Berlandier wrote, and "it conducts to the tomb three or four newborn babies a week or two old." Puerperal fever, as it was called at the time, commonly struck convalescing mothers as well.[26]

Cholera was, however, the disease that concerned Berlandier the most. He lived through several terrible epidemics, such as in 1833. He carefully noted the initial symptoms of the stricken person, which began with "looseness in the intestines, which is perhaps considered as the general precedent of the dangerous period of the disease. Sometimes during this first period, illness does not spare the person and strikes him down to the grave, but this is rare." Typically, "the intestinal looseness is generally accompanied by a little sharp suffering kept in abeyance over several hours or days; the pain is so slight as to be insignificant," yet the result for the hapless person was the same. Nevertheless, Berlandier recommended aggressive action both in terms of a prescribed regimen of medicines and the implementation of an active public health agenda. Of the former, he recommended opium-based concoctions, mustard plasters, and purgatives. Locals swore

by a sagebrush-leaf tea known colloquially as *estafiat*. But more important, Berlandier believed that a system of public health and sanitary measures were most important to address the initial stages of the epidemic.
"Immediately when the disease breaks out," he wrote, "the authorities
should . . . take measures and use methods to visit daily the most poor habi-
tations/neighborhoods." Physicians would then dispense "proper medicine
to arrest the initial malevolent symptoms." Berlandier believed that preventing cholera epidemics was relatively simple, if difficult to organize on a
large scale. Since he subscribed to the miasmic theory of disease, Berlandier
believed that public health officials must act to clean up all forms of animal waste, whether human urine and feces lying in the streets and gutters,
dead animals decaying in dried-up lagoons, or offal from the slaughter of
animals. Cleanliness of streets, good drainage, and proper attention to the
location and use of outhouses, especially in places with hot, heavy air, were
the chief means of combating epidemic sickness.[27]

Berlandier's house and office that he rented in Matamoros, called
Lojere, was, as Darius Couch discovered when he visited Berlandier's
widow in 1853, filled with scientific instruments, natural specimens, Indian
artifacts, maps, and manuscripts. Berlandier's fecundity in drawing and
map-making was exceeded only by his manuscript writings. His maps of
coastal and inland regions and routes are clear and illustrative of the landscape and trails. Examples abound in his handwritten manuscript journals as well as isolated in the various manuscript holdings at Harvard's
Gray Herbarium, Yale's Beinecke Library, and the Smithsonian Institution
Archives—as collected by Darius Couch in 1853. In a folder (labeled #47)
of maps, drawings, and itineraries at the Beinecke Library, one finds drawings of cacti, an accurate pencil drawing of the coastline from the mouth
of the Rio Grande to Matagorda Bay and the mouth of the Texas Colorado
River, and another pencil drawing of the coastline from Matagorda Bay to
Galveston Bay. This latter map includes soundings in fathom for Galveston
and Trinity bays and inlets, and lists the various bayous that flow into the
bay, rivers such as the Trinity, and forts erected by the Mexicans to defend
the bay and east Texas. Berlandier also drew maps of Aransas Bay and
the coast from San Bernardo (also called Matagorda) Bay to the Laguna
Madre. This folder also contains a brief itinerary and accompanying map
of a journey Berlandier made from Laredo to San Antonio in November
and December of 1834.[28]

Berlandier's interest in meteorology, hydrology, and astronomy required that he possess a host of various instruments to measure atmospheric and water temperature, humidity, dew point, atmospheric pressure, and blueness of the sky. He used "the hygrometer of Saussure, and another of Poullet, with an accompanying Fahrenheit thermometer by Pool of New York; the bulb," made of gold, was "submerged in ether." Berlandier used a cyanometer to measure the color of the atmosphere, and a barometer by Gay-Lussacs, with an attached Celsius thermometer. He had a specially made heliothermometer. Most of his thermometers registered degrees in Celsius. One had a golden bulb, which he used along with a psychrometer to measure temperature and moisture. Another, the standard mercury thermometer "constructed by Pixie, father & son, of Paris," had a scale engraved on a glass tube. He possessed several pocket Celsius thermometers, one of which had a scale engraved on ivory, another was mounted on a mahogany back. His collection of Fahrenheit thermometers included one constructed by Pastorelli of London, the scale engraved on ivory, set in a case. One day in December 1847, Berlandier performed an elaborate experiment in the courtyard of his house at Matamoros to gauge the temperature of the sun's rays on Earth with as few impeding environmental variables as possible. He set up six large alcohol thermometers along a line from east to west, two feet apart. Each thermometer was firmly held in a carbon mold in a box; a hole, one inch in diameter, allowed the rays of the sun to strike successively the spherical bulbs of each thermometer. The carbon was meant to remove any variables in the surrounding environment. Also on a daily basis, Berlandier took the water temperature in his two wells as well as the atmospheric temperature, humidity, and pressure.[29]

Berlandier kept live as well as dead specimens. A savant of his singular reputation, the only one for miles around in southern Texas and northern Mexico, attracted the attention of all sorts of would-be scientists, people who were interested in natural phenomena but without the training to form hypotheses and to collect and analyze data. Berlandier also had an easy way with hunters and soldiers, which often led these untrained, ad hoc naturalists to assist the savant in his collecting. Hunters sometimes brought him specimens, such as the caiman, which Berlandier kept to observe and study; the animals refused captivity, would not eat, and if not released would eventually starve themselves. Berlandier also kept for study Mexican wolves and coyotes, the former also for the purposes of watching and companionship.

The Mexican wolf, which Berlandier christened *Canis mexicanus* (now called *Canis lupus baileyi*) was prevalent throughout the valley of the Rio Grande. The wolf was quite large, readily mated with domestic dogs in the neighborhood of Matamoros, could become quite tame, and was useful as a watchdog and shepherd dog. Berlandier trained quite a few of these wolves. He was less successful training coyotes, which were less loyal and more intelligent than the wolves. The coyote was ubiquitous throughout Texas and Mexico, ravenous and willing to approach towns to satisfy hunger or to mate with domestic dogs. In his manuscript *Mammalia*, Berlandier described the coyote as "about the size of a . . . fox or a little larger: of a rustyish, gray color, with a blackish gray mane along the back." The coyotes he kept barked at night like a dog, whereas the wolves howled. The distinction between the coyote and the various species of fox were, he realized, confusing, and naturalists had theretofore been very unclear how exactly to categorize these animals. Berlandier categorized wolves, coyotes, foxes, and canines according to their eyes, whether round, like the dog and wolf, or vertically slanted, like the coyote and fox. The dogs that Berlandier encountered at Matamoros were largely mixed-breeds; indigenous dogs had once existed throughout Mexico and still did in some parts. The Aztecs bred dogs in part for food, a characteristic continued among the Charitica Indians.[30]

Some of the more remarkable live specimens that Berlandier sometimes kept in his collection were fish dropped from clouds during rainstorms. These fish were very small but plentiful over a space of hundreds of meters; Berlandier could not determine their species, which did not appear to be native to northern Mexico and southern Texas. He assumed they were marine fish caught up in a storm over the Gulf and brought inland. The rainwater in which they were carried and deposited was completely fresh, without a saline content. Some of the fish that fell into pools of water survived the fall; these Berlandier kept until they died (perhaps because of their saltwater origin). Such a phenomenon of falling fish was reportedly not unique in the valley of the Rio Grande. Berlandier learned from a trustworthy source that early in the nineteenth century at Laredo a storm dropped a "fresh water turtle . . . , a shrimp . . . & a bagre," or catfish. "In 1847 a woman, residing upon the left bank of the Rio del Norte in the vicinity of Matamoros, found after a shower in the branches of an Acacia [tree], about 6 or 7 feet from the ground, a live fish, weighing about ten pounds, quite large enough for an ordinary repast."[31]

Berlandier's office at Lojere made room for crates, boxes, and catalogues of specimens preserved in alcohol, glass, paper, and on canvas by means of Berlandier's pencil and paintbrush. Berlandier kept numerous snakes, preserved in alcohol, which he had captured on his travels. On his journeys into Tamaulipas in 1830 and 1831, for example, and into Texas in 1834, he and his companions were confronted with rattlesnakes, which in Tamaulipas were so plentiful that it would have been difficult not to catch specimens for preservation. The catalogue of his zoological collection, for example, preserved at the Smithsonian Institution Archives, lists the varied vipers that he collected, with descriptions of where found and scientific versus colloquial names. Berlandier was a collector of fossils and mollusks, and kept extensive descriptions of where found, accompanied by exact drawings of particular shells. He maintained notes and executed drawings of anatomical features of different animals, some based on precise dissections of specimens. His zoological drawings include beautiful images of the bat, frigate bird, beaver, armadillo, raccoon, hamster, opossum, coyote, snowshoe hare (which he named *Lepus chowelli berl.*, now called *Lepus americanus*), peccary, pronghorn, weasel (which he named *Putorius mexicanus* Berl., now included in genus *Mustela*), badger, and cougar (which he named *Felis unicolor* Berl., called the *onza* by the Apache Indians, now called *Puma concolor*). Berlandier was a prolific writer of natural history; the Smithsonian Institution Archives contain massive manuscript tomes on birds and mammals.[32]

CHAPTER NINE

River of Death

⚜

✢ HAVING COME TO KNOW MANY AMERICANS, SUCH AS STEPHEN AUSTIN,
during his journeys to Texas before 1836, and having been convinced by
General Terán's viewpoint that it was just a matter of time before the greedy
Americans would push Texas into a declaration of independence, Berlandier
had not been surprised that the Texas Revolution occurred or that the disor-
ganized and squabbling Mexican authorities and generals had allowed Texas
to slip away from their control. Neither did it surprise Berlandier to learn
that the United States was, by the mid-1840s, serious about annexing the
Republic of Texas. When Gen. Francisco Mejia in the summer of 1845 determined that he should send a small expedition to reconnoiter Texas positions
and Mexican strength along the Nueces River to its mouth, including Brazos
de Santiago and Fronton de Santa Isabela (Point Isabel), there was no more
knowledgeable explorer and cartographer than the Frenchman Jean Louis
Berlandier. Berlandier had journeyed to Brazos de Santiago numerous times
and knew the routes, landscapes, and scattered peoples.

At General Mejia's request, Berlandier set out for Brazos de Santiago
on the same day, July 4, 1845, that Texas voted in favor of annexation by the
United States. As Mexico considered Texas still in rebellion and refused to
recognize the independent so-called Republic of Texas, American attempts
to annex Mexico had to yield a forceful response. General Mejia enjoined
Berlandier to reconnoiter the landscape to know how best to respond to
aggression from Texas or the United States and to hold on to control of the

Figure 14.
Zachary Taylor,
half-length portrait,
facing slightly left,
in uniform, holding
telescope engraved
by Alexander Hay
Ritchie. Library of
Congress.

Nueces River. Berlandier discovered on this journey that Mexico had done little to encourage population growth and the development of an infrastructure that would help retain control over the area between the Rio Grande and the mouth of the Nueces River. He returned for a second visit to Point Isabel in September. Believing that politics must give way to science, Berlandier constructed an experiment to measure the speed of sound. Berlandier knew that every year on September 15, Mexico celebrated independence from Spain; at Point Isabel, as elsewhere, soldiers fired artillery in celebration. Berlandier arranged with an officer in charge of the artillery to allow for an experiment to be set up to measure, from a distance, the time difference between the flash of light of the cannon explosion and the report of the cannon. Working with a few assistants, he took meticulous readings of his chronometer as to the exact moment of the flash of the cannon and the exact moment of the boom. Once he had the range of time, he divided the distance by these figures.

The cannon went off a dozen times. The average time was 4.66 seconds, with a range between 4.0 and 5.0 seconds. Berlandier doubtless knew of like experiments in France and elsewhere in preceding centuries but was characteristically seeking to discover what might be the unique impact of the latitude, longitude, climate, atmosphere, and winds of the Gulf Coast.[1]

During the autumn and winter of 1845 to 1846, negotiations over Texas broke down between the Mexican and American governments; Gen. Zachary Taylor had invested Corpus Christi with dragoons and artillery; Mexican troops under Francisco Mejia from Fort Guerrero adjacent to Matamoros ranged over the land between the Rio Grande and the Nueces, ready to respond to any American incursion into northern Tamaulipas. In March, in response to an order from the secretary of war, Taylor had his troops moved out of Corpus Christi, marching toward the Rio Grande. As the American army approached the estuary of the Arroyo Colorado, Mexican troops occupied the opposite side, threatening to resist the American advance. At this point Berlandier, General Mejia's adjutant, arrived, crossed the Arroyo, asked to be presented to General Taylor, and handed him a letter from General Mejia warning that an American attempt to ford the Arroyo would be considered an act of war, which the Mexicans would resist. Taylor ignored the warning, and the Army of Occupation crossed the Arroyo on March 22—the Mexicans, along with Jean Louis Berlandier, retreated. By the end of March, Taylor's army had reached the Rio Grande and had taken up positions on its northern bank. In early April, Taylor faced a new counterpart, Gen. Mariano Arista, who took command of Mexico's northern forces. After several weeks of fortifying positions, isolated skirmishes, and failed negotiations, the first significant battle of the Mexican War occurred on May 8 at Palo Alto, on the northern side of the Rio Grande. The two armies were similarly manned by infantry, dragoons (mounted infantry), and artillery; the United States, with greater wealth, had more sophisticated rifles and cannon; poverty and disorganization characterized the courageous but ill-trained and ill-equipped Mexican force. Berlandier, who served during the battle as an officer-surgeon, wrote that the Mexican esprit de corps was weak, as the common soldier served only under compulsion; many were convicts, and most were impoverished, homeless, or luckless men impressed by the Mexican government to serve. The Mexican army was officer-heavy, and though these officers were willing to fight, they often had little military training, and jealousy among them was rampant. Berlandier, meanwhile, manned the field hospital at the rear of the Mexican position. The location of the hospital changed during the course of the battle as it was bombarded by American artillery. The hospital had inadequate medical supplies, and conditions were filthy. Neither army used anesthetics, as ether was not introduced into surgery until 1846, in Massachusetts. Surgeons had no choice but to amputate the limbs of seriously injured men, of which there were many; surgeons offered liquor or opium to dull the pain; the dressing of severed limbs was inadequate to encourage healing, and infection and gangrene were often the result. During such chaos, suffering, screams of pain, and moans of the dying, surgeons such as Berlandier had to become spiritual counselors to mortally wounded and disillusioned men. Somehow or other Berlandier, even amid the burden of his surgical work, contrived to glimpse the battlefield and to gain intelligence from soldiers as to the positions of the two armies, their strengths and weaknesses, and the course of the battle.[2]

After Mexico's defeat at Palo Alto, and subsequently at Resaca de la Palma, Mexican soldiers fled the battlefield across the river to Matamoros. Late the night of May 17, into the early morning of May 18, Arista and his troops prepared to depart west for Monterrey, then silently exited the town before dawn. Berlandier, who kept a diary of the American occupation, wrote that the streets of Matamoros were deserted as the people waited for the

Figure 15. "A little more grape Capt. Bragg"—General Taylor at the Battle of Buena Vista, Feby 23d, 1847 / Cameron; lith. & pub. by N. Currier. Library of Congress.

inevitable occupation of the city. American troops, the morning of the eighteenth, occupied Fort Guerrero y Paredes outside of Matamoros. This fort, the construction of which was begun, if not completed, under Gen. Manuel Mier y Terán, was known variously as Guerrero or Paredes; today, as a museum, it is Fort Casamata. The prefect of the city sent a delegation, which included Berlandier, to meet with General Taylor to ask that during the occupation the American troops respect religious ceremonies, personal property, the judicial system, and local police enforcement. Taylor in turn asked the delegation questions about the countryside, particularly distances to the Sierra Madre, in preparation for pursuing Arista's army. Berlandier met later that afternoon with Taylor respecting the condition of the hospitals and the injured. He particularly sought to find out whether American surgeons were willing to consult with him about the advisability of amputating the leg of Captain don Barragan, who had been badly wounded by a gunshot; the surgeons recommended against the amputation. The military occupation deteriorated during the course of the day and night. Notwithstanding General Taylor's assurances, volunteers under his command from the militias of such states as Texas and Louisiana roamed about the town, respecting neither property nor the rights of citizens. Some citizens were forced to quarter American troops. Berlandier treated a city watchman named Mendiola, who had been stabbed by an unknown assailant. At the same time there was a prison revolt that the Americans could not put down. May 19, more American troops arrived at Matamoros. Armed and unarmed, they caroused about the city. Some troops came to the hospital looking for wounded Mexican officers. Undisciplined troops entered the homes of Mexicans, carrying off booty and terrifying families; Berlandier did hear that American officers punished soldiers who were guilty of such actions. At eight o'clock that night a fire broke out, set (it was assumed) by a drunken American soldier. Mexicans and Americans worked together to put out the flames and eventually succeeded. The morning of May 20, with the help of a Mexican traitor, American troops discovered hidden armaments; henceforth, the soldiers could not rest until they found all sources of arms, which increased their searches of private property. Berlandier credited General Taylor with trying to prevent the disorder and thievery of American soldiers, though with limited success. Berlandier's diary, which abruptly ends after twelve pages, concludes with the news that American ships were bringing a thousand troops to the Rio Grande, five hundred of whom were volunteers from Louisiana. A camp near the mouth of the river on the southern shore, at Burrita, was to hold two thousand troops.[3]

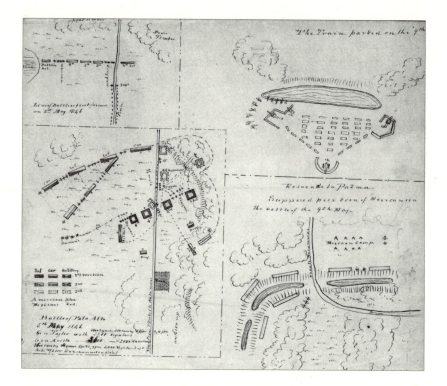

Figure 16. Battle of Palo Alto, 8th May 1846, by
Charles R. Glynn. Library of Congress.

One assumes, without any clear evidence from the Berlandier papers, that Berlandier's life was the same for the next few months, during the spring and early summer of 1846. Matamoros served as the headquarters for Taylor's army as it accumulated men and supplies, as well as steamboats, to make the advance into the interior to face the regrouped Mexican forces. During the summer, another revolution swept through Mexican politics; Santa Anna returned from exile and assumed control of the defense of Mexico against the United States. More troops had already been put on their way to the north; contrary to Santa Anna's wishes, General Mejia, and after him General Ampudia, determined to defend Monterrey from the American advance. During July, Taylor and the Army of Occupation journeyed upriver on their way to Monterrey to engage the Mexican army. Although an American garrison remained at Matamoros, and the Rio Grande had become an American river, day-to-day existence for the apothecary, physician, and scientist Berlandier must have returned to normal. What was normal for Berlandier was to journey, to explore, to feel the excitement of the scientific vagabond. Even though war was engulfing parts of Mexico, other parts were relatively untouched, hence fair game for the exploring scientist. Berlandier, intent on continuing his accumulation of data on the latitude of various places in Tamaulipas, decided to journey south once again, to visit various locales in the Mexican state of Tamaulipas, some of which he had seen on previous journeys, to use the best scientific instruments he could muster to determine exact geographic measurements, and, if possible, to pursue his quest into the states of Nuevo León and San Luis Potosí, west of Tamaulipas, for the same purpose.[4]

Berlandier's notes on the journey are restricted to scientific measurements, though his record allows us to see where and when he journeyed during the winter of 1846 to 1847. On this journey he retraced the route he had taken with Constantino Tarnava in 1830 from Matamoros to Ciudad Victoria, and from this city into the Sierra Madre toward Tula. He passed through Palmilla on November 30 and arrived at Tula four days later. The nights were clear, allowing for astronomical measurements. Berlandier used the sextant

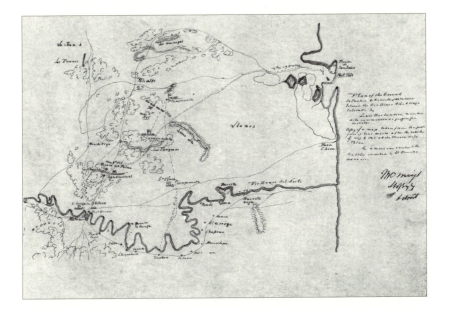

Figure 17. Plan of the ground situated to the north of Matamoras between the Rio Bravo & the Arroyo Colorado by Luis Berlandier. Library of Congress.

and an azimuth compass to take bearings on such celestial objects as Sirius, the Dog Star, and Rigel, the point of the southern foot of the constellation Orion, to determine latitude. After a few days taking measurements at Tula, he journeyed southwest into a region of the Sierra in which he had never been (at least according to extant manuscripts). Journeying for several days across an arid plateau, he arrived at Rancho de la Viga, where he took a measurement of Rigel in the clear December sky. On the ninth he arrived at the Ranchos de Buena-Vista, situated on the same arid plateau. It took several days of hard travel to cross a range of forbidding peaks that separated one flat tableland from another; he arrived at Peotillos on the twelfth. It took almost a week to travel through the inhospitable landscape from Peotillos to the Rancho de los Atascaderos, then the "Villa de la Soledad de los ranchos," and finally Ciudad de San Luis Potosí. It had been nineteen years since Berlandier had seen the city, which was on a cool, windy plateau that in December was not, thankfully, so subject to the blinding sun as in summer. Berlandier tarried for four days at San Luis Potosí, then proceeded north following the same trail that the Comisión de Límites had followed in 1827. Five leagues of travel brought him on Christmas Day, 1846, to the Hacienda del Peñasco. This hacienda was aptly named because of random craggy hills with stark cliffs nearby. Berlandier had explored these with General Terán in 1827, but he appears not to have taken the time in 1846; he was on the trail toward the Hacienda de Bocas the next day. The route passed through a canyon and an isolated rancho named for St. Anthony. From Hacienda de Bocas to Hacienda de Charcos was a journey of about a dozen leagues, which Berlandier accomplished in two days. At Charcos, Berlandier departed from the route of 1827 and turned northeast toward Matehuala. He traveled for three days through an arid land of ranchos dependent on grazing animals, and haciendas dependent on growing crops such as chili peppers. Berlandier appears to have stayed at Matehuala for over a month, taking a variety of celestial measurements and engaging in other unknown business. Matehuala was an old Spanish city not very far from the mines of Real de Catorce, which could have drawn Berlandier on visits of scientific interest. Departing Matehuala in February 1847, Berlandier journeyed east-northeast, crossing again the Sierra Madre, arriving after a fortnight to San Fernando. Berlandier stayed at San Fernando for perhaps a month or more before setting out for the Gulf Coast. The last entry in his journal is the note that he arrived at "Rancho du Mezquital sur la cote du Golfe du Mexique."[5]

By most accounts, the Mexicans had gone to war against the United States with optimism and confidence, fed by the rhetoric of their leaders, that the weak rabble north of the Nueces could not hope to be victorious. Defeat, that crushing blow to ideals and expectations experienced by vanquished Mexico, ensured that political chaos, already so prevalent in Mexican local, regional, and national affairs, grew in rancor and bitterness as old rivalries and unrequited jealousies infected social and political relationships in towns such as Matamoros. Jean Louis Berlandier, a leading citizen of the town, sufficiently wealthy and knowledgeable to be a force in local politics, moderate and humanistic enough to forbear engaging in character assassination and vengeance, found himself in the immediate postwar years victim of accusations by individuals not so discerning. Berlandier's character as a leading scientist of the valley of the Rio Grande was one reason for the rancor that he attracted. Just a few months after the conclusion of the war, Berlandier received a letter from Lt. J. D. Webster of the Topographical Corps of Engineers of the U.S. Army requesting that he respond to a series of questions regarding the meteorological conditions of life along the valley and coastline, especially the port at Brazos de Santiago. Based on the previous contacts the officers of the U.S. Army had with Berlandier, Webster knew that the Frenchman could read English. Whether or not Berlandier knew that Webster and his superior Colonel Davenport could read French is less certain; nevertheless, Berlandier wrote a lengthy response in French to the lieutenant's questions. He described in detail the various storms that had destroyed life and property along the river mouth and Gulf Coast during recent decades. Berlandier identified and described in detail what meteorologists today know as the hurricanes of 1829, 1831, 1835 (the Antigua Hurricane), 1837 (the Racer's Storm), and 1844. His matter-of-fact discussion with a recent enemy, providing scientific information to help the United States more effectively govern what until very recently had been under Mexican control, must have raised some eyebrows among diehard patriots and personal enemies.[6]

During the course of the day on Tuesday, November 20, 1849, while Berlandier was experimenting with a new meteorological instrument, the sympiesometer, a barometer without mercury invented by Scotsman Alexander Adie in the early 1800s, a messenger arrived from the consistory, interrupting the scientist with an official note from the chief of police, don Leonardo Manse. Berlandier, in an extensive journal of the event and its aftermath, wrote that when he saw who the note was from he was very worried, for he believed that the police chief was an infamous traitor of a past generation during the "epoch of independence," who held his position because of his willingness to participate in the crimes of the governor, don Jesús Cárdenas. With trepidation, Berlandier reluctantly heeded the official summons to go to the consistory (a building that formed the center of government in Matamoros); upon arriving he found himself under arrest for treason. In reality, according to his journal, the governor was avenging himself on Berlandier, a magistrate (alcalde) in Matamoros in 1849, for refusing to loan municipal funds to government officials and for suing to obtain redress after said officials endorsed a bill in his name for which he and the town of Matamoros became legally responsible. Berlandier found that he was not alone among important Matamoros residents charged with treason or other such vague crimes. Joining him were opposition editor Andres Trevino as well as the French vice-consul, the latter of whom was doubtlessly accused because of involvement on the wrong side in the endless conspiracies involving adventuring filibusters from Texas who had designs on northern Mexico. The vice-consul had not yet presented himself at the consistory. The instigator of the arrest of Berlandier and the other two men, Jesús Cárdenas, was himself an active conspirator in these affairs, having been almost a decade earlier the president of the short-lived Republic of the Rio Grande. Berlandier knew Cárdenas's history, of course, and in his journal branded him a traitor. The detained men were informed that they were to be escorted to the capitol of Tamaulipas, Ciudad Victoria, to face charges. While they awaited the escort, the three men wrote a petition to the governor protesting their arrest and the refusal of authorities to allow them to appear before a magistrate to learn the exact nature of the charges. Berlandier likewise requested the legal right to post bail, agreeing to appear under his own recognizance at Ciudad Victoria, but was refused. The delay in beginning the march continued because the French vice-consul refused to surrender to the authorities, claiming diplomatic immunity; the governor, chief of police, and commander of the military forces, Gen. Francisco Arelos, were afraid to force the issue and allowed the vice-consul to cross the Rio Grande to Brownsville. In his journal Berlandier derided the ludicrousness of the entire episode; General Arelos refused to set out for Ciudad Victoria until a sufficient force arrived; a few troops of infantry and cavalry were insufficient; he had to await the arrival of Lt. Col. Nicolás de la Portilla, in command of a cavalry regiment as well as three pieces of artillery. With such a formidable army, the two prisoners, Trevino and Berlandier, began a journey under coercion to Ciudad Victoria.[7]

Notwithstanding his concern for the illegality of the action and trepidation for what the future might bring, Berlandier, ever the scientist, took advantage of the journey to record his observations. They set out on November 20, journeying south through Tamaulipas, their initial destination being San Fernando. Berlandier had come this way on previous occasions, such as nineteen years before, also in autumn, under completely different circumstances, then traveling with his friend Constantino Tarnava under orders from General Terán. Nature knows little of politics, and science must eschew such temporal distractions. Berlandier's journal reveals something like joy in the beauties of late autumn evenings, the serenity of the sky and gentle zephyrs arriving from the south. He experienced a "great morning" on November 21; they journeyed to the small Laguna de Quijano, at which they bivouacked for the rest of the day because the trail south would offer little water or pasturage. While encamped at Quijano, Berlandier explored the environs. He noted that the huisache trees appeared abnormal, their branches perpendicular to the trunk; no other trees in the area mirrored this peculiar phenomenon. He also noted that the vegetation of trees appeared quite decimated; searching for the cause, he discovered numerous beetles, over an inch long, which he identified as part of the Longicornes family (order of Coleoptera). The night of November 22 was also tranquil, save for a strong breeze that blew in from the south-southeast. They bivouacked that evening at a hamlet, Saint Teresa, next to a small pond. The twenty-third began in like fashion, warm and dry after a cool and serene night in which the coyotes howled in the distance and the rippling pond water lapped at the banks next to the men's camp. But by the end of the day the wind had changed to the north and blew "furiously," heralding a storm. They took cover under the lee of a grove of trees. November 24, they arrived at the town of San Fernando, where luckily for Berlandier he was allowed the hospitality of a friend, Joaquin Garcia. Even so, Berlandier learned that the commander of the troops guarding him received a note by express courier from General Arelos warning that friends might help the scientist escape; Berlandier, however, was much too interested in clearing his name and casting infamy on his accusers to consider such an option. The morning of November 25, they proceeded on the route to Ciudad Victoria, initially descending toward a small, largely waterless creek, Las Chorreras. They found a small canyon in which to camp to shield them from the continuing strong breezes of the night. Water along the route was scarce, and that found was usually not potable; pasturage for the horses was similarly scant. They stayed the night of the twenty-sixth at the Rancho del Encinal, the hospitality of which Berlandier had enjoyed on the trail in previous years. Drought had prevailed for some time, and water and fodder were hard to come by, but the rancheros told them that the Mesa del Encinal, a broad plateau to the south, might afford some pasturage for the animals, which they found, during the course of the journey south, to be true. The evening of November 27 they arrived at Santander, where they visited "the ruins of the ancient palace of the Count de Sierra Gorda"; descendants of the first settlers showed the inquisitive visitors the sword of the count. The next day the escort and prisoners continued on to Padilla, traversing a wooded landscape that during the wet season would be marshy. Soon the elevation of the trail ascended to the Mesa de Solis, which spanned three leagues; on the other side was the Rancho de San Antonio, after which they came to the Río del Pílon, a pretty stream flowing through a deep gully with banks lined with elm trees. Crossing the river was especially difficult because of the steep bank on the opposite side. After a few leagues of travel through a wooded plain, they arrived at the Río Soto La Marina, also lined with beautiful arboreal vegetation. Arriving at Padilla, Berlandier and escort stayed in the same quarters as had representatives to the state congress when Padilla had been the capital of Tamaulipas, and where the emperor Iturbe had awaited execution in 1824. At Padilla, Berlandier requested and was given the chance to be escorted to the sepulcher of General Terán, where he meditated on the greatness and tragedy of his former friend and leader. The route from Padilla to the Río de Güemez was through a hilly, wooded landscape. After ascending and descending the deep, tree-lined banks of the Río de Güemez, they crossed a plain dotted with large cacti until they could spy in the distant valley the capital, Ciudad Victoria. As they awaited another military escort from the city, a sergeant was ordered to the city to ensure that the prisoners' quarters were made ready.[8]

Berlandier had during his journey to Mexico in the previous twenty years entered many towns and cities as part of a military procession; his entry into Ciudad Victoria was different only in that he was under escort, a prisoner. Fortunately, he got along with the dragoons charged with his detention; they mercifully hurried him to his quarters rather than to the alternative, to stand before His Excellency the Governor of the State of Tamaulipas. Berlandier and his partner in crime Trevino were retained in secure quarters to await their appearance before the governor, along with their accusers; several officers stayed with them acting as security guards. The soldiers and officers were, unlike the accusers, friendly to Berlandier, less a military escort than "travel companions." During their stay, friends from Ciudad Victoria visited the two men; others, with less benevolent motives, visited them as well, seeking dirt by which to earn the respect and monetary well-wishes of their duplicitous patrons. Another, more welcome, visitor was a member of the state senate, a well-known and generous lawyer, G. N. de Casares, who told Berlandier and Trevino that false correspondence, allegedly between them and revolutionaries in Matamoros, had been contrived to prove ostensibly their treasonous designs. Lawyer de Casares claimed to have evidence to prove the falsity of the accusations, which he would present to the authorities. De Casares said that he had discovered a web of forgery, including weapons sales to revolutionaries that involved individuals, including statesmen, in Tampico, Victoria, and Matamoros. Still Berlandier awaited justice. The prison guards departed, but he was to stay put without bail, without clear charges. Berlandier petitioned the governor "not to continue to violate the constitution" and to drop the charges. The governor, of course, did not respond; however, the local newspaper did, branding Berlandier and his associate guilty. A "few days after," Berlandier wrote, "we received by mail from Mexico, the newspapers of the capital." One paper, *El Guardia Nacional*, maintained by General Arista, the minister of war, included a letter by one Quintero Flores, deceased, upon which some of the charges against Berlandier were based; Raphael Chowell, who later investigated the matter in response to a secret letter sent to him by his imprisoned friend, discovered that the Flores letter had been forged. Meanwhile, Berlandier appealed to get some sort of legal judicial process to hear his defense. The trial kept being delayed, Berlandier wrote in his journal, because alcaldes that were to serve as judges refused to ingratiate themselves with the governor by holding trials on trumped-up charges. The supreme court, composed of three judges who were supporters of the governor, Berlandier believed, evaded and questioned and never quite recognized the plight of Berlandier and Trevino. Meanwhile, people and the press in Brownsville were providing counterevidence of the charges against Berlandier and Trevino, and the French foreign minister demanded answers as to why the French vice-consul had been implicated and had fled Matamoros to evade arrest. A few days after Christmas, Berlandier had dinner with several people, including Juan Molano, the principal alcalde of Victoria, who though a partisan of the governor, nevertheless told Berlandier that he was clearly innocent, and that he would arrange a meeting with the governor for Berlandier to make his defense. This Berlandier did, wading through the nonsensical charges and evidence that the governor presented; in the end, the governor finally relented and allowed the scientist his freedom.[9]

Berlandier made good use of his easy imprisonment and lengthy stay in Victoria by making a series of meteorological measurements. He considered the situation of Victoria at the foot of the Sierra Madre, and how it was very hot in summer and cold in winter, and blamed the winds for the phenomenon: summer equatorial winds proved very hot, and the winds of winter blowing from the peaks proved very cold. Berlandier had brought with him a Celsius thermometer and a cyanometer with which he recorded observations of temperature and the color of the sky. He analyzed the course and speed of the winds; changes in atmospheric conditions; moisture in the air, fogs, and frosts; and the relative impact of coastal and inland (mountain) winds on the climate of Ciudad Victoria. Berlandier interviewed locals about what they typically experienced, noting that untrained weather-watchers could provide accurate observations for scientists. Berlandier used his own experience of observing snow-covered peaks in Savoy to make an assessment respecting the infrequent snowfall of the Sierra Madre; he believed relative snow on different peaks had something to do with the direction of the range and the impact of the winds. The mountains also influenced the direction and the course of the winds and their effect on the people of Victoria and surrounding communities.[10]

After a forced stay of about a month at Ciudad Victoria, Berlandier was finally allowed to depart on January 2, 1850; he and Trevino journeyed north to Matamoros in the coming days. They hurried along, traveling by day and at night under the illumination of the moon, for fear that the governor's duplicity would manifest itself in the appearance of his "janissaries." They allowed themselves one good night's rest at Palmillas, where a local priest, remarkably well informed about the politics and lies involving Governor Cardenas and Berlandier, told the latter that the letter implicating Berlandier had indeed been forged. When Berlandier arrived at Matamoros on January 7, he went immediately to the federal district judge indicating his availability to answer questions (and clear his name) should the issue be raised in the future, and since he had not yet had the chance to answer the charges in a court of law.[11]

This entire episode had a profound, even fatal, impact upon Berlandier. That he had not been able to clear himself wholly of all the false charges, but rather had to suffer the lack of finality of Governor Cardenas's decision to drop charges, could hardly be tolerated by a man of Berlandier's ilk. To be sure, as a scientist he had a sense of the broad patterns of time, of the transcendence of existence, not as readily perceived by a person, such as the governor, who lives for the day and for whatever the day might bring him in power and wealth. Berlandier showed as well time and again during his many journeys throughout Mexico and Texas that he had the patience to wait for a rational conclusion. But this incident had been so numbingly irrational! His arrest and imprisonment had distorted reality, disrupted his life, made the political machinations and chaos that had practically destroyed Mexico part of his own experience. He could not but think badly about his adopted country and the government under which he lived. Somehow it must be put right. If he could not find justice in Tamaulipas, then perhaps at the capital of Mexico, where he had old friends who could support him in his appeals for justice. After the passage of a year, he began to make plans for a journey to Ciudad Mexico.[12]

Jean Louis Berlandier set out on his final journey with perhaps a guide or two, in mid-spring of 1851—on what date, even what month, is unclear. Berlandier's proclivity to record his experiences on the trail finally came to a halt; if he kept a journal of this trip, it succumbed to the elements with him. Berlandier had never returned to the capital of Mexico after his initial visit there in 1827; then the path taken by the Comisión de Límites was north of the city across the Mexican Plateau of Anahuac to San Luis Potosí, Monterrey, and Laredo. Berlandier knew the path to Ciudad Victoria much better, so he set out south of Matamoros through Tamaulipas toward San Fernando. The journey to San Fernando, which could take a few days to a week of travel depending on the haste of the traveler, the weather, and the level of streams and rivers, took Berlandier through Moquete and across the Arroyo del Tigre, south through ranchos and haciendas rarely visited by travelers, ultimately to the village of San Fernando. Berlandier was usually careful about crossing rivers, choosing ferries or rafts when available, especially during the flood season. The foolhardiness of crossing a swollen river on horseback can hardly be explained, save that Berlandier must have felt an urgency to reach his destination. The current of rushing water is deceptive, and during flooding the water is brown, not transparent. Neither horse nor rider can see what hazards lie in wait. Berlandier had seen enough horses drown on his journeys to know the danger; yet he took the risk, and died.

As the ayudante told Couch two years later, "Berlandier left Matamoras sometime in 1851 . . . for the purpose of visiting the City of Mexico to obtain a claim of his against the general government. When crossing on horseback the Rio San Fernando at a town of the same name 90 miles south of Matamoras, he was drowned, aged about 45 years."[13]

Finality came only after years of observation, experiences, experiments, travels, and trials and errors. Jean Louis Berlandier was a collector par excellence, possessed of a mind fascinated with the grand as well as the minutiae, maintaining a child's fascination for human and natural history long after he was considered a savant. Typical of his time, he was out to gain knowledge of everything natural, which meant, of course, that he was knowledgeable about much but an expert at little. He was an able but not a superb botanist, as revealed by the exasperation and impatience of the Swiss botanists who received some fruits of his collecting. He was a good physician for the people of Matamoros because of his knowledge of regional materia medica and his generous personality, yet he had no formal medical training. He was interested in geology but lacked the training in mineralogy of his friend Raphael Chowell. He made astronomical and meteorological observations but not with the expertise of the leader of the Comisión de Límites, General Terán. Not a trained historian, he had nevertheless a general historical interest in the Mexican past, and he had the heart of an antiquarian.

Berlandier's greatest gift was his ability to wonder and his willingness to try new experiences. Having never journeyed beyond the Rhône River valley, in 1826 he departed the places of his youth for a journey to Mexico that would last a lifetime. Arriving at the Pánuco River on Mexico's eastern coast, he journeyed to Mexico City, then north across the Mexican Plateau paralleling the Sierra Madre to the Rio Grande. From 1828 until his death in 1851, Berlandier lived in the Rio Grande valley and traveled into Texas as far as the Trinity River. He made numerous excursions in Mexico and southern Texas, exploring, gathering, examining, and recording. All the while he observed northern Mexico and southern Texas through the eyes of a newcomer, a person not quite prepared for what he is about to see. This fascination and wonder mark the many writings of Jean Louis Berlandier.

Berlandier was a prolific writer, penning works not only in his native French but also in his adopted language of Spanish. Trained as a botanist, he was proficient in Latin as well, and he knew how to carry on a conversation in English. His published manuscripts are few and include accounts of the scientific and botanical discoveries of the Comisión de Límites, narrative accounts of the Comisión, a descriptive analysis of the Indian tribes of Texas, and an account of bear and buffalo hunting in Texas. More extensive are Berlandier's handwritten manuscripts neatly prepared for distribution or publication. He wrote and copied in a clear hand his many narratives of journeys in notebooks. His notebooks also include clearly written records and accounts of medical, botanical, astronomical, meteorological, and zoological phenomena. His encyclopedic writings reveal a savant uninterruptedly interested in every facet of information that came within his purview, and the compulsive need to record all that he saw, studied, analyzed, and considered. The office of his apothecary shop in Matamoros, when Lieutenant Couch first saw it almost two years after the savant's death, was crowded with knowledge and attempts to know.

Berlandier's youth and young adulthood growing up in extreme eastern France and Geneva, studying pharmaceuticals, plants, animals, and other topics of scientific interest to the early-nineteenth-century naturalist, prepared him for the extremes in climate and geography that he found in the Rio Grande valley. Many of the flora and fauna specimens that he discovered in Texas had a recognizable genus, even if the specific species escaped his recognition. The mountainous environment of central and northern Mexico was drier, the landscape more forbidding, than what he experienced in the Alps, yet he felt sufficiently acclimated to the mountains to find a sense of familiarity with and understanding of the Mexican cordilleras. The waters of the Sierra Madre flowing east toward the Gulf of Mexico were as clear as the waters of mountain streams descending from the western slopes of the Alps. The zigzag thalwegs of the creeks west of San Antonio and among the cordilleras of Tamaulipas were like the many gorges of the Jura Mountains and Alps of Savoy. The extremes of heat and humidity of the Pánuco, Rio Grande, Brazos, and Trinity River valleys were unexpected, to be sure; but the environment of the Rhône valley, Lake Geneva, and the Alps was also moist if cold. Bright blue days when the skies were clear over the Alps were like the startling blue of a cloudless day during the Texas winter.

Berlandier's experiences in France and Geneva had not quite prepared him, however, for the varieties of human habit, custom, and behavior that he experienced in Mexico and Texas. Even if he had read Baron Humboldt's account of Mexico or perused the various idealistic ponderings about the "noble savage" by Rousseau and Montaigne, books could hardly prepare a person of culture and learning for the uninhibited nakedness; gaudily painted and tattooed bodies; strange combination of ferocity and timidity;

contradictory expressions of honor and duplicity; unexpected hospitality, friendliness, and passivity in a people at times given to bloodlust, even cannibalism, toward enemies; and naïveté toward the intentions of other humans at the same time that they could show an unequaled understanding of the natural environment—all of which characteristics he found in the American Indian. The culture of these people seemed out of place and from a different time. Reading Plutarch could never prepare a person to meet a living Caesar. Likewise reading about distant cultures in time, when the Europeans were in their infancy, paled next to the experience of riding with on the hunt, standing next to examining the stars, and sitting with smoking the pipe such persons struggling to survive in the stingy environment of northern Mexico and southern Texas. Berlandier's journals, drawings, and maps document his experiences on the verge of space and time, of the known and unknown, of civilization and wilderness. "Mingling with the confusion of nomadic men," he wrote in November 1828, about his joining the Comanche hunt up the Guadalupe River, "I believed myself to have been transported to those remote eras in which men lived in the fields, being still in the infancy of a future civilization." If the Comanches were like the Europeans of centuries past, at the same time their character, customs, and humanness suggested that these people would in time develop a society and culture akin to that of the western Europeans.[14]

The Indian's physical nakedness, Berlandier discovered, was akin to the bareness of human character and emotions. What clothes the Indian wore were stripped from the animals he killed and ate. The manufacture of cloaks, moccasins, and breechcloths was done on the spot; garments were neither purchased nor sold. The blood of the buffalo as well as that of slain enemies, mixed with the dirt of everyday living, clung to the bodies of Indian men and women. Their oil was bear grease, their makeup was taken directly from earth. Privacy was scarcely a concern; bodily functions were too normal and regular to hide; sexuality lay just behind the breechcloth and was exerted without formality, often without forethought. Passion, anger, joy, and fear were quickly revealed rather than pent up to exude in greater force later. Friendship and hatred were spontaneous expressions, which cut to the quick of human relations, eschewing the facade and mystery of the more sophisticated. Codes of behavior came not from scriptures, philosophers, and teachers, but from the writings and teachings of nature. Warriors wore the feathers of the eagle, dignified and majestic in flight, caring for and protecting its young, fierce in battle and tireless in the hunt; the woolly head and horns of the buffalo, unwilling to surrender, fighting to the last breath, meeting death with unequaled courage; the skin of the wolf, sly and aggressive, unrelenting in its pursuit of prey, dominating and controlling the pack; and the magical pouhahantes, the medicine of nature, the reliance upon which could guide the warrior's missiles to their target and check those of the enemy.

The indigenous people that Berlandier got to know through study and experience lived along the courses of streams and rivers, as have most humans throughout time. The seemingly endless flow of water from highlands to lowlands oriented, provided a sense of direction for people who lacked maps, save those in their minds. Descending waters through hot and arid lands attracted beasts and their prey, who with lance, bow and arrow, or carbine provided sustenance in a land that was stingy in its blessings. Rivers were meeting places of peoples, friends to communicate and trade with as well as foes to steal from, scare away, and kill. In a land with few trees, riverbanks provided shade and comfort. When scattered pools gave out in late summer, streams and rivers offered water, even if but a trickle, to quench thirst. Hunters and explorers, travelers and discoverers, warriors and messengers, traders and trappers, ascended and descended such rivers as the Pánuco, Rio Grande, Nueces, San Antonio, Guadalupe, Colorado, Brazos, Trinity, San Fernando, and Purificación.

John Louis Berlandier's earliest memories were of the river. The existence, course, origins, nature, and mysteries of the river gave meaning, purpose, and continuity to his life. Berlandier's youth and young adulthood were spent living in eastern France on the border with Switzerland and Savoy and in Geneva, the Rhône River emerging from Lake Geneva after its rush west from the Swiss Alps. The Rhône carved a channel into his memory that remained with him during his many travels, when he would examine the rivers of America in light of his memories of the Rhône and the other important river of his youth, the Arve, flowing from the highlands that reach a pinnacle in Mount Blanc. Berlandier spent half of his life living next to the Rhône and Arve, growing up at the frontier Fort l'Ecluse and pursuing science in Geneva, and half of his life living next to the Río Bravo del Norte, the Rio Grande, exploring the rivers north into Texas and south into Mexico, and practicing medicine at the frontier town of Matamoros. The valleys of the Rio Grande and Rhône were vastly different in the look and taste of the water, in the surrounding environs, in the peoples who inhabited the valleys, in history and culture. Yet rivers arrive from a similar

source, highlands, the descending waters of the Alps of Switzerland forming the Rhône, and the waters of the southern Rockies of America forming
the Rio Grande.

A drowning man can hardly think clearly of what is most fitting in
death as in life. Berlandier died as he lived, among river waters. Throughout
his life, the river yielded knowledge both tacit and explicit. Even as a child
he realized that his society of the early nineteenth century was dependent
upon the river for so much: political and cultural boundaries; water to
quench the thirst of the land; the means to send and receive information, to
transport oneself by boat to and from. The river was a route and a barrier,
a giver and taker of life, beautiful and always the same, yet dangerous and
never tame. Where the water came from and where it went were questions
never adequately answered, for Berlandier knew that within the shifting
riverbanks were countless and unique varieties of life and refuse—some
things good and pure, other things old and decayed. The contrariness and
variety that never halted, continuing on over the years, from long ago in the
past extending far into the future, suggested metaphors of life and being,
creation and destruction, and analogies to one's own existence, one's birth
and death, coming from somewhere uncertain, returning to a place equally
unknown. The mysteries of nature suggested by the river and its valley, its
source in the mountains and conclusion at the sea, drove Berlandier to seek
answers as traveler and scientist. His training was as a botanist, but his avo-
cation was explorer, observer, and recorder of experience.

Death is an experience for which no one can adequately prepare; nevertheless, humans spend a lifetime anticipating this one moment in time. To
learn about, to observe, to witness the deaths of others are means of anticipating and preparing for one's own death. As a well-traveled physician, Jean
Louis Berlandier had many experiences with the deaths of others. Cholera
and yellow fever carried off scores of people in the valley of the Rio Grande
during the 1830s and 1840s, when Berlandier was a physician at Matamoros.
Berlandier often treated infants who developed infantile tetanus, which was
generally fatal. The most compelling story of death found in the writings of
Berlandier involved the death of his friend the Quicapú—when and where
the death occurred is unclear, but probably in the early 1830s in Matamoros.
This man, who had presented such a fierce appearance when Berlandier first
saw him in the spring of 1828, who was a skilled hunter, who was generous
with his game, who taught Berlandier so much about indigenous life and culture, who exacted terrible revenge against his wife and her lover—this friend

lay dying. Berlandier wrote about his friend's demise as an aside to a discussion about indigenous religious beliefs in "Indigenes nomades." Possibly the Quicapú succumbed to the yellow fever epidemic of 1829 or the cholera epidemic of 1833 that swept through the Rio Grande valley. The Quicapú did not die instantly, as there was a deathbed scene at which Berlandier was present. By this time the Quicapú had grown tired of his indigenous religion, which had allowed him to justify murderous revenge; he had given up those ways where, "once offended" by treachery, he believed his soul "to be defiled" and sought "at any cost and at every moment to destroy those who" had injured him. Guilt engendered by a growing knowledge of Christianity and the behavior and teachings of his friend Berlandier convinced the Quicapú to repent and to convert. How long he believed in Christ's redemption before he accepted baptism is not recorded; perhaps he had been coming to the belief for some time; perhaps it occurred when he realized the nearness of death. The brief account in Berlandier's "Indigenes nomades" indicates that the Quicapú was under Berlandier's care, indeed resided in the physician's house. Berlandier encouraged his mortally ill friend to be baptized. The Quicapú consented, and Berlandier sent for the only sanctioned baptizer in Matamoros, a Catholic priest. Berlandier watched as his friend "rejoiced at the sight of the priest" who was to administer the sacrament. Berlandier, who was not a proselyte, recorded what he observed: a former "savage" of the plains had willingly accepted the sacrament that would cleanse his sins and mark him as Christ's own. Missionaries and other commentators before, during, and after this time tended to explain Indian conversion to Christianity as superficial, even inspired by mercenary reasons. The Quicapú, however, believed that he had nothing to gain from baptism but his eternal soul. Berlandier observed his dying friend to "invoke the Most High" when the priest sprinkled the holy water upon his head. The invocation was "in his own way," in his own language and according to the beliefs of his youth, "indicating the sky as His place of residence."[15]

Twenty years later, in a baptism of sorts, Berlandier joined his friend. Rushing water surrounded, then darkness overcame, the final thoughts of the savant of Matamoros.

Appendix One

Fauna and Flora Named for Jean Louis Berlandier

Fauna

Rana berlandieri: Rio Grande Leopard Frog
Gopherus berlandieri: Texas Tortoise
Taxidea taxus berlandieri Baird: Mexican badger
Thryothorus ludovicianus berlandieri Baird: Berlandier's wren

Flora

Abutilon berlandieri: Berlandier's Indian mallow
Acacia berlandieri guajillo: Berlandier acacia
Acleisanthes obtusa (Choisy) Standl.: Berlandier's trumpets
Astragalus crassicarpus var. berlandieri Barneby: Berlandier's groundplum
Berlandiera lyrata Benth.: lyreleaf greeneyes
Berlandiera texana: Texas greeneyes
Calia erythrosperma Terán & Berland.: Sophora secundiflora (Ortega) DC, Texas mountain laurel
Calylophus berlandieri Spach: Berlandier's sundrops
Citharexylum berlandieri B.L. Rob.: Berlandier's fiddlewood
Ebenopsis ebano Berl. Barneby & Grimes: Texas ebony
Echinocereus berlandieri (Engelm.) Haage: Berlandier's hedgehog cactus
Ehretia anacua (Terán & Berl.) I. M. Johnst.: anacua
Esenbeckia berlandieri Baill. ex Hemsl.: Berlandier's jopoy
Fraxinus berlandieriana: Berlandier ash
Hamatocactus bicolor (Terán & Berl.) I. M. Johnst.: twisted-rib cactus
Jatropha cathartica Terán & Berl.: Berlandier's nettlespurge

Juglans microcarpa Berl.: little walnut
Leucophyllum frutescens (Berl.) I. M. Johnst.: Texas barometer bush
Linum berlandieri var. berlandieri: Berlandier's yellow flax
Lobelia berlandieri A. DC.: Berlandier's lobelia
Lycium berlandieri Dunal: Berlandier's wolfberry
Mahonia tinctoria (Terán & Berl.) I. M. Johnst.: mahonia
Mimosa pigra L. var. berlandieri: giant sensitive plant

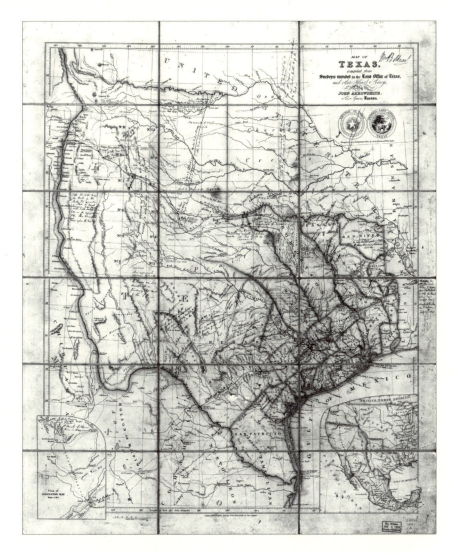

Figure 18. Map of Texas, compiled from surveys recorded in the Land Office of Texas and other official surveys by John Arrowsmith. Library of Congress.

Appendix Two

◯

Chronology of the Journeys of Jean Louis Berlandier

1826

October 14: Departed Le Havre de Grace, France, for Mexico, aboard the *Hannah Elizabeth*.

December 24: Arrived at Tampico, Mexico.

1827

February–March: Round-trip journey from Tampico to Tuxpan via Laguna de Tamiahua.

May 3: Departed Tampico for Mexico City.

May: Journeyed up the Pánuco River into the Huasteca, the mountains and valleys of the Sierra Madre Oriental, to the towns of Tantoyuca, Zacualtipán, Real del Monte, and Mexico City.

June–September: Small journeys in and about Mexico City.

October: Journeyed west to Toluca, south to Tenancingo, east to Cuernavaca, and north, returning to Mexico City.

November 10: Departed Mexico City for Texas on El Camino Real de Tierra Adentro.

November: Journeyed across the Mexican Plateau from Mexico City to San Juan del Río, Querétaro, San Miguel de Allende, Dolores Hidalgo, Guanajuato, and San Felipe.

December: Continued journeying across the Mexican Plateau from San Luis Potosí, Charcas, Catorce, Ventura, to Saltillo.

1828

January: Journeyed through Sierra Madre from Saltillo east to Monterrey.

February: Journeyed from Monterrey north to Villaldama, Carrizal, Lampazos, to the Río Salado.

March: Journeyed from the Río Salado to the Rio Grande and across into Texas, then on the Old Béxar Road from Laredo to the Nueces River, the Frio River, and the Medina River, to San Antonio (Béxar). Journeyed up the San Antonio River to its source.

April: Journeyed from San Antonio east on the Gonzales Road to Gonzales on the Guadalupe River, after which continued on the Atascosito Road, crossing the Colorado River to San Felipe de Austin on the Brazos River.

May: Journeyed east from the Brazos River on Camino de la Magdalena to the Trinity River.

June: Return journey west from the Trinity River on the Camino de Arriba, crossing the Little Brazos, Brazos, Colorado, and Guadalupe Rivers to San Antonio.

Late summer: Journeyed from San Antonio to Laredo and from Laredo to Matamoros, Mexico.

October–November: Journeyed from Matamoros to San Antonio.

November–December: Journeyed in company with Comanche Indians up the San Antonio River to the Medina River valley, northwest to the Guadalupe River valley, south to upper Frio River, through the Cañon de don Juan de Ugalde, then northeast following the Medina back to San Antonio.

1829

February: Journeyed from San Antonio to Goliad on the San Antonio River and Guadalupe Victoria on the Guadalupe River, then back to San Antonio.

March: Journeyed from San Antonio to Cópano on Aransas Bay; boarded schooner *Paumone* for New Orleans; arrived at New Orleans in late March.

May: Return journey from New Orleans to Cópano to Goliad to San Antonio.

July to August: Journeyed from San Antonio to Matamoros by way of Laredo.

December: Journeyed from Matamoros to Boca Chica, then across the Rio Grande to Brazos de Santiago.

1830

April: Journeyed from Matamoros to Monterrey.

August–September: Journeyed from Matamoros to Brazos de Santiago.

October–November: Journeyed from Matamoros through Tamaulipas to Moquete on the Arroyo del Tigre, San Fernando on the Río San Fernando, Santander Jiménez, Padilla, and Güemez, crossing the Río del Pilon and Río Purificación, and Río de Santa Engracia, to Ciudad Victoria.

November: Journeyed from Ciudad Victoria into the Sierra Madre to Jaumave, Palmillas, and Tula.

November–December: Journeyed from Tula through the Sierra Madre, halting to explore Cerro Partido on the way to Santa Bárbara, then on to Ciudad de Horcasitas, stopping to try to ascend Bernal de Horcasitas, continuing along the Tamesí River to the Pánuco River and Tampico.

December 1830–January 1831: Journeyed from Tampico south to Tantoyuca.

1831

January–February: Journeyed from Tampico up the Pánuco and Tamesí Rivers and along Laguna de Altamira to Altamira, from which proceeded north to Aldama past the Sierra de Tamaulipas and Sierra de los Maratines to Bejarano, then Soto La Marina, from which followed the descending Río Soto La Marina across Mesa del Encinal to Encinal, then San Fernando to Matamoros.

December: Journeyed from Matamoros south to Ciudad Victoria.

1834

April–May: Journeyed from Matamoros across Rio Grande to Arroyo Colorado, across the Nueces River to San Patricio, then Goliad, and up the San Antonio River to San Antonio.

June: Journeyed from San Antonio across the Medina River, Arroyo Hondo, Frio, and Nueces, continuing on past Laguna Espantosa to and across the Rio Grande to San Juan Bautista.

June–July: Journeyed from San Juan Bautista along the descending Rio Grande past Palafox and Laredo, across the Río Salado to Revilla, on to Mier, Camargo, Reynosa, then Matamoros.

November–December: Journeyed from Matamoros to Laredo to San Antonio.

1835

October–November: Journeyed from Matamoros across the Moquete River to San Fernando.

1838

June: Journeyed from Matamoros south to Moquete and Barreales, then east following the Moquete River past Caracal to the Gulf of Mexico.

1845

July and September: Journeyed from Matamoros to Point Isabel.

1846

March: Journeyed from Matamoros to Arroyo Colorado to meet with Gen. Zachary Taylor.

November–December: Journeyed from Matamoros to Ciudad Victoria into the Sierra Madre to Tula, Peotillos, and San Luis Potosí, then on to Matehuala.

1847

Febuary–March: Journeyed from Matehuala to San Fernando to Matamoros.

1849

November–December: Journeyed from Matamoros south to San Fernando, then Santander, across the Río del Pílon and Río de la Marina to Padilla, across Río de Güemez to Ciudad Victoria.

1850

January: Journeyed from Ciudad Victoria to Palmillas to Matamoros.

1851

Spring: Journeyed from Matamoros to Río San Fernando, where Berlandier drowned.

Notes

Introduction

1. Jean Louis Berlandier, *Journey to Mexico During the Years 1826 to 1834*, trans. Sheila M. Ohlendorf, Josette M. Bigelow, Mary M. Standifer, 2 vols (Austin: Texas State Historical Association, 1980). The only modern biographical study, (though not a full biography) of Berlandier in English is Samuel Wood Geiser, *Naturalists of the Frontier* (Dallas, TX: Southern Methodist University Press, 1948). A brief biographical study in Spanish is Luis Sánchez Osuna, *Explicando a Berlandier* (Programa de Apoyo a las Culturas Municipales y Comunitarias, 2004). Berlandier's life has been put to fiction in James Kaye, *Berlandier—A French Naturalist on the Texas Frontier* (Bloomington, IN: Trafford, 2010).

2. "Indigenes nomades des Etats Internes d'Orient et d'Occident des territoires du Nouveau Mexique et des deux Californies," in the possession of Gilcrease Museum, has been translated as *The Indians of Texas in 1830*, edited by John C. Ewers (Washington, D.C.: Smithsonian Institution Press, 1969). Berlandier and Chowell's collaboration was published as *Diario de viage de la Comision de Limites* (Mexico City: Juan R. Navarro, 1850).

3. A similar example comes from the life and journeys of the English botanist Thomas Nuttall, who relied on the guide, Mr. Lee, who had the intuitive ability to survive the Oklahoma wilderness of 1819. See Russell M. Lawson, *The Land between the Rivers: Thomas Nuttall's Ascent of the Arkansas, 1819* (Ann Arbor: University of Michigan Press, 2004).

4. Berlandier, *Journey to Mexico*, 10, 421, 464; Louis Agassiz, *Contributions to the Natural History of the United States of America* (Boston, MA: Little Brown, 1857), 447; Smithsonian Institution Archives Record Unit 7052, Jean Louis Berlandier Papers (hereafter cited as SIAJLB): Jean Louis Berlandier Watercolor Paintings, Drawings, and Photographs Taken of These Works, Boxes 12 and 13.

5. SIAJLB has a tremendous amount of material on Berlandier's work in the physical sciences and meteorology. For his theories about changes in rivers and coastal waters, see Berlandier, *Journey to Mexico*, 58–59, 465.

6. Many of Berlandier's maps have been reproduced digitally by Yale University's Beinecke Library at digital images from the Jean Louis Berlandier Papers, Beinecke Library, Yale University: http://hdl.handle.net/10079/fa/beinecke.berlandi (hereafter cited as DIBL).

7. See Ewers, *Indians of Texas*.

Chapter One

1. Biographical portraits of Couch include Edward F. Kennedy Jr., *Lt. Darius Nash Couch in the Mexican War* (Taunton, MA: Old Colony Historical Society, 1977), and A. M. Gambone, *Major-General Darius Nash Couch: Enigmatic Valor* (Baltimore, MD: Butternut and Blue, 2000). For information on Couch's arrival to Texas and Mexico in 1846, see Kennedy, *Lt. Darius Nash Couch*, 5–6. Manuscript documents describing Couch's journey to Mexico are found in the Spencer Fullerton Baird Papers, Unit 7002, Box 18, Smithsonian Institution Archives (hereafter cited as SIA), and Couch manuscripts at the Old Colony Historical Society, Taunton, Massachusetts. For Comanche unrest, see David J. Weber, *The Mexican Frontier, 1821–1846: The American Southwest under Mexico* (Albuquerque: University of New Mexico Press, 1982), chap. 5.

2. For Drummond and other nineteenth-century botanists, see Geiser, *Naturalists of the Frontier* and Russell M. Lawson, ed., *Research and Discovery: Landmarks and Pioneers in American Science*, vol. 1, sec. 3, "Botany" (Armonk, NY: Sharpe, 2008). Martino Sessé and Josepho Mociño, *Flora mexicana*, 2nd ed. (Mexico City: Oficina Tipográfica de la Secretaría de Pomento, 1894).

3. William H. Emory, *Report on the United States and Mexican Boundary Survey*, vol. 1 (Washington, D.C.: Nicholson, 1857), 54.

4. *Encyclopedia Americana*, (New York: Encyclopedia Americana, 1920), 26: 99–100; Spencer Baird to George B. McClellan, November 6, 1852, in *Spencer Fullerton Baird: A Biography*, ed., William H. Dall, (Philadelphia, PA: Lippincott, 1915), 282–83; Darius Couch to Spencer Baird, February 16, 1853, SIA.

5. Couch to Baird, February 16, 1853, March 14, 1853, November 16, 1854, SIA. According to Osuna, *Explicando a Berlandier*, 14, the widow's name was Beatriz Concepción Villaseñor. Osuna writes (p. 55) that Joseph Henry had heard about Berlandier and his death and had sent Couch to purchase the collection. There is, however, no evidence upon which to base this conclusion; indeed, Couch's letters to Baird indicate that the discovery of the collection was through happenstance and the decision to purchase it was his own. Berlandier's manuscripts in natural and human history are found at the Smithsonian Institution Archives and Yale's Beinecke Library.

6. Couch to Baird, February 16, 1853, March 14, 1853, November 16, 1854, SIA.

7. Baird to Couch, March 1 and March 17, 1853, SIA. An edited version of the March 1 letter appears in Dall, *Spencer Fullerton Baird*, 296–97.

8. Couch to Baird, March 14, 1853, SIA; Ewers, *Indians of Texas*, 20.

9. Couch to Baird, March 14, 1853, and January 30, 1855, SIA.

10. Couch to Baird, March 14 and April 17, 1853, SIA; Darius Nash Couch, "Notes of Travel," Old Colony Historical Society, 23 (1), 23 (3), 26, 32, 33 (1), 33 (2), 33 (4), 33 (5), 37, 40–41, 43–45. The social organization of ranchos and haciendas is discussed in Armando C. Alonzo, *Tejano Legacy: Rancheros and Settlers in South Texas, 1734–1900* (Albuquerque: University of New Mexico Press, 1998), 44–45, 80–81.

11. Couch, "Notes of Travel," 42, 49, 50; Couch to Baird, April 17, 1853, January 30, 1855, SIA.

12. Couch, "Notes of Travel," 53; Couch to Baird, November 16, 1854, SIA; Berlandier, *Journey to Mexico*, 282.

13. Kennedy, *Lt. Darius Nash Couch*, 6, 9–11, 14, 17, 23, 24; John R. Bartlett, *Personal Narrative of Explorations and Incidents in Texas, New Mexico, California, Sonora, and Chihuahua, Connected with the United States and Mexican Boundary Commission*, vol. 2 (New York: D. Appleton, 1854), chap. 42. Captain Hitchcock was "Chief Director of the Hospitals at Buena Vista," according to William H. Robarts, *Mexican War Veterans* (Washington, D.C.: Brentanos, 1887), 7.

14. Couch to Baird, November 16, 1854, January 30, 1855, SIA; Bartlett, *Personal Narrative*, chap. 42.

15. Couch to Baird, May 14, 1853, January 30, 1855, SIA; Kennedy, *Lt. Darius Nash Couch*, 7. For Comanche raids into the Chihuahuan Desert, see Pekka Hämäläinen, *The Comanche Empire* (New Haven, CT: Yale University Press, 2008), 222–24.

16. Couch to Baird, November 16, 1854, SIA.

17. Ibid.

18. Couch to Baird, May 16, 1853, November 16, 1854, SIA.

19. Couch's translation of Berlandier, "Hunting the Bear and Buffalo in North Western Texas," is found at the Old Colony Historical Society. Couch's "Notes on Travel" has editorial comments indicating the intent to prepare a formal manuscript.

20. Couch to Baird, November 16, 1854, SIA; Ewers, *Indians of Texas*, 20–21. The jealous politics of the American and Swiss scientific communities relating to Berlandier and his collection are recounted in C. H. Muller, "Introduction," in Berlandier, *Journey to Mexico*, xvii–xxi.

Chapter Two

1. Contemporary accounts of the Alps and the Rhône include Robert Bakewell, *Travels*, vol. 2 (London: Longman, 1823); William B. Sprague, *Letters from Europe in 1828* (New York: Leavitt, 1828); K. Baedeker, *Switzerland and the Adjacent Portions of Italy, Savoy and the Tyrol* (Coblenz: Baedeker, 1864); Daniel Wilson, *Letters from an Absent Brother*, vol. 2 (London: Wilson, 1827); W. E. Frye, *After Waterloo* (London: Heinemann, 1908).

2. William Siborne, *The Waterloo Campaign, 1815* (Westminster, UK: Constable, 1895), 775–77; Frederick Beach and George Rines, eds., *The Americana: A Universal Reference Library* (New York: Scientific American, 1912); Caesar, *The Conquest of Gaul*, trans. S. A. Handford (Harmondsworth, UK: Penguin Books, 1951).

3. Augustin Pyramus de Candolle, *Mémoires et souvenirs* (Geneva: Cherbuliez, 1862), 336–38; Siborne, *Waterloo Campaign*, 775–77.

4. Sources to recreate the history of Fort l'Ecluse include the site of Fort L'Ecluse, http://www.lesitedefortlecluse.org/; Fort L'Ecluse, http://www.leaz.fr/webleaz/mairies.leaz/leaz/fortlecluser.htm; Fort l'Ecluse: Site Officiel, http://www.fortlecluse.fr/.

5. For Gesner, see Daniel J. Boorstin, *The Discoverers* (New York: Random House, 1983), 429. The experiences of American scientists upon the highest peak in northeastern America are recreated in Russell M. Lawson, *Passaconaway's Realm: Captain John Evans and the Ascent of Mount Washington* (Hanover, NH: University Press of New England, 2002).

6. Information on Geneva as a timepiece-making center of Europe comes from David S. Landes, *Revolution in Time: Clocks and the Making of the Modern World* (Cambridge, MA: Harvard University Press, 1983), 237–44.

7. Frye, *After Waterloo*, 107–9; *Encyclopedia Britannica*, 4th ed., s.v. "Geneva"; *Encyclopedia Britannica*, 11th ed., s.v. "Pierre Prévost"; Clarissa Campbell Orr, "Romanticism in Switzerland," in *Romanticism in National Context*, ed. Roy Porter and Mikuláš Teich (Cambridge: Cambridge University Press, 1988); "Letter of 1 June 1816," Mary Shelley, University of Pennsylvania, Department of English, http://www.english.upenn.edu/Projects/knarf/MShelley/1jun16.html#geneva.

8. Berlandier, *Journey to Mexico*, 159, 185, 293.

9. *American Journal of Science and Arts* 2, vol. 35 (1863): 1–16; Julius von Sachs, *History of Botany*, trans. Henry Garnsey (Oxford: Clarendon Press, 1890), 126–39.

10. Boorstin, *Discoverers*, 442–44; Jacob Jones, "Linnaeus in America," in Lawson, *Research and Discovery*, 138–40; Muller, "Introduction," in Berlandier, *Journey to Mexico*, xvii–xxi.

11. Muller, "Introduction," in Berlandier, *Journey to Mexico*, xvii–xviii. Berlandier's paper is found at the Gray Herbarium Library, Harvard University. Campanulaiees, or Campanulales, are a subclass of Asteridae.

12. The history of American botany is found in Lawson, *Research and Discovery*, 1:133–81.

13. Fred W. Stauffer, Rodrigo Duno de Stefano, and Laurence J. Dorr, et al., "Contribución del Dr. José María Vargas a las ciencias botánicas en Venezuela," *Acta Botánica Venezuelica* 29, no. 1 (2006): 135–64; Muller, "Introduction," in Berlandier, *Journey to Mexico*, xvii–xviii; Sessé and Mociño, *Flora mexicana;* Paul C. Standley, *Trees and Shrubs of Mexico*, Contributions from the United States National Herbarium, vol. 23, pt. 1. (Washington, D.C.: Government Printing Office, 1920), 13–15.

14. Wilfrid Blunt, *The Art of Botanical Illustration: An Illustrated History* (New York: Dover, 1992), 169–72; Standley, *Trees and Shrubs*, 15–17.

15. Muller, "Introduction," in Berlandier, *Journey to Mexico*, xvii–xviii.

16. Candolle, *Mémoires et Souvenirs*, 337.

17. Sprague, *Letters from Europe*, 45–46; Berlandier, *Journey to Mexico*, 1; Geiser, *Naturalists of the Frontier*, 34.

Chapter Three

1. Berlandier, *Journey to Mexico*, 1–2.
2. Ibid., 2–4.
3. Ibid., 4–9.
4. Ibid., 10–12, 14. French naturalist the Comte de Lacépède wrote *Histoire naturelle des poissons*. The Smithsonian Institution Archives possesses a watercolor sketch by Berlandier of a dorado.
5. Ibid., 12–19, 24; "Journal Descriptive of the Route from New York to Real Del Monte by Way of Tampico," *London Magazine*, February 1826, 146–47.
6. Berlandier, *Journey to Mexico*, 20–21; Herbert E. Bolton and Thomas M. Marshall, *The Colonization of North America, 1492–1783* (New York: Kessinger, 2005), 37; Hubert H. Bancroft, *History of the North Mexican States and Texas* (San Francisco, CA: Bancroft, 1884), 11–12; Lyman D. Platt, "The Escandón Settlement of Nueva España," http://www.rootsweb.ancestry.com/~mextam/escando1.htm; David J. Weber, *The Spanish Frontier in North America* (New Haven, CT: Yale University Press, 1992), 34–35; "Tamaulipas," http://www.vsalgs.org/stnemgenealogy/tamaul.html#Tampico; Arthur C. Benke and Colbert E. Cushing, *Rivers of North America* (Maryland Heights, MO: Academic Press, 2005), 1032.
7. Paul Horgan, *Great River: The Rio Grande in North American History* (Austin: Texas Monthly Press, 1984), 422–40.
8. Berlandier, *Journey to Mexico*, 20–26. The Beinecke Library at Yale University possesses several drawings executed by Berlandier that detail Tampico and its adjacent lagoon and river. In one drawing, "Plan de la ville de Tampico province de Tamaulipas," Berlandier incorrectly identified the lagoon to the north of Tampico as the Lagune de Tampico. The drawing notes its source as an earlier drawing by the alcalde of Tampico. On another drawing, however, "Ville de Santa Anna de Tampico," Berlandier correctly identified the lagoon as the Laguna del Carpintero. See DIBL.
9. Berlandier, *Journey to Mexico*, 20–34. The poverty of many inhabitants of the lower Pánuco is illustrated in a drawing executed by Lino Sánchez y Tapia, "Barra del Rio de Panuco," DIBL. This drawing, based on Berlandier's observations, and perhaps sketches, shows a fort at the mouth of the river built by the Spanish when they invaded Mexico in 1829.
10. Berlandier, *Journey to Mexico*, 34–38.
11. Ibid., 22, 24; "Vue des fortifications de Tampico," "Untitled map depicting fortifications in Tampico," "Borrador de los vistas de los fortines de Tampico," DIBL.
12. Berlandier, *Journey to Mexico*, 39–46. Berlandier's watercolor of the huisache is found between pp. 42 and 43.
13. Ibid., 46–52.
14. Ibid., 56–59.
15. Ibid., 60–61; "Berlandier's Records of Shipments and Collections," in appendix 2, vol. 2, Berlandier, *Journey to Mexico*.

16. My comments on Berlandier's equipment are informed by the Berlandier Papers and Couch Papers, Smithsonian Institution Archives, as well as Spencer F. Baird, *Directions for Collecting, Preserving, and Transporting Specimens of Natural History* (Washington, D.C.: Smithsonian Institution, 1852).

17. Berlandier, *Journey to Mexico*, 62–63.

18. Ibid., 64.

19. Ibid., 64–65. For "nighuas," see John C. Phillips, "A Year's Collecting in the State of Tamaulipas, Mexico," *Auk: Quarterly Journal of Ornithology* 28 (1911): 67–89.

20. Berlandier, *Journey to Mexico*, 66–69. Berlandier's discussion of mimosa, mesquite, and huisache trees is found in "A estudiar en viajes: Histoire naturelle des plantes employees dans la matiere medicals les arts, etc. des Mexicains anciens et modernes," Papers of Jean Louis Berlandier, Archives, Gray Herbarium Library, Harvard University (hereafter cited as GHA). Lino Sánchez y Tapía's watercolor of mesquite is reproduced in Berlandier, *Journey to Mexico*, between pp. 186 and 187.

21. Berlandier, *Journey to Mexico*, 70–81; Joseph Burkart, "Residence and Travels in Mexico," in *Foreign Quarterly Review* 19 (1837): 270–71.

22. Berlandier, *Journey to Mexico*, 81–90; Benke and Cushing, *Rivers of North America*, 1039; Alexander de Humboldt, *Political Essay on the Kingdom of New Spain* (London: Longman, 1811), 2:107.

23. Berlandier, *Journey to Mexico*, vol. 2, chaps. 1–2; Berlandier, "Observations Cyanometriques," no. 1, 1827–1830, SIAJLB, Box 1, Folder 12; William E. Burns, *Science in the Enlightenment: An Encyclopedia* (Santa Barbara, CA: ABC-Clio, 2003), 252–53; Mechthild Rutsch, "Natural History, National Museum and Anthropology in Mexico," *Perspectivas Latinoamericanas* (2004), 94, 101, http://www.nanzan-u.ac.jp/LATIN/4rutsch.pdf; Graciela Zamudio, "El Real Jardín Botánico del Palacio Virreinal de la Nueva España," *Ciencias* 68 (December 2002), http://www.ejournal.unam.mx/cns/no68/CNS06803.pdf; Humboldt, *Political Essay*, 43, 49, 51; Standley, *Trees and Shrubs*, 13.

24. Berlandier, *Journey to Mexico*, 121–31; Humboldt, *Political Essay*, 22.

25. Berlandier, *Journey to Mexico*, 147–71; "Berlandier's Records of Shipments and Collections," in appendix 2, vol. 2, Berlandier, *Journey to Mexico*; Berlandier, "A estudiar en viajes," GHA. For Francisco Hernández, see Simon Varey, ed., *The Mexican Treasury: The Writings of Dr. Francisco Hernández* (Palo Alto, CA: Stanford University Press, 2000).

26. Berlandier, *Journey to Mexico*, 171–74. Humboldt, *Political Essay*, 121ff, provides a detailed history of the Desagüe.

Chapter Four

1. A good discussion of the politics of the Boundary Commission is Ohland Morton, "Life of General don Manuel de Mier y Terán," *Southwestern Historical Quarterly Online* 47 (July 1943–April 1944), 29–47, http://texashistory.unt.edu/ark:/67531/metapth146054/m1/33/?q=ohland.

2. Berlandier, *Journey to Mexico*, 180–207; José María Sánchez, "A Trip to Texas in 1828," trans. Carlos E. Castañeda, *Southwestern Historical Quarterly Online* 29, no. 4 (1926), http://www.tshaonline.org/shqonline/apager.php?vol=029; Morton, "Life of General don Manuel de Mier y Terán," 41–42, http://texashistory.unt.edu/ark:/67531/metapth146054/m1/45/?q=ohland. Berlandier's beautiful watercolor of *Passiflora* is found in Berlandier, *Journey to Mexico*, between pp. 202 and 203.

3. Berlandier, *Journey to Mexico*, 208–10.

4. Ibid., 207–28. Hacienda de Buenavista was the site of the American victory over Mexican troops in February 1847.

5. Ibid., 228–42.

6. Ibid., 242–46; Ewers, *Indians of Texas*, 51, 165, fig. 17, painting by Lino Sánchez y Tapía after a sketch by Berlandier, original at Gilcrease Museum.

7. Berlandier, *Journey to Mexico*, 246–61; T. N. Campbell and T. J. Campbell, *Indian Groups Associated with Spanish Missions of the San Antonio Missions National Historical Park*, Special Report No. 16 (San Antonio: Center for Archaeological Research, University of Texas, 1985), http://www.nps.gov/history/history/online_books/saan/campbell/contents.htm; Gill Ediger, "The Bustamante Area," http://www.cavetexas.org/mexico/PDF/carriza11.pdf; Sánchez, "Trip to Texas," 250.

8. Berlandier, *Journey to Mexico*, 257.

9. Ibid., 257, 265–68, 287.

10. Manuel de Mier y Terán, *Texas by Terán: The Diary Kept by General Manuel de Mier y Terán on his 1828 Inspection of Texas*, ed. Jack Jackson, trans. John Wheat, with botanical notes by Scooter Cheatham and Lynn Marshall (Austin: University of Texas Press, 2000), 139, 209.

11. Sánchez, "Trip to Texas," 267, 277–78. Osuna, *Explicando a Berlandier*, 94–95, writes that José María Sánchez y Tapia was brother to Lino Sánchez y Tapia, that the former died in 1834, and that the latter died in 1838.

12. Berlandier, *Journey to Mexico*, 257–58, 268–70; Ewers, *Indians of Texas*, 42, 65, 156, pl. 1, original at Gilcrease Museum.

13. Berlandier, *Journey to Mexico*, 303.

14. Ibid., 271–79, 415; Sánchez, "Trip to Texas," 251–53; Geiser, *Naturalists of the Frontier*, 37; Birds, trans. C. B. R. Kennerly, SIAJLB, Box 14. Berlandier's sketch of Tasajillo, *Opuntia leptocaulis* is found in Berlandier, *Journey to Mexico*, between pp. 424 and 425.

15. Berlandier, *Journey to Mexico*, 278–80; Sánchez, "Trip to Texas," 254–55.

16. Berlandier, *Journey to Mexico*, 281–82; Sánchez, "Trip to Texas," 255.

17. Berlandier, *Journey to Mexico*, 122, 283; Sánchez, "Trip to Texas," 257; Geiser, *Naturalists of the Frontier*, 37.

18. Berlandier, *Journey to Mexico*, 285, 289–97, 413; Sánchez, "Trip to Texas," 257–59; "The Five Spanish Missions of Old San Antonio," *Lone Star Junction*, http://www.lsjunction.com/facts/missions.htm.

19. Berlandier, *Journey to Mexico*, 293–97, 302; Sánchez, "Trip to Texas," 266. Berlandier's drawing of persimmon (*Diospyros*) is found in Berlandier, *Journey to Mexico*, between pp. 424 and 425.

20. Mier y Terán, *Texas by Terán*, 27–39, 96–101, 207–9.

21. Berlandier, *Journey to Mexico*, 301–5, 310; Sánchez, "Trip to Texas," 266; Mier y Terán, *Texas by Terán*, 43–45; Geiser, *Naturalists of the Frontier*, 38.

22. Berlandier, *Journey to Mexico*, 303–7; Sánchez, "Trip to Texas," 267; Mier y Terán, *Texas by Terán*, 45–46. Berlandier's drawing of *Clematis* is found in Berlandier, *Journey to Mexico*, between pp. 274 and 275. American Indians referred to some species of *Clematis* as the pepper vine, which had reputed medicinal qualities. See Lady Bird Johnson Wildflower Center, www.wildflower.org/plants/result.php?id_plant=CLLI2.

23. Berlandier, *Journey to Mexico*, 307–13; Sánchez, "Trip to Texas," 267–70; Mier y Terán, *Texas by Terán*, 47–52; Ewers, *Indians of Texas*, 158, pl. 5, painting by Lino Sánchez y Tapía based on a sketch by José María Sánchez, original at Gilcrease Museum.

24. Berlandier, *Journey to Mexico*, 313–16; Sánchez, "Trip to Texas," 270; Mier y Terán, *Texas by Terán*, 52–56.

25. Berlandier, *Journey to Mexico*, 317–18; Sánchez, "Trip to Texas," 271; Mier y Terán, *Texas by Terán*, 56–57.

26. Berlandier, *Journey to Mexico*, 321; Sánchez, "Trip to Texas," 271; Morton, "Life of General don Manuel de Mier y Terán," 122, http://texashistory.unt.edu/ark:/67531/metapth146054/m1/140/.

27. Berlandier, *Journey to Mexico*, 316; Sánchez, "Trip to Texas," 271–72; Kenneth E. Hendrickson Jr., "Brazos River," Handbook of Texas Online, http://www.tshaonline.org/handbook/online/articles/BB/rnb7.html; "An Analysis of Texas Waterways," Texas Parks and Wildlife, http://www.tpwd.state.tx.us/publications/pwdpubs/pwd_rp_t3200_1047/14_c_tx_brazos.phtml. On Terán's return through the area the following winter, he wrote of the potential of the Brazos to host ships of all sizes; he heard and believed that the source of the Brazos was near the Red River (indeed, both rivers rise in eastern New Mexico). Mier y Terán, *Texas by Terán*, 145.

28. A description of Terán's wagon is found in Mier y Terán, *Texas by Terán*, 221–22.

29. Berlandier, *Journey to Mexico*, 322–23; Sánchez, "Trip to Texas," 272–73; Mier y Terán, *Texas by Terán*, 61–62.

30. Berlandier, *Journey to Mexico*, 323.

31. Ibid., 323–24; Sánchez, "Trip to Texas," 273.

32. Berlandier, *Journey to Mexico*, 323; Sánchez, "Trip to Texas," 273; Mier y Terán, *Texas by Terán*, 62–63; Zoe Merriam Kirkpatrick, *Wildflowers of the Western Plains* (Austin: University of Texas Press, 1992), 94.

33. Berlandier, *Journey to Mexico*, 323–24; Sánchez, "Trip to Texas," 273–74; *Texas by Terán*, 63–64, 144–45, 222. When Terán visited Groce's plantation the following winter, he saw no evidence that Groce mistreated his slaves.

34. Berlandier, *Journey to Mexico*, 325–26; Sánchez, "Trip to Texas," 274–75; Mier y Terán, *Texas by Terán*, 64–66.

35. Berlandier, *Journey to Mexico*, 320, 326–28; Ewers, *Indians of Texas*, 45; Sánchez, "Trip to Texas," 275–77; Mier y Terán, *Texas by Terán*, 67–68; Steven Foster and James A. Duke, *A Field Guide to Medicinal Plants and Herbs of Eastern and Central North America*, 2nd ed. (Boston, MA: Houghton Mifflin, 2000), 18, 89, 304–5. The history of the use of dogwood and creosote for healing is traced in Virgil J. Vogel, *American Indian Medicine* (Norman: University of Oklahoma Press, 1970), 296–97, 299–301.

36. Berlandier, *Journey to Mexico*, 327–28; Sánchez, "Trip to Texas," 277; Mier y Terán, *Texas by Terán*, 69–70.

37. Berlandier, *Journey to Mexico*, 328–30; Sánchez, "Trip to Texas," 277–79; Mier y Terán, *Texas by Terán*, 70–71; Morton, "Life of General don Manuel de Mier y Terán," 126, http://texashistory.unt.edu/ark:/67531/metapth146054/m1/144/; Elliott Coues, ed., *The Expeditions of Zebulon Montgomery Pike*, 3 vols. (New York: Harper, 1895), 2:708.

Chapter Five

1. For Thomas Nuttall, see Lawson, *Land Between the Rivers*. The example of the Kickapoos hunting with Lewis and Clark comes from Arrell M. Gibson, *The Kickapoos: Lords of the Middle Border* (Norman: University of Oklahoma Press, 1975), 92.

2. Sánchez, "Trip to Texas," 280–81; Mier y Terán, *Texas by Terán*, 73.

3. Berlandier, *Journey to Mexico*, 330–31; Sánchez, "Trip to Texas," 279; Mier y Terán, *Texas by Terán*, 71; Geiser, *Naturalists of the Frontier*, 38.

4. Berlandier, *Journey to Mexico*, 331–32, 334; Ewers, *Indians of Texas*, 158–59, pl. 6, painting by Lino Sánchez y Tapía based on a sketch by José María Sánchez, original at Gilcrease Museum.

5. For information on the Kickapoos, see Gibson, *Kickapoos*.

6. Berlandier, *Journey to Mexico*, 332–33.

7. Ibid., 333–35; Ewers, *Indians of Texas*, 52, 105–7, 112–13, 126, 144, 149, 159–60, pls. 7 and 9, painting by Lino Sánchez y Tapía based on a sketch by José María Sánchez, originals at Gilcrease Museum; Mier y Terán, *Texas by Terán*, 61.

8. Berlandier, *Journey to Mexico*, 335–37.

9. Ibid., 339–40; Ewers, *Indians of Texas*, 143–44. For the Mexican poppy, see Berlandier, "Des plantes usuelles chez les Indiens du Mexique," GHA.

10. Berlandier, *Journey to Mexico*, 340–42.

11. Ewers, *Indians of Texas*, 89, 94–95, 143–44. Berlandier's portrait of the mountain laurel is found in Berlandier, *Journey to Mexico*, between pp. 524 and 525.

12. Ibid., 5, 31, 32–33, 43, 44, 50, 51, 63, 156, 157, pls. 2 (painting by Lino Sánchez y Tapía based on a sketch by José María Sánchez) and 3 (painting by Lino Sánchez y Tapía based on a sketch by Berlandier), originals at Gilcrease Museum; Berlandier, *Journey to Mexico*, 343, 345; Geiser, *Naturalists of the Frontier*, 39; Brian Delay, "The Wider World of the Handsome Man: Southern Plains Indians Invade Mexico, 1830–1848," *Journal of the Early Republic* 27 (Spring 2007), 92.

13. Berlandier, *Journey to Mexico*, 331–32, 343.

14. Ibid., 344. Berlandier and Chowell's *Diario de viage* provides a similar account of the journey. Darius Nash Couch at some point translated the Spanish (somewhat freely) in the manuscript "Hunting the Bear and Buffalo in North Western Texas." Translated from the Spanish of Louis Berlandier of the Mexican Boundary Commission. The Beinecke Library, Yale University, has the manuscript account— "Voyage a les parties N. O. du Texas, Nov–Dec, 1834" (WA MSS S-330, #47)— of the journey published in *Diario de viage*. It is, however, inexplicably misdated as 1834; the journey took place in 1828. A recent account of this journey in the context of Comanche history is Gerald Betty, *Comanche Society: Before the Reservation* (College Station: Texas A&M University Press, 2005), chap. 2.

15. Berlandier, *Journey to Mexico*, 344–45, 460; Ewers, *Indians of Texas*, 90–91.

16. Berlandier, *Journey to Mexico*, 345–47.

17. Ibid., 348–49; Foster and Duke, *Medicinal Plants*, 281; Ewers, *Indians of Texas*, 46.

18. Foster and Duke, *Medicinal Plants*, 248; Berlandier, *Journey to Mexico*, 349–51; Hämäläinen, *Comanche Empire*, 169.

19. Berlandier, *Journey to Mexico*, 351–53; English botanist and explorer John Bradbury had a similar experience with skunk prepared by French voyageurs; Bradbury was unwilling to try the delicacy. See John Bradbury, *Travels in the Interior of North America in the Years 1809, 1810, and 1811* (London: Sherwood, Neely, & Jones, 1817). For another account of Berlandier's views of the skunk, see Elliot Coues, *Fur-Bearing Animals: A Monograph of North American Mustelidæ* (Washington, D.C.: Government Printing Office, 1877), 236.

20. Berlandier, *Journey to Mexico*, 353–57; Robert H. Thonhoff, "Arredondo, Joaquin de," *Handbook of Texas Online*, http://www.tshaonline.org/handbook/online/articles/AA/far18.html.

21. Berlandier, *Journey to Mexico*, 355–64; T. R. Fehrenbach, *Comanches: The Destruction of a People* (Cambridge, MA: Da Capo Press, 1994), 228.

22. Berlandier, *Journey to Mexico*, 364–65.

Chapter Six

1. Couch, "Notes of Travel," 55, 60; Emory, *Report*, 69.

2. Belknap's comment is quoted in Russell M. Lawson, *The American Plutarch: Jeremy Belknap and the Historian's Dialogue with the Past* (Westport, CT: Praeger, 1998), 125.

3. Montaigne, "Of Cannibals," in *The Complete Essays of Montaigne*, trans. Donald M. Frame (Stanford, CA: Stanford University Press, 1958).

4. Ewers, *Indians of Texas*, 33, 37, 41, 48, 55–58, 62; Berlandier, *Journey to Mexico*, 460; Jedidiah Morse, *A Report to the Secretary of War of the United States on Indian Affairs* (New Haven, CT: Converse, 1822), 69.

5. Berlandier, *Journey to Mexico*, 348, 450–61. An example of a colonial account of New England Indian remedies for rattlesnake bite is John Josselyn, *New-Englands Rarities Discovered* (London: G. Widdowes, 1672), and *Two Voyages to New-England* (London, 1674); John Josselyn, *Colonial Traveler: A Critical Edition of Two Voyages to New-England*, ed. Paul Lindholdt (Hanover, NH: University Press of New England, 1988).

6. Arrowsmith's map is reproduced at http://www2.1ib.virginia.edu/exhibits/lewis_clark/exploring/ch4-30.html. Humboldt's map is reproduced by the Library of Congress at http://memory.loc.gov/cgi-bin/map_item.pl?data=/home/www/data/gmd/gmd4/g4410/g4410/ct000554.sid&style=gmd&itemLink=r?ammem/gmd:@field(NUMBER+@band(g4410+ct000554))&title=General%20chart%20of%20the%20kingdom%20of%20New%20Spain%20betn.%20parallels%20of%2016%20%26%2038%3csup%3e0%3c%2fsup%3e%20N.%20from%20materials%20in%20Mexico%20at%20commencement%20of%20year%20of%201804%20%2f%20by%20Humboldt. Zebulon Pike's maps are reproduced in Coues, *Expeditions*. The University of Tulsa archives and special collections have Tanner's map of North America, which can be accessed online at "Maps of the American West," http://www.lib.utulsa.edu/Speccoll/collections/maps/tanner/tanner1.htm. Berlandier discussed these maps in Berlandier, *Journey to Mexico*, 365–66.

7. Berlandier, *Journey to Mexico*, 369–71.

8. Ibid., 370, 373.

9. Ibid., 373–82, 552; Ewers, *Indians of Texas*, 7, 14–15, 162, 165, fig. 16, pl. 15, painting by Lino Sánchez y Tapía, and pl. 16, painting by Lino Sánchez y Tapía based on a sketch by Berlandier, originals at Gilcrease Museum; Mier y Terán, *Texas by Terán*, 152; Berlandier, "Vista del Presidio de Golia antes Bahia del Espiritu Santo" and "Plan de la caserne de la Compaignie Presidiale," DIBL. See also Albert S. Gatschet, *The Karankawa Indians, The Coast People of Texas* (Cambridge, MA: Peabody Museum of American Archeology and Ethnology, 1891).

10. Berlandier, *Journey to Mexico*, 369–72, 382–84; Mier y Terán, *Texas by Terán*, 149–50. Berlandier had visited a Tonkawa village up the Guadalupe River the preceding April. Berlandier, "Ruta de Goliad a Guadalupe y la Vaca," DIBL.

11. Berlandier, *Journey to Mexico*, 384–90.

12. Ibid., 390–92; Carol A. Lipscomb, "Karankawa Indians," The Handbook of Texas Online, http://www.tshaonline.org/handbook/online/articles/KK/bmk5.html.

13. Berlandier, *Journey to Mexico*, 391–94, 396.

14. Ibid., 394–98; François-René vicomte de Chateaubriand, *Atala; or the Love and Constancy of Two Savages in the Desert*, trans. Caleb Bingham, 2nd ed. (Boston, MA: Samuel Armstrong, 1814), 6–7.

15. The historical background of New Orleans is found in Berlandier, *Journey to Mexico*, 399–403.

16. Berlandier, *Journey to Mexico*, 396–400, 404–5.

17. Ibid., 400, 405.

18. Ibid., 400–4.

19. Ibid., 402–3.

20. Ibid., 405–6.

21. Ibid., 407–10. The herb of the Chenopodiaceae family that Berlandier discovered was perhaps *Rivina vernalis*, which he described in *Memorias de la Comision De Limites. Historia natural. Botanica*, written by himself and Manuel Mier y Terán (Matamoros, 1832), reproduced in the appendix of Berlandier, *Journey to Mexico*, 1980 edition. Berlandier executed a watercolor of the species of *Lantana*, which he named *Lantana rubra*, reproduced in Berlandier, *Journey to Mexico*, between pp. 410 and 411.

Chapter Seven

1. Berlandier, *Journey to Mexico*, 412.

2. Ibid., 412–14.

3. Ibid., 414–22; Geiser, *Naturalists of the Frontier*, 36–37; *Memorias de la Comision de Limites. Jatropha cathartica* Terán & Berl. is now called Berlandier's nettlespurge.

4. Berlandier, *Journey to Mexico*, 423–26; Weber, *Spanish Frontier*, 194. Information about José de Escandón comes from Alonzo, *Tejano Legacy*, chap. 2, and Lyman D. Platt, "The Escandón Settlement of Nueva España," http://www.rootsweb.ancestry. com/~mextam/escand01.htm.

5. Berlandier, *Journey to Mexico*, 429–32.

6. Berlandier, *Journey to Mexico*, 426–29; Ewers, *Indians of Texas*, 165 and fig. 17— painting by Lino Sánchez y Tapía—original at Gilcrease Museum; Mier y Terán, *Texas by Terán*, 169. Emory, *Report*, 67.

7. Berlandier, *Journey to Mexico*, 433–44; Mier y Terán, *Texas by Terán*, 176.

8. Berlandier, *Journey to Mexico*, 439–44; "Journal, Aug. 13/30–Feb. 28/31," GHA; Berlandier, "Miscellaneous Documents Pertaining to Jean Louis Berlandier," Uncat WA MS 178, Beinecke Rare Book and Manuscript Library (hereafter cited as BRBML).

9. Berlandier, *Journey to Mexico*, 462; Edward O. Moll, "Gopherus berlandieri (Agassiz, 1857)—Texas Tortoise," *Sonoran Herpetologist* 16 (2003): 38–39. Brazos de Santiago changed very little over the space of twenty years, between when Berlandier saw it and William Emory described it. See Emory, *Report*, 54, 58–59.

10. Berlandier, *Journey to Mexico*, 442, 444–46.

11. Ibid., 449–50.

12. Berlandier, *Journey to Mexico*, 449–55; Berlandier and Chowell, *Diario de viage*, 236; Berlandier, "Vue des Cerro de la Silla prise de la Ciudad de Cadereyta" and "Le Cerro de la Silla vue prise entre Monterey et la parage nommé la Parra," DIBL.

13. Berlandier, *Journey to Mexico*, 67, 421, 449–50, 456–61. A reproduction of Berlandier's guayacán is found in Berlandier, *Journey to Mexico*, between pp. 456

and 457. For the Texas ebony, see USDA, Natural Resources Conservation Service, *Plants Database*, http://plants.usda.gov/java/profile?symbol=EBEB.

14. Berlandier, *Journey to Mexico*, 463–65, 521; Berlandier, "Etat de Tamaulipas," "Llanos del Sacramento," "Jurisdiction de la ville de Matamoros," "Matamoros," "Marais sales situes dans les environs de Matamoros," "Untitled map depicting the route between San Fernando and Matamoros," DIBL. Berlandier's manuscript "Voyage pour reconnoitre les principaux points de l'Etat de Tamaulipas," GHA, includes field sketches he made of the topography of various places along the route, not included in the published *Journal to Mexico*. SIAJLB, Box 1, Folders 6 and 10. See also John W. Tunnell Jr. and Frank W. Judd, *The Laguna Madre of Texas and Tamaulipas* (College Station: Texas A&M, 2002).

15. Berlandier, *Journey to Mexico*, 465–67; Berlandier, "Untitled map depicting the route between San Fernando and Matamoros," DIBL; John W. Thieret et al., *National Audubon Society Field Guide to North American Wildflowers, Eastern Region* (New York: Knopf, 2001), 477. Seventeenth-century English scientist John Josselyn learned from the Abenaki Indians of Maine that the fat of the rattlesnake was a useful application to relieve joint and muscle pains. Berlandier journeyed on this route again in October and November 1835, as recorded in his astronomical notes, SIAJLB, Box 1, Folders 6 and 10. Berlandier, *Journey to Mexico*, between pp. 466 and 467, reproduces Berlandier's drawing of tornilla.

16. Berlandier, *Journey to Mexico*, 467–68; Berlandier, "Untitled map depicting the route between San Fernando and Matamoros," DIBL. SIAJLB, Box 1, Folder 10.

17. Berlandier, *Journey to Mexico*, 468–69; Berlandier, "Untitled map depicting the route between San Fernando and Matamoros," DIBL. Berlandier's sketch of San Fernando was the basis for a well-executed drawing of San Fernando by his Matamoros friend Lino Sánchez y Tapia—"Villa de San Fernando tomado del Norte," DIBL.

18. Berlandier and Chowell, *Diario de viage*, 182–90; Berlandier, "Voyage pour reconnoitre les principaux points de l'Etat de Tamaulipas," GHA; Platt, "Escandón Settlement of Nueva España," http://www.rootsweb.ancestry.com/~mextam/escando2.htm; Berlandier, *Journey to Mexico*, 535–36; Oakah L. Jones, *Los Paisanos* (Norman: University of Oklahoma Press, 1996), 65; Gobierno Municipal de Jimenez (official site), http://www.jimenez.gob.mx/municipio.asp. The Smithsonian National Museum of American History has a Blunt theodolite in its physical sciences collection: http://americanhistory.si.edu/collections/surveying/object.cfm?recordnumber=997496. Berlandier's brief note on the mountains he could see from Santander is at SIAJLB, Box 1, Folder 4, No. 2. Berlandier, "Untitled map depicting roadways between Victoria and Santander," DIBL.

19. Berlandier and Chowell, *Diario de viage*, 190–94.

20. Ibid., 194–99; Berlandier, *Journey to Mexico*, 449–50. Berlandier, "Untitled map depicting roadways between Victoria and Tula," DIBL; "Observations barometriques faites durant l'expedition de Tamaulipas," SIAJLB, Box 1, Folder 10. Berlandier's cenizilla is now known as the Texas barometer bush. Berlandier's beautiful

watercolor is reproduced in Berlandier, *Journey to Mexico,* between pages 246 and 247. Mexican Route 101 mirrors Berlandier's route.

21. Platt, "Escandón Settlement," http://www.rootsweb.ancestry.com/~mextam/ escando2.htm; Berlandier and Chowell, *Diario de viage,* 199–202; Berlandier, "Untitled map depicting roadways between Victoria and Tula" and "Untitled map depicting roadways between Santa Barbara and Tula," DIBL.

22. Berlandier and Chowell, *Diario de viage,* 202–3; Berlandier, *Journey to Mexico,* 472– 75, 477; Berlandier, "Untitled map depicting roadways between Victoria and Tula" and "Untitled map depicting roadways between Santa Barbara and Tula," DIBL.

23. Berlandier, *Journey to Mexico,* 172, 475–81, and for Xochicalco, see 166–67; Berlandier, "Untitled map depicting roadways between Santa Barbara and Tula" and "Puerto de Boquillas," DIBL; Botanica, *Trees & Shrubs* (San Diego, CA: Laurel Glen, 1999), 152–54, 666; Thieret et al., *Field Guide to North American Wildflowers,* 492–93. Berlandier's drawings of the artifacts at Tula are found at BRBML.

24. Berlandier, *Journey to Mexico,* 481–84; Berlandier, "Untitled map depicting roadways between Santa Barbara and Tula" and "Observations barometriques faites durant l'expedition de Tamaulipas," SIAJLB, Box 1, Folder 10.

25. Berlandier, *Journey to Mexico,* 484–89. For Prévost and Lyell, see Gabriel Gohan, *A History of Geology,* rev. and trans. Albert V. Carozzi and Marguerite Carozzi (New Brunswick, NJ: Rutgers University Press, 1991), 140. For D'Aubuisson, see Archibald Geikie, *The Founders of Geology* (London: Macmillan, 1905), chap. 8. Berlandier's sketch "Cerro Partido: Volcan del Charburo cerca de la villa de Sta Barbara" is found at DIBL.

26. Berlandier, *Journey to Mexico,* 489–91; Berlandier, "Vista del Bernal y valle de Orcasitas tomada desde la Sierra de Santa Barbara," DIBL.

27. Berlandier, *Journey to Mexico,* 491–93; Berlandier, "Observations barometriques faites durant l'expedition de Tamaulipas," SIAJLB, Box 1, Folder 10.

28. Berlandier, *Journey to Mexico,* 494–96; Burns, *Science in the Enlightenment,* 196; Lawson, *Passaconaway's Realm,* 88, 103; Berlandier, "Vista del Mont-Bernal desde el Camino al W. de los ranchos de San Juan," DIBL.

29. Berlandier, *Journey to Mexico,* 496–99.

30. Berlandier and Chowell, *Diario de viage,* 227–32. Was Micheltorena, otherwise unidentified, Manuel Micheltorena, Santa Anna's companion and chief of staff in the Mexican War? See Cadmus M. Wilcox, *History of the Mexican War* (Washington, D.C.: Church News, 1892), 218. Micheltorena was also for a time governor of California before the Mexican War, see Theodore H. Hittell, *History of California,* vol. 2 (San Francisco, CA: Stone, 1898).

31. Berlandier, *Journey to Mexico,* 500–503; Berlandier, "Untitled map depicting roadways and landmarks around El Carrizo and Altamira," DIBL.

32. Berlandier, *Journey to Mexico,* 500–508; Berlandier, "Untitled map depicting roadways and landmarks between Presas and La Palma," DIBL. Berlandier's *Quercus tropicae* was not published; the accepted name is *Quercus oleoides,*

common name *Encino prieto*. See Victoria Schlesinger, *Animals and Plants of the Ancient Maya* (Austin: University of Texas Press, 2002), 264–65.

33. Berlandier, *Journey to Mexico*, 508–11; Berlandier, "Untitled map depicting roadways and landmarks between Presas and La Palma," DIBL.

34. Berlandier, *Journey to Mexico*, 511–12. Berlandier's beautiful and precise sketch "Barra de Soto La Marina" is found at the DIBL.

35. Berlandier, *Journey to Mexico*, 512–16; Berlandier, "Untitled map depicting roadways and landmarks between Soto La Marina and Encinal," DIBL.

36. Berlandier, *Journey to Mexico*, 470, 516–17; Berlandier, "Untitled map depicting roadways between Santander and San Fernando," DIBL.

37. Berlandier, *Journey to Mexico*, 517–35; Platt, "Escandón Settlement," http://www.rootsweb.ancestry.com/~mextam/escando4.htm; Berlandier, "Camino de Hoyos a San Carlos," DIBL; Botanica, *Trees & Shrubs*, 541–42.

38. Berlandier, *Journey to Mexico*, 535–37.

Chapter Eight

1. Mier y Terán, *Texas by Terán*, 149.

2. Berlandier, *Journey to Mexico*, 339–40, 541; Berlandier, "Ruta de Matamoros a Goliad," DIBL.

3. Berlandier, *Journey to Mexico*, 541–47; Berlandier, "Ruta de Matamoros," DIBL.

4. Berlandier, *Journey to Mexico*, 547–49; Berlandier, "Croquis de la cote du Texas depuis la barre de Corpus Christi," DIBL.

5. Berlandier, *Journey to Mexico*, 550–55; Berlandier, "Vista del Presidio de Golia antes Bahia del Espiritu Santo," DIBL. Osuna, *Explicando*, 40–41, writes that Chowell stayed at Goliad on Terán's orders, and that he married in Matamoros in 1836, where he served as a magistrate in the 1850s.

6. Berlandier, *Journey to Mexico*, 557–65; Ewers, *Indians of Texas*, 124; Berlandier, "Itinerario del Presidio de Bexar," DIBL; George and Eve Delange, "Blackbrush Acacia," Xeriscape Landscaping Plants for the Arizona Desert, http://www.delange.org/AcaciaBlackbrush/AcaciaBlackbrush.htm; Foster and Duke, *Medicinal Plants*, 247–50.

7. Berlandier, *Journey to Mexico*, 419, 565–70; Botanica's *Trees & Shrubs*, 369; Berlandier, "Itinerario del Presidio de Bexar," DIBL. For Laguna Espantosa, see "Espantosa Lake," Handbook of Texas Online, http://www.tshaonline.org/handbook/online/articles/EE/roe9.html.

8. Berlandier, *Journey to Mexico*, 570–75; Berlandier, "Itineraire de Rio Grande a Laredo," DIBL; Robert S. Weddie, "San Bernardo," Handbook of Texas Online, http://www.tshaonline.org/handbook/online/articles/uqs52; Robert S. Weddie, "San Juan Bautista," Handbook of Texas Online, http://www.tshaonline.org/handbook/online/articles/uqs24.

9. Berlandier, *Journey to Mexico*, 575–77; Berlandier, "Itineraire de Rio Grande a Laredo," DIBL. Santa Anna's supporters proclaimed the Plan of Cuernavaca in 1834 to halt congressional power and return Santa Anna to his rightful leadership

as president of the Republic. See Will Fowler, *Santa Anna of Mexico* (Lincoln: University of Nebraska Press, 2007), 154.

10. Berlandier, *Journey to Mexico*, 577–82; Berlandier, "Itineraire de Rio Grande a Laredo." Berlandier drew two separate maps of the route from San Juan Bautista to Laredo; the first traced the route from the former to Arroyo el Amole; the second traced the route from Palafox to Laredo. Berlandier, "Vista de las masa de avenisca que se observan en el paraje llamado las Iglesias cerca villa Guerrero" and "Palafox," DIBL.

11. Berlandier, *Journey to Mexico*, 582–91; Berlandier, "Cours du Río Bravo del Norte," "Map depicting Río Bravo and road between Camargo and Reynosa," DIBL; "Coahuiltecan Indians," Handbook of Texas Online, http://www.tshaonline.org/handbook/online/articles/CC/bmcah.html. Couch wrote in his "Notes on Travel" that "Berlandier in his investigations states that at Linares bones of the extinct Mastodon have been found in large quantities." Couch did not indicate the source in the Berlandier papers for this statement.

12. "Voyage a les Parties N. O. du Texas, Nov–Dec, 1834," BRBML.

13. Berlandier, "Etat de Tamaulipas," "Llanos del Sacramento," "Jurisdiction de la ville de Matamoros," "Matamoros," "Marais sales situes dans les environs de Matamoros," BRBML. SIA, RU 7052, Box 1, Folder 6. See also Tunnell and Judd, *Laguna Madre*.

14. For nineteenth-century French medicine, see George Weisz, *Medical Mandarins: The French Academy of Medicine in the Nineteenth and Early Twentieth Centuries* (Oxford: Oxford University Press, 1995).

15. Berlandier, "A estudiar en viajes," GHA.

16. Ibid.; Berlandier, Miscellaneous Documents on Medicine, BRBML; Berlandier, *Journey to Mexico*, 32, 76, 165.

17. Berlandier, "A estudiar en viajes," GHA.

18. Berlandier, *Journey to Mexico*, 239, 241, 354; Berlandier, "A estudiar en viajes," GHA.

19. Berlandier, "Des plantes usuelles chez les Indiens du Mexique," GHA; Berlandier, *Journey to Mexico*, 246, 421, 449, 450; Charles W. Kane, *Herbal Medicine of the American Southwest* (Tucson, AZ: Lincoln Town Press, 2006), 121.

20. Berlandier, "A estudiar en viajes," GHA; Manuel Aguilar-Moreno, *Handbook to Life in the Aztec World* (Oxford: Oxford University Press, 2007), 346.

21. Berlandier, Miscellaneous Documents on Medicine, BRBML, is an indispensable source to understand Berlandier's ideas about medicine and health.

22. Ibid.

23. SIAJLB, Box 14, Folder 14.

24. Miscellaneous Documents Pertaining to Jean Louis Berlandier, BRBML, Uncat WA, MS 178; Berlandier, *Journey to Mexico*, 224, 350, 424, 434, 449.

25. "Chirurgie et medecine," in Miscellaneous Documents, BRBML.

26. Berlandier, *Journey to Mexico*, 436–37.

27. "Medecine practique: Traitement du cholera," Miscellaneous Documents on Medicine, BRBML. For the use of sagebrush in treating cholera, see William H. Emory, *Report on the United States and Mexican Boundary Survey*, vol. 2 (Washington, D.C.: Nicholson, 1859), 17.

28. WA MSS S-330: #47, BRBML.

29. "Meteorologie—Observations et calculs de moyennes," trans. by Cleveland Abbe; "Instruments dont je me suis servi pour les observations journallieres"; "Note sur les instruments qui serviront durant le cours de la presente anneé [1847]"; "Temperature du Sol," SIAJLB, RU 7052, Box 14, Folders 14, 15.

30. Berlandier, *Journey to Mexico*, 337; "Translation of Dr. Berlandier's Letter and Descriptions" of January 5, 1851, and "Translation of Dr. Berlandier's Paper, Feb. 25th, 1851," Academy of Natural Sciences; "Mammalia," trans. C. B. R. Kennerly, SIAJLB, RU 7052, Box 14.

31. "Astronomie geographique," 1843–1850, SIAJLB, RU 7052, Box 1.

32. Berlandier, "Catalogue de ma collection zoologique et d'anatomie compare faite au Mexique," SIAJLB, RU 7052, Box 12. Drawings and paintings are found in Box 13, and manuscripts in Box 14. Berlandier claimed to have studied the badger at length, so much so that later zoologists appended his name to the scientific classification for the Mexican badger, *Taxidea taxus berlandieri* Baird. See Coues, *Fur-Bearing Animals*, 289–90; and David J. Schmidly, *Texas Natural History: A Century of Change* (Lubbock: Texas Tech University Press, 2002), 184.

Chapter Nine

1. Berlandier, "Excursion au Fronton de Sa Isabel," GHA; Berlandier, "Astronomie geographique," 1843–1850, SIAJLB, RU 7052, Box 1.

2. Accounts of the events leading up to the initial battles of the Mexican War are found in J. Reese Fry, *A Life of General Zachary Taylor* (Philadelphia, PA: Grigg, Elliot, 1848); K. Jack Bauer, *Zachary Taylor: Soldier, Planter, Statesman of the Old Southwest* (Baton Rouge: Louisiana State University Press, 1993); Justin H. Smith, *The War with Mexico*, vol. 1 (New York: Macmillan, 1919); Cadmus M. Wilcox, *History of the Mexican War* (Washington, D.C.: Church News, 1892). Berlandier's maps of the Battle of Palo Alto are reproduced in Charles M. Haecker, *A Thunder of Cannon: Archeology of the Mexican War: Battlefield of Palo Alto* (Santa Fe, NM: National Park Service, 1994). A brief account of Berlandier's meeting with General Taylor is in T. B. Thorpe, *Our Army on the Rio Grande* (Philadelphia, PA: Cary and Hart, 1846), 14. A good recent treatment of the Mexican War is K. Jack Bauer, *The Mexican War, 1846–1848* (Lincoln: University of Nebraska Press, 1992).

3. Berlandier, "Extracto de un diario de la ocurrido durante la occupacion de Matamoros por las tropas Americanas," BRBML; Thorpe, *Army on the Rio Grande*.

4. A good overview of the events during the summer of 1846 is Smith's *War with Mexico*, vol. 1, chaps. 10–11. Osuna, *Explicando*, 41, writes that Berlandier visited Santa Anna in 1846 to request funds to pay for medical expenses incurred at the military hospital in tending the wounded.

5. "Voyage de Matamoros de Tamaulipas a San Luis Potosi," SIAJLB, RU 7052, Box 1, Folder 13; Berlandier, *Journey to Mexico*, 211–13.

6. Correspondence, SIA, RU 7052, Box 1, Series 2, Folder 3; David Roth, "Texas Hurricane History," National Weather Service, http://www.hpc.ncep.noaa.gov/research/txhur.pdf. Osuna, *Explicando*, 96, writes that Berlandier organized a spy network during the American occupation of Matamoros and that as a consequence General Taylor retaliated against the scientist and his family.

7. Berlandier's journal at the Gray Herbarium Archives, Harvard University, is "Prison; notification, escorte jusqu'a la capitale de l'Etat; attentats du Gouverneur Don Jesus Cardenas: confiance de ce fonctionnaire dans ses autes inconstitutionnels: nullite de la commission permanente du Congres—reponde absurde de la supreme cour de justice: notre passeport; redour a Matamoros." For the sympiesometer, see the article by Marco Frontijn at http://www.antique-horology.org/_editorial/sympiezometerfontijn/. Andres Trevino became in time governor of Tamaulipas. See also Joseph A. Stout Jr., *Schemers & Dreamers: Filibustering in Mexico, 1848–1921* (College Station: Texas A & M Press, 2002).

8. "Prison; notification," GHA; Berlandier, "Untitled map depicting roadways between Victoria and Santander," DIBL. General Terán committed suicide July 3, 1832.

9. "Prison; notification," GHA.

10. Ibid.

11. Ibid.

12. Couch to Baird, November 16, 1854, SIA.

13. Ibid.

14. Berlandier, *Journey to Mexico*, 344; Couch to Baird, November 16, 1854, SIA.

15. Berlandier, *Journey to Mexico*, 331–32, 434, 437; Ewers, *Indians of Texas*, 94.

Sources Consulted

Manuscript Works by Jean Louis Berlandier

Papers of Jean Louis Berlandier, Archives, Gray Herbarium Library, Harvard University

"Voyage pour reconnoitre les principaux points de l'Etat de Tamaulipas."

"Journal, Aug. 13/30–Feb. 28/31."

"A estudiar en viajes: Histoire naturelle des plantes employees dans la matiere medicals les arts, etc. des Mexicains anciens et modernes."

"Des plantes usuelles chez les Indiens du Mexique."

"Excursion au Fronton de Sa Isabel."

"Prison; notification, escorte jusqu'a la capitale de l'Etat; attentats du Gouverneur Don Jesus Cardenas: confiance de ce fonctionnaire dans ses actes inconstitutionnels: nullite de la commission permanente du Congres—reponse absurde de la supreme cour de justice: notre passeport; retour a Matamoros."

Jean Louis Berlandier Papers. Yale Collection of Western Americana, Beinecke Rare Book and Manuscript Library

"Calculos de observaciones hechas desde el 16 de oct hasta el 31 de dicho, 1832," WA MSS S-330, #47.

"Estracto de un diario de la ocurrido durante la ocupacion de Matamoros por las tropas Americanas," WA MSS S-321.

Miscellaneous Documents Pertaining to Jean Louis Berlandier, Uncat WA, MS 178.

"Nota medico-statistique de Matamoros," WA MSS S-330, #47.

"Voyage a les parties N.O. du Texas, Nov–Dec, 1834 [1828]," WA MSS S-330, #47.

Digital images from the Jean Louis Berlandier Papers, Beinecke Library, Yale University: http://hdl.handle.net/10079/fa/beinecke.berlandi.

Smithsonian Institution Archives Record Unit 7052, Jean Louis Berlandier Papers.

Jean Louis Berlandier General Correspondence, Box 1, Folder 3.

Astronomical Calculations and Observations, Nos. 1–2, 1827–1832, Box 1, Folder 4.

Astronomical Calculations and Observations, No. 4, 1834–1838 (Addenda), Box 1, Folder 6.

Astronomical Observations, Nos. 1–2, 1832–1833, by Berlandier and Raphael Chowell, Box 1, Folder 8.

Cyanometrical Observation Journal No. 1, 1827–1830, Box 1, Folder 12.

Geographic Astronomy, 1843–1850, Box 1, Folder 13.

Means of Meteorological Observations, Goliad, Texas, 1832–1833, Box 1, Folder 14.

Means of Meteorological Observations, Matamoros, 1843, Box 1, Folder 15.

Catalog of Manuscripts kept by Jean Louis Berlandier, Box 12, Folder 3.

Catalogue de mes collections d'histoire naturalle, Box 12, Folder 4.

Catalogs of Geological Collections kept by Jean Louis Berlandier, Box 12, Folder 5.

Catalogs of Paintings and Drawings kept by Jean Louis Berlandier, Box 12, Folder 6.

Catalogs of Zoological Collections kept by Jean Louis Berlandier, Box 12, Folder 7.

Jean Louis Berlandier Watercolor Paintings, Drawings, and Photographs Taken of These Works, Boxes 12 and 13.

"Vocabulario de las plantas medicinales espanol-latino," Box 14, Folder 4.

"Meteorologie—Observations et calculs de moyennes." Translated by Cleveland Abbe. Box 14, Folder 14.

Walter L. Nicholson's copy of Berlandier's notes on instruments that he used during 1847. Copied in French. Collected by Cleveland Abbe, Box 14, Folder 15.

C. B. R. Kennerly Translations of Berlandier's Zoological Manuscripts, Box 14, Folder 16, Birds, Box 14, Folder 17, Mammalia.

Gilcrease Museum

"Journal de voyage aux limites N. E. de la Republicque Mexicano sous les ordres du General Terán commence le 9 novembre, 1827."

"Indigenes nomades des Etats Internes d'Orient et d'Occident des territoires du Nouveau Mexique et des deux Californies."

Academy of Natural Sciences

"Translation of Dr. Berlandier's Letter and Descriptions," of January 5, 1851, and "Translation of Dr. Berlandier's Paper, Feb. 25th, 1851."

Manuscript Works by Darius Nash Couch

Smithsonian Institution Archives

Spencer Fullerton Baird Papers, Unit 7002, Box 18.

Old Colony Historical Society

Darius Nash Couch, "Notes of Travel."

Darius Nash Couch. Translator. "Hunting the Bear and Buffalo in North Western Texas." Translated from the Spanish of Louis Berlandier of the Mexican Boundary Commission.

Published Works by Jean Louis Berlandier

Berlandier, Jean Louis. *The Indians of Texas in 1830*. Edited by John C. Ewers. Washington, D.C.: Smithsonian Institution Press, 1969.

———. *Journey to Mexico During the Years 1826 to 1834*. Translated by Sheila M. Ohlendorf, Josette M. Bigelow, Mary M. Standifer. 2 vols. Austin: Texas State Historical Association, 1980.

Berlandier, Luis, and Raphael Chowell. *Diario de viage de la Comision de Limites*. Mexico City: Juan R. Navarro, 1850.

Berlandier, Luis, and Manuel Mier y Terán. *Memorias de la Comision de Limites. Historia Natural. Botanica*. Matamoros: 1832.

Published Contemporary Sources

Agassiz, Louis. *Contributions to the Natural History of the United States of America*. Boston, MA: Little Brown, 1857.

American Journal of Science and Arts. 2nd ser. Vol. 35 (1863).

Arrowsmith, Aaron. "A Map Exhibiting All the New Discoveries in the Interior Parts of North America." University of Virginia Library. Lewis and Clark: The Maps of Exploration 1507–1814. 1795. http://www2.iib.virginia.edu/exhibits/lewis_clark/exploring/ch4–30.html.

Baedeker, K. *Switzerland and the Adjacent Portions of Italy, Savoy and the Tyrol*. Coblenz: Baedeker, 1864.

Baird, Spencer F. "Birds." In *Reports of Explorations and Surveys*, vol. 9. Washington, D.C.: Tucker, 1858.

———. *Directions for Collecting, Preserving, and Transporting Specimens of Natural History*. Washington, D.C.: Smithsonian Institution, 1852.

Bakewell, Robert. *Travels*. Vol. 2. London: Longman, 1823.

Bartlett, John R. *Personal Narrative of Explorations and Incidents in Texas, New Mexico, California, Sonora, and Chihuahua, Connected with the United States and Mexican Boundary Commission*. Vol. 2. New York: D. Appleton, 1854.

Blodget, Lorin. *Climatology of the United States*. Philadelphia, PA: J. P. Lippincott, 1857.

Bradbury, John. *Travels in the Interior of North America in the Years 1809, 1810, and 1811*. London: 1819.

Burkart, Joseph. "Residence and Travels in Mexico." *Foreign Quarterly Review* 19 (1837): 270–71.

Candolle, Augustin Pyramus de. *Mémoires et souvenirs*. Geneva: Cherbuliez, 1862.

———. *Prodromus Systematis Naturalis Regis Vegetabilis*. Paris: Masson, 1847.

Chateaubriand, François-René, vicomte de. *Atala; or the Love and Constancy of Two Savages in the Desert*. Translated by Caleb Bingham. 2nd ed. Boston, MA: Samuel Armstrong, 1814.

Coues, Elliott, ed. *The Expeditions of Zebulon Montgomery Pike*. 3 vols. New York: Harper, 1895.

Emory, William H. *Report on the United States and Mexican Boundary Survey*. Vol. 1. Washington, D.C.: Nicholson, 1857.

———. *Report on the United States and Mexican Boundary Survey*. Vol. 2. Washington, D.C.: Nicholson, 1859.

Fry, J. Reese. *A Life of Gen. Zachary Taylor*. Philadelphia, PA: Grigg, Eliot, 1848.

Gray, Asa. *Scientific Papers of Asa Gray*. Edited by Charles S. Sargent. Vol. 2. Boston, MA: Houghton Mifflin, 1889.

"Henry S. Tanner's 1822 Map of North America." University of Tulsa McFarlin Library. Maps of the American West. http://www.lib.utulsa.edu/Speccoll/collections/maps/tanner/tanner1.htm.

Humboldt, Alexander de. *Political Essay on the Kingdom of New Spain*. Vol. 2. London: Longman, 1811.

Josselyn, John. *Colonial Traveler: A Critical Edition of Two Voyages to New-England*, ed. Paul Lindholdt. Hanover, NH: University Press of New England, 1988.

———. *New-Englands Rarities Discovered*. London: G. Widdowes, 1672.

———. *Two Voyages to New-England*. London: 1674.

"Journal Descriptive of the Route from New York to Real Del Monte by Way of Tampico." *London Magazine*. February 1826.

Mier y Terán, Manuel de. *Texas by Terán: The Diary Kept by General Manuel de Mier y Terán on his 1828 Inspection of Texas*. Edited by Jack Jackson. Translated by John Wheat. With botanical notes by Scooter Cheatham and Lynn Marshall. Austin: University of Texas Press, 2000.

Morse, Jedidiah. *A Report to the Secretary of War of the United States on Indian Affairs*. New Haven, CT: Converse, 1822.

Sánchez, José María. "A Trip to Texas in 1828." Translated by Carlos E. Castañeda. *Southwestern Historical Quarterly Online* 29, no. 4 (1926). http://www.tshaonline.org/shqonline/apager.php?vol=029.

Sessé, Martino, and Josepho Marianno Mociño, *Flora mexicana*. 2nd ed. Mexico City: Oficina Tipográfica de la Secretaría de Pomento, 1894.

Shelley, Mary. "Letter of 1 June 1816." University of Pennsylvania, Department of English. http://www.english.upenn.edu/Projects/knarf/MShelley/1jun16.html#geneva.

Sprague, William B. *Letters from Europe in 1828*. New York: Leavitt, 1828.

Thorpe, Thomas Bangs. *Our Army on the Rio Grande*. Philadelphia, PA: Cary and Hart, 1846.

Tylor, Edward B. *Anahuac; or, Mexico and the Mexicans, Ancient and Modern*. London: Longman, 1861.

Varey, Simon, ed. *The Mexican Treasury: The Writings of Dr. Francisco Hernández.* Palo Alto, CA: Stanford University Press, 2000.

Wilson, Daniel. *Letters from an Absent Brother.* Vol. 2. London: Wilson, 1827.

Secondary Sources: Books, Articles, Reference, Internet

Jean Louis Berlandier

Campbell, T. N. "Journey to Mexico During the Years 1826 to 1834: A Review." *Southwestern Historical Quarterly Online* 86, no. 3 (1983): 401–12. http://www.tshaonline.org/shqonline/apager.php?vol=086&pag=418.

Geiser, Samuel Wood. *Naturalists of the Frontier.* Dallas, TX: Southern Methodist University Press, 1948.

Osuna, Luis Sánchez. *Explicando a Berlandier.* Programa de Apoyo a las Culturas Municipales y Comunitarias, 2004.

Darius Nash Couch

Gambone, A. M. *Major-General Darius Nash Couch: Enigmatic Valor.* Baltimore, MD: Butternut and Blue, 2000.

Kennedy, Edward F., Jr. *Lt. Darius Nash Couch in the Mexican War.* Taunton, MA: Old Colony Historical Society, 1977.

Rhône Valley, Geneva, and the Alps

Caesar. *The Conquest of Gaul.* Translated by S. A. Handford. Harmondsworth, UK: Penguin Books, 1951.

Fort l'Ecluse. http://www.leaz.fr/webleaz/mairies.leaz/leaz/fortlecluser.htm.

Fort l'Ecluse: Site Officiel. http://www.fortlecluse.fr/.

Frye, William E. *After Waterloo.* London: Heinemann, 1908.

Orr, Clarissa Campbell. "Romanticism in Switzerland." In *Romanticism in National Context,* edited by Roy Porter and Mikuláš Teich. Cambridge: Cambridge University Press, 1988.

Siborne, William. *The Waterloo Campaign, 1815.* Westminster, UK: Constable, 1895.

The Site of Fort L'Ecluse. http://www.lesitedefortlecluse.org/.

Natural History and Science

The Americana: A Universal Reference Library. Edited by Frederick Beach and George Rines. New York: Scientific American, 1912.

"An Analysis of Texas Waterways." *Texas Parks and Wildlife.* http://www.tpwd.state.tx.us/publications/pwdpubs/pwd_rp_t3200_1047/14_c_tx_brazos.phtml.

Benke, Arthur C., and Colbert E. Cushing. *Rivers of North America.* Maryland Heights, MO: Academic Press, 2005.

Blunt, Wilfrid. *The Art of Botanical Illustration: An Illustrated History.* New York: Dover, 1992.

Boorstin, Daniel J. *The Discoverers.* New York: Random House, 1983.

Botanica. *Trees & Shrubs.* San Diego, CA: Laurel Glen, 1999.

Brune, Gunnar. *Springs of Texas.* College Station: Texas A&M University Press, 2002.

Burns, William E. *Science in the Enlightenment: An Encyclopedia.* Santa Barbara, CA: ABC-Clio, 2003.

Cartron, Jean-Luc E., Gerardo Ceballos, and Richard Stephen Felger. *Biodiversity, Ecosystems, and Conservation in Northern Mexico.* Oxford: Oxford University Press, 2005.

Cartron, Jean-Luc E., David C. Lightfoot, Jane E. Mygatt, Sandra L. Brantley, and Timothy K. Lowrey. *A Field Guide to the Plants and Animals of the Middle Rio Grande Bosque.* Albuquerque: University of New Mexico Press, 2008.

Coues, Eliot. *Fur-Bearing Animals: A Monograph of North American Mustelidæ.* Washington, D.C.: Government Printing Office, 1877.

Dall, William H., ed. *Spencer Fullerton Baird: A Biography.* Philadelphia, PA: Lippincott, 1915.

Delange, George and Eve. "Blackbrush Acacia." *Xeriscape Landscaping Plants for the Arizona Desert.* http://www.delange.org/AcaciaBlackbrush/AcaciaBlackbrush.htm.

Encyclopedia Americana. Vol. 26. New York: Encyclopedia Americana Corp., 1920.

Fontijn, Marco. "The Sympiesometer Designed by Alexander Adie: An Unusually Short 'Barometer' without Mercury." http://www.antique-horology.org/_editorial/sympiezometerfontijn/.

Foster, Steven, and James A. Duke. *A Field Guide to Medicinal Plants and Herbs of Eastern and Central North America.* 2nd ed. Boston, MA: Houghton Mifflin, 2000.

Geikie, Archibald. *The Founders of Geology.* London: Macmillan, 1905.

"Giant Hyssop." Innvista. http://www.innvista.com/health/herbs/gianthys.htm.

Gohan, Gabriel. *A History of Geology.* Translated by Albert V. Carozzi and Marguerite Carozzi. New Brunswick, NJ: Rutgers University Press, 1991.

Hayden, F. V. *Bulletin of the United States Geological and Geographical Survey.* Vol. 4. Washington, D.C.: Government Printing Office, 1878.

Kane, Charles W. *Herbal Medicine of the American Southwest.* Tucson, AZ: Lincoln Town Press, 2006.

Kirkpatrick, Zoe Merriam. *Wildflowers of the Western Plains.* Austin: University of Texas Press, 1992.

Landes, David S. *Revolution in Time: Clocks and the Making of the Modern World.* Cambridge, MA: Harvard University Press, 1983.

Lawson, Russell M. *The American Plutarch: Jeremy Belknap and the Historian's Dialogue with the Past.* Westport, CT: Praeger, 1998.

———. *The Land Between the Rivers: Thomas Nuttall's Ascent of the Arkansas, 1819.* Ann Arbor: University of Michigan Press, 2004.

———. *Passaconaway's Realm: Captain John Evans and the Ascent of Mount Washington.* Hanover, NH: University Press of New England, 2002.

———, ed. *Research and Discovery: Landmarks and Pioneers in American Science*. Vol. 1. Armonk, NY: M. E. Sharpe, 2008.

Library of Congress. American Memory. http://memory.loc.gov/.

Lipscomb, Carol A. "Karankawa Indians." The Handbook of Texas Online. http://www.tshaonline.org/handbook/online/articles/KK/bmk5.html.

Miall, L. C. *The Early Naturalists: Their Lives and Work, 1530–1789*. London: Macmillan, 1912.

Moll, Edward O. "Gopherus berlandieri (Agassiz, 1857)—Texas Tortoise." *Sonoran Herpetologist* 16 (2003): 38–39.

Phillips, John C. "A Year's Collecting in the State of Tamaulipas, Mexico." *Auk: Quarterly Journal of Ornitthology* 28 (1911): 67–89.

Proceedings of the American Academy of Arts and Sciences. New series. Vol. 20. Boston, MA: University Press: John Wilson and Son, 1893.

Roth, David. "Texas Hurricane History." *National Weather Service*. http://www.hpc.ncep.noaa.gov/research/txhur.pdf.

Sachs, Julius von. *History of Botany*. Translated by Henry Garnsey. Oxford: Clarendon Press, 1890.

Schlesinger, Victoria. *Animals and Plants of the Ancient Maya*. Austin: University of Texas Press, 2002.

Schmidly, David J. *Texas Natural History: A Century of Change*. Lubbock: Texas Tech University Press, 2002.

Smithsonian National Museum of American History. "Theodolite." Physical Sciences Collection—Surveying and Geodesy. http://americanhistory.si.edu/collections/surveying/object.cfm?recordnumber=997496.

Standley, Paul C. *Trees and Shrubs of Mexico*. Contributions from the United States National Herbarium, vol. 23, pt. 1. Washington D.C.: Government Printing Office, 1920.

Stauffer, Fred W., Rodrigo Duno de Stefano, and Laurence J. Dorr, Fernand Jacquemoud, and Nicolas Fumeaux. "Contribución del Dr. José María Vargas a las ciencias botánicas en Venezuela." *Acta Botánica Venezuelica* 29, no. 1 (2006): 135–64.

Texas Parks and Wildlife Department. *An Analysis of Texas Waterways*. College Station: The Texas Agricultural Extension Service, Texas A&M University System, 1974. http://www.tpwd.state.tx.us/publications/pwdpubs/pwd_rp_t3200_1047/index.phtml.

Thieret, John W. *National Audubon Society Field Guide to North American Wildflowers, Eastern Region*. Original authors William A. Niering and Nancy C. Olmstead. New York: Knopf, 2001.

Tilford, Gregory L. *Edible and Medicinal Plants of the West*. Missoula, MT: Mountain Press, 1997.

Tunnell, John W., Jr., and Frank W. Judd, eds. *The Laguna Madre of Texas and Tamaulipas*. College Station: Texas A&M Press, 2002.

University of Texas at Austin. Ladybird Johnson Wildflower Center. http://www.wildflower.org.

USDA. Plants Database, Natural Resources Conservation Service. http://plants.usda.gov/java/profile?symbol=EBEB.

Vogel, Virgil J. *American Indian Medicine*. Norman: University of Oklahoma Press, 1970.

Weisz, George. *Medical Mandarins: The French Academy of Medicine in the Nineteenth and Early Twentieth Centuries*. Oxford: Oxford University Press, 1995.

Zamudio, Graciela. "El Real Jardín Botánico del Palacio Virreinal de la Nueva España." *Ciencias* 68 (December 2002). http://www.ejournal.unam.mx/cns/no68/CNS06803.pdf.

History of Indigenous Peoples

Campbell, Lyle, and Marianne Methun. *The Languages of Native America: Historical and Comparative Assessment*. Austin: University of Texas Press, 1979.

"Coahuiltecan Indians." Handbook of Texas Online. http://www.tshaonline.org/handbook/online/articles/CC/bmcah.html.

Delay, Brian. "The Wider World of the Handsome Man: Southern Plains Indians Invade Mexico, 1830–1848." *Journal of the Early Republic* 27 (Spring 2007): 83–113.

Fehrenbach, T. R. *Comanches: The Destruction of a People*. Cambridge, MA: Da Capo Press, 1994.

Gatschet, Albert S. *The Karankawa Indians, the Coast People of Texas*. Cambridge, MA: Peabody Museum of American Archeology and Ethnology, 1891.

Gibson, Arrell M. *Kickapoos: Lords of the Middle Border*. Norman: University of Oklahoma Press, 1976.

Hämäläinen, Pekka. *The Comanche Empire*. New Haven, CT: Yale University Press, 2008.

Kavanagh, Thomas W. *The Comanches: A History, 1706–1875*. Lincoln: University of Nebraska Press, 1999.

Latorre, Felipe A., and Dolores L. Latorre. *The Mexican Kickapoo Indians*. New York: Dover, 1991.

Montaigne, Michel de. "Of Cannibals." In *The Complete Essays of Montaigne*, vol. 1, 150–58. Translated by Donald M. Frame. Stanford, CA: Stanford University Press, 1958.

Pritzker, Barry M. *A Native American Encyclopedia: History, Culture, Peoples*. Oxford: Oxford University Press, 2000.

Salinas, Martin. *Indians of the Rio Grande Delta: Their Role in the History of Southern Texas*. Austin: University of Texas Press, 1990.

History of Mexico, Texas, and the Gulf Coast

Aguilar-Moreno, Manuel. *Handbook to Life in the Aztec World*. Oxford: Oxford University Press, 2007.

Alonzo, Armando C. *Tejano Legacy: Rancheros and Settlers in South Texas, 1734–1900*. Albuquerque: University of New Mexico Press, 1998.

Bancroft, Hubert H. *History of the North Mexican States and Texas*. San Francisco, CA: Bancroft, 1884.

Bauer, K. Jack. *The Mexican War, 1846–1848*. Lincoln: University of Nebraska Press, 1992.

———. *Zachary Taylor: Soldier, Planter, Statesman of the Old Southwest.* Baton Rouge: Louisiana State University Press, 1993.

Bolton, Herbert E., and Thomas M. Marshall. *The Colonization of North America, 1492–1783.* New York: Kessinger, 2005.

Campbell, T. N., and T. J. Campbell. *Indian Groups Associated with Spanish Missions of the San Antonio Missions National Historical Park.* Special Report No. 16. San Antonio: Center for Archeological Research, University of Texas. http://www.nps.gov/history/history/online_books/saan/campbell/contents.htm.

Ediger, Gill. "The Bustamante Area." http://www.cavetexas.org/mexico/PDF/carriza11.pdf.

"Espantosa Lake." Handbook of Texas Online. http://www.tshaonline.org/handbook/online/articles/EE/roe9.html.

"The Five Spanish Missions of Old San Antonio." Lone Star Junction. http://www.lsjunction.com/facts/missions.htm.

Foster, William C. *Spanish Expeditions into Texas, 1689–1768.* Austin: University of Texas Press, 1995.

Fowler, Will. *Santa Anna of Mexico.* Lincoln: University of Nebraska Press, 2007.

Fry, J. Reese. *A Life of Gen. Zachary Taylor.* Philadelphia, PA: Grigg, Elliot, 1848.

Gobierno Municipal de Jimenez. Official website, http://www.jimenez.gob.mx/municipio.asp.

Guerra, Guillermo. "Tamaulipas." History and Genealogy of South Texas and Northeast Mexico. http://www.vsalgs.org/stnemgenealogy/tamaul.html#Tampico.

Haecker, Charles M. *A Thunder of Cannon: Archeology of the Mexican War: Battlefield of Palo Alto.* Santa Fe, NM: National Park Service, 1994.

Hendrickson, Kenneth E., Jr. "Brazos River." Handbook of Texas Online. http://www.tshaonline.org/handbook/online/articles/BB/rnb7.html.

Hittell, Theodore H. *History of California.* Vol. 2. San Francisco, CA: Stone, 1898.

Horgan, Paul. *Great River: The Rio Grande in North American History.* Austin: Texas Monthly Press, 1984.

Jones, Oakah L. *Los Paisanos.* Norman: University of Oklahoma Press, 1996.

Morton, Ohland. "Life of General don Manuel de Mier y Terán." *Southwestern Historical Quarterly Online* 47 (1943). http://www.tshaonline.org/shqonline/apager.php?vol=047.

Pierce, Franklin C. *A Brief History of the Lower Rio Grande Valley.* Menasha, WI: George Banta, 1917.

Platt, Lyman D. "The Escandón Settlement of Nueva España." http://www.rootsweb.ancestry.com/~mextam/escando1.htm.

Robarts, William H. *Mexican War Veterans.* Washington, D.C.: Brentanos, 1887.

Rutsch, Mechthild. "Natural History, Natural Museum and Anthropology in Mexico." *Perspectivas Latinoamericanas* no. 1 (2004): 89–122. http://www.nanzan-u.ac.jp/LATIN/4rutsch.pdf.

Smith, Justin H. *The War with Mexico.* Vol. 1. New York: Macmillan, 1919.

Stout, Joseph A., Jr. *Schemers & Dreamers: Filibustering in Mexico, 1848–1921.* Fort Worth: Texas Christian University Press, 2002.

Teja, Jesús F. de la, and John Wheat. "Bexar: Profile of a Tejano Community, 1820–1832." *Southwestern Historical Quarterly* 89, no. 1 (1985): 7–34. http://ecommons.txstate.edu/histfacp/14.

Thonhoff, Robert H. "Arredondo, Joaquin de." Handbook of Texas Online. http://www.tshaonline.org/handbook/online/articles/AA/far18.html.

Weber, David J. *The Spanish Frontier in North America.* New Haven, CT: Yale University Press, 1992.

Wilcox, Cadmus M. *History of the Mexican War.* Washington, D.C.: Church News, 1892.

Index